Praise for
A Teacher's Guide to
ONLINE LEARNING

"This comprehensive and engaging book provides everything a teacher would want for effective online teaching, including an exploration of tools, examples of instructional techniques, ideas for motivating students, and more. Plus it's fun to read. Lindy is a teacher's teacher and has written the best guide to online teaching and learning available."

~ Pamela (Livingston) Gaudet,

Author of *Like No Other School Year* and
1-to-1 Learning: Laptop Programs That Work

"Lindy takes all her experience helping learning practitioners leverage technology and packages it up in an easy-to-read and handy manual. This year as teachers have pivoted back and forth from in-person to online, they have all struggled to figure out how to utilize technology in a meaningful way. This book gives you the appropriate background and foundation to begin to make a difference in your students' online learning endeavors."

~ Tom Lademann, LuminEd

"A Teacher's Guide to Online Learning looks at all of the elements of online learning and provides insight for teachers that are looking to design the best online learning possible. This book can be a great introduction to online learning for teachers new to the practice while also helping more experienced teachers check their practice and identify blind spots from past practices. This book also introduces a number of tools that can help make online learning both effective and efficient. Online learning will continue to grow as a part of K–12, and this book can help educators prepare and provide excellent instruction."

~ Dr. Robert Dillon, School Designer at Sustainable Education Solutions
Author of *The Space: A Guide for Educators*

"These practical strategies to improve K–12 student engagement in virtual learning come from a highly respected, hands-on practitioner, Lindy Hockenbary. An excellent read and a long-term handbook for teachers."

~ Wayne Poncia, CEO of Hāpara

InTECHgratedPD.org

A
Teacher's Guide to
ONLINE LEARNING

Practical Strategies to Improve K-12 Student Engagement in Virtual Learning

BY LINDY HOCKENBARY

A Teacher's Guide to Online Learning:
Practical Strategies to Improve K–12 Student Engagement in Virtual Learning

InTECHgrated Professional Development
www.intechgratedpd.org

Book and cover design: Rebecca Stanton

Line editor: Lindsee Tauck

Copy editor: Betsy Palmerston

Proofreader: Samantha Held

Indexer: CC Thomas

First Edition
eBook ISBN: 978-1-7363503-0-0
Paperback ISBN: 978-1-7363503-1-7
Hardback ISBN: 978-1-7363503-2-4

Library of Congress Control Number: 2021909772

Printed in the United States of America

Lindy Hockenbary
www.intechgratedpd.org

TABLE OF CONTENTS

TABLE OF CONTENTS

PART 4: BEST PRACTICES

BRING LINDY TO YOUR SCHOOL OR EVENT!

Acknowledgments

The only person who has read this book as many times as I have is my husband, Chad. Thank you for the unwavering support and confidence, as well as reviews of endless book drafts.

I wanted this book to bring in multiple perspectives of stakeholders in education, and it wouldn't be what it is without the contributors who volunteered their time. Thank you to the chapter authors: Nikki Vradenburg for sharing your knowledge of caregiver support, Traci Piltz for sharing your expertise of everything primary, and Bill Bass for bringing in the school leader perspective. Thank you to the educators who shared their best practices in online learning: Keyleigh Hennessy, Tracey Nesrallah, Billie Johnson, Lana Hekkel, Rebecca Recco, Lindsee Tauck, Brittany Mosher, Keturah Rush and Sarah Hagans. Thank you to Lynn Silbernagel and Esther Jensen for sharing your perspectives on teaching students with special needs. Thank you to Shelly Stanton for the wonderful recommendations! Finally, thank you to the students and parents who completed the anonymous surveys.

I had numerous alpha and beta readers who provided invaluable feedback. Pamela Livingston Gaudet provided publishing guidance. Thank you to Lindsee Tauck for both the editing assistance and reviews from the teacher perspective. Last but not least, Rebecca Stanton sprinkled her artistic magic to bring the cover and interior graphics to life.

I LOVE TO HEAR FROM EDUCATORS

and would enjoy hearing your thoughts on the book.

How are you **IMPLEMENTING THE STRATEGIES** in your classroom?

What information from the book has been the most **HELPFUL**?

What **TIPS** and **STRATEGIES** do you have to share?

Share your takeaways on social media using
#TeachersGuideToOnline

**Connect with me
in any of the following ways:**

- **Website:** intechgratedpd.org

- **LinkedIn:** linkedin.com/in/lindyhockenbary

- **TikTok:** tiktok.com/@lindyhockenbary

- **Twitter:** twitter.com/lindyhockenbary

- **Facebook:** facebook.com/lindyhockenbary

- **Email:** lindy@intechgratedpd.org

When it comes to educational technology, my motto is **"use the tool that is right for the job."** Therefore, I try to be well versed in the educational technology field and hold several certifications, including:

- *Google for Education Certified Trainer and Educator Level 2*

- *Microsoft Innovative Educator (MIE) Master Trainer and Expert*

- *Minecraft Certified Trainer*

- *Hāpara Champion Trainer*

- *Raspberry Pi Certified Educator*

Part 1:

INTRODUCTION

Chapter 1: My Story

You will learn in this book how important it is in online learning for your learners to get to know you, not only as their teacher but also as a person. I am all about modeling, and even though you are learning via a book and not an online course, I feel it is important to start with you getting to know me.

My name is Lindy Hockenbary, and I have spent my career in education in various roles. I started as a middle and high school teacher, where I was lucky that my classroom was a computer lab! Through this experience, it became clear to me that technology, if leveraged correctly, can help to create powerful learning experiences. I also developed a curriculum for a personal finance project. As part of this job, we trained teachers how to use the curriculum. I began to really enjoy the professional development side of education. This led to working as a technology integration specialist for a regional education service center, and that is what started my current career path of supporting teachers as an instructional technology consultant.

As someone who loves to learn, I spend my spare time pondering **how to make learning better.**

I never planned to write a book, but when the world turned upside down in early 2020, I began writing about my experiences as an online learner and teacher. Over the course of 2020, I continued to lead training sessions for teachers on best practices for online learning. These experiences and writings culminated in this book, and thus, *A Teacher's Guide to Online Learning* was born.

Online learning and I go way back. My graduate degree in educational technology was completed entirely online through Boise State University, and I loved every minute of it. I would never have been able to complete a face-to-face graduate program at that point in my life due to my travel schedule, so I am incredibly thankful to have had the ability to complete my degree online.

When it comes to educational technology, my motto is "use the tool that is right for the job." Therefore, I try to be well versed in the educational technology field and hold several certifications, including Google for Education Certified Trainer and Educator Level 2, Microsoft Innovative Educator (MIE) Master Trainer and Expert, *Minecraft* Certified Trainer, Hāpara Champion Trainer, and Raspberry Pi Certified Educator.

I have assisted schools across the world with varying initiatives with focuses on specific technologies to large pedagogical shifts. I am the go-to person for questions related to integrating technology into classroom instruction. My goal is to provide effective teacher training so every student can thrive.

I live with my husband and our pack of squishy-faced dogs in Bozeman, Montana, USA, where we enjoy exploring the beauty of Montana. We have a small camper that we enjoy taking out in the summer. In the winter, we enjoy a ski trip every now and then. Lately, we have spent every spare minute remodeling our house.

I love to hear from educators and would enjoy hearing your thoughts on the book. How are you implementing the strategies in your classroom? What information from the book has been the most helpful? What tips and strategies do you have to share? Share your takeaways on social media using the hashtag **#TeachersGuideToOnline**. Connect with me in any of the following ways:

- Website: intechgratedpd.org
- LinkedIn: linkedin.com/in/lindyhockenbary
- TikTok: tiktok.com/@lindyhockenbary
- Twitter: twitter.com/lindyhockenbary
- Facebook: facebook.com/lindyhockenbary
- Email: lindy@intechgratedpd.org

Contact Lindy

Chapter 2: About This Book

This book began in March of 2020 when almost every school in the entire world was forced to move to online learning due to COVID-19. I began receiving pleas for help from teachers across the globe. I started to research resources for online learning in K–12. Guess what? There was virtually nothing focused on K–12. I set out to share my knowledge of teaching online in hopes of helping even a little. This book was a labor of love and is a gift to the resilient teachers of the world.

As an educator, if you find this book helpful, please consider leaving a review on Amazon (bit.ly/teachersguidetoonline). This will help get this knowledge in the hands of more educators.

Who Is This Book For?

This book was designed with K–12 teachers in mind, but most information can be applied to postsecondary/higher education learning environments as well.

This book was *not* designed for online learning that has few or no instructor touchpoints, such as **massive open online courses (MOOCs)**. The information shared is designed to help you create engaging, active digital learning experiences, whether you are a full-time online instructor or are suddenly forced to move your course online due to an emergency.

What Is This Book?

This book is called a "guide" to online learning for a reason. Online learning has no step-by-step instructions. Every online teacher has to find what works best for their unique mix of teaching style, content area, learner demographics, and individual learner personalities. With that being said, the subtitle of the book starts with "Practical Strategies," as its focus is on the how-tos of online learning.

Just as resources for K–12 online learning are scarce, so is the research. The literature on online learning is fairly extensive but mostly focused on higher education. Therefore, the how-to elements of the book are backed by the research that is available for K–12 online learning, research on online learning in higher education, and personal experiences with online learning.

How To Use This Book

I know your time is limited and valuable, so the book is organized into four parts to ensure you can find the information you need:

- **"Part 1: Introduction"** sets the stage for the remainder of the book with important definitions, key takeaways, and the learner perspective.

- **"Part 2: Foundations"** focuses on foundational elements at the base of the online learning pyramid. Without this base, your online learning pyramid will crumble!

- **"Part 3: Strategies"** dives into the day-to-day instructional strategies of an online course.

- **"Part 4: Best Practices"** digs deeper into specific groups of learners.

The end of each chapter includes pre-populated reflection questions. Use these reflection questions to determine your top takeaways and create a plan for implementation. If you thrive with accountability, use the hashtag #TeachersGuideToOnline to share your reflections via social media. If you need guidance on how to implement the strategies or would like to share these strategies with others, contact me at intechgratedpd.org to discuss training options.

For easy access, I have curated all resources provided throughout the book, including examples and templates, on a single web page at intechgratedpd.org/vip. In addition to the resources, all graphics from the book are available for download in full color on the same web page.

If you take away one thing from this book, reading it will have been a successful learning experience.

Grade-Level Terminology

I am based in the United States, but I work with educators all over the world. The terminology describing grade and age levels of students varies from country to country. To create uniformity, I will use the descriptions below:

- **Elementary school** refers to grades kindergarten–5 with students typically aged 5–11. Elementary school can be split into primary (grades K–2, ages 5–8) and intermediate (grades 3–5, ages 8–11).
- **Secondary school** refers to grades 6–12 with students generally aged 11–18. Secondary can be split into middle school (grades 6–8, ages 11–14) and high school (grades 9–12, ages 14–18).
- **Higher education** or **postsecondary** refers to continuing adult education, typically at universities or colleges.

Icons

Icons have been added throughout the book to call attention to specific types of content:

EQUITY

Content where equity could be discussed

ACCESSIBILITY

Content specific to the accessibility of learning materials

REFLECTION QUESTIONS

Questions throughout to help you reflect on how the content can be applied to your unique learning environment

STUDENT DATA PRIVACY AND SECURITY

Content that relates to student data privacy and security

TIPS

Any suggestions or best practices

Chapter 3: A Pep Talk

As I begin to write this it is early August 2020. Every school in the United States is grappling with the decision of whether to return to face-to-face school or go back to the full-time online learning that was forced upon them in early 2020. I have heard only a handful of positive experiences from this unexpected time of online learning from teachers, students, and parents; few want to return to the same remote learning scenario. Before we start into the book, I think we all need a little pep talk.

Online learning can be really great! For real. I completed my entire master's degree online, and I loved it.

Because of the crisis learning we experienced in early 2020, online learning seems to have gotten a bad rap. In "The Difference Between Emergency Remote Teaching and Online Learning," it is stated that "well-planned online learning experiences are meaningfully different from courses offered online in response to a crisis or disaster."[1]

John Hattie reviewed meta-analyses to evaluate the effect size of different influences on the learning process.[2] The higher the effect size, the greater the positive effect on learning. According to *The Distance Learning Playbook*, the effect size of distance learning is 0.14.[3] This means that online learning does not significantly improve the learning process, but it doesn't have a negative effect either. However, it is important to note that the studies used to determine the effect size of online learning involved well-planned online courses, not crisis learning or emergency remote learning.

> ## What we experienced in 2020 was not online learning.
> ## It was crisis learning.

---

1   Charles Hodges et al., "The Difference Between Emergency Remote Teaching and Online Learning," EDUCAUSE, March 27, 2020, https://er.educause.edu/articles/2020/3/the-difference-between-emergency-remote-teaching-and-online-learning.

2   John Hattie, *Visible Learning: A Synthesis of Over 800 Meta-Analyses Relating to Achievement* (New York: Routledge, 2009).

3   Douglas Fisher, Nancy Frey, and John Hattie, *The Distance Learning Playbook, Grades K-12: Teaching for Engagement and Impact in Any Setting* (Thousand Oaks, CA: Corwin, 2021), 5.

This is my plea to you: go into this book with an open mind, having wiped from your brain any preconceived notions of online learning. Can online learning be a bad experience? You bet. And so can face-to-face learning. I am sure everyone reading this has had a bad face-to-face learning experience.

I have had countless bad face-to-face learning experiences! There is good and bad online learning just as there is good and bad face-to-face learning. In fact, you will find that you have students who thrive in online learning just as you have students who thrive in face-to-face learning.

Here is the fact of the matter. To create quality online learning experiences, can you re-create a typical face-to-face learning day for K–12 students? Absolutely not. I am not saying it is easy to create online learning experiences, but it is doable. It requires an open mind and a willingness to change. **You can do this.**

Chapter 4: The Learning Continuum

Before we dive into the world of facilitating online learning, let's make sure we are all on the same page regarding some definitions. Bear with me here, because this is important information.

Online learning is learning that occurs over the internet with no face-to-face interaction between the teacher and learner. Online learning may also be referred to as e-learning, remote learning, virtual learning, or distance learning. Online learning means all content, learning tasks, communication, and collaboration occur virtually.

Face-to-face learning is learning that occurs with the learner and teacher in the same physical space. Face-to-face learning may also be referred to as in-person learning or brick-and-mortar learning. If we were to make a continuum of learning models, face-to-face learning would be on one end and online learning would be on the other end, as shown in *Figure 4.1*.

What about the middle? That is where **blended learning** comes in. Blended learning is any combination of face-to-face learning and online learning. What does that do to our continuum of learning environments? *Figure 4.2* shows the final learning continuum. Everything in the middle is some form of blended learning.

You may have heard the phrase **hybrid learning**; this term exploded in 2020. The Aurora Institute (formerly iNACOL) defines blended learning as follows: "Blended learning, also referred to as hybrid learning, combines the best features of traditional schooling with the advantages

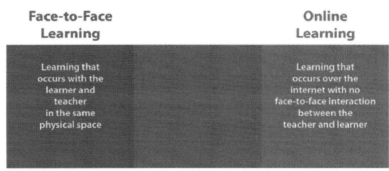

Figure 4.1: Face-to-Face and Online Learning

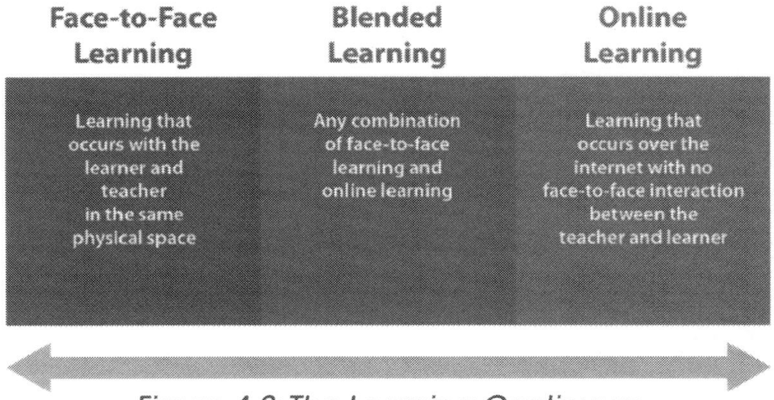

Figure 4.2: The Learning Continuum

of online learning to deliver personalized, differentiated instruction across a group of learners."[4] Therefore, any mention of blended learning will encompass hybrid learning and vice versa.

Almost every person in the world understands face-to-face learning because that is what the vast majority of people have experienced. Are there many different ways to teach face-to-face? Not many . . . millions! However, most people can picture what face-to-face learning *generally* looks like.

Similarly, online learning is fairly clear. Although, if you have never experienced a *good* online course, it may be hard to see how this is an awesome, meaningful, engaging learning experience.

Blended learning is much fuzzier. "Any combination of online and face-to-face learning" covers a lot! Because of this, it helps to have blended learning models. I am going to take a small detour into the world of blended learning. I promise it will soon make sense why.

Blended Learning

As noted in the Aurora Institute's definition of blended learning, a large focus of blended learning is on differentiating, individualizing, or personalizing learning:

- **Differentiated learning** utilizes the differences and similarities among learners to provide learning options in terms of process, product, and/or content for *groups* of learners.
- **Individualized learning** is a learning environment where learners move at their own pace to accomplish the *same* learning goals.
- **Personalized learning** is learning that is tailored specifically to the needs, preferences, and interests of *individual* learners.

On the surface, these terms may sound almost the same, but in fact, they are very different. Differentiated learning is equivalent to groups of learners and pieces of learning. Individualized learning adds the element of pace. Personalized learning is the entire learning process. ***Figure 4.3*** summarizes the differences in each.

According to the Christensen Institute (another leader in blended learning research), there are seven blended learning models. The best explanation of these seven

---

4   Allison Powell et al., *Blending Learning: The Evolution of Online and Face-to-Face Education from 2008–2015* (International Association for K–12 Online Learning, 2015), https://aurora-institute.org/wp-content/uploads/iNACOL _Blended-Learning-The-Evolution-of-Online-And-Face-to-Face-Education-from-2008-2015.pdf.

	Learning Goals	Pace	Content	Process	Product
Differentiated			X	X	X
Individualized		X	X	X	X
Personalized	X	X	X	X	X

Figure 4.3: Differentiated versus Individualized versus Personalized Learning

models that I have found is on the Blended Learning Universe website (blendedlearning.org/models) from the Christensen Institute.[5] Each model is briefly summarized below, but refer to the Blended Learning Universe website for more details:

- **Station rotation**—Learners rotate through stations with at least one station focusing on an online learning component. Since stations group learners together, this model supports differentiated instruction. Focus is mostly on the face-to-face time.
- **Lab rotation**—Similar to the station rotation, learners rotate through stations, but the online learning component is completed in a specific location, usually a lab environment. Lab rotation models typically support differentiated environments.
- **Individual rotation**—Learners rotate through stations on individualized schedules rather than in groups. The individual rotation model can support an individualized or personalized environment.
- **Flipped classroom**—Learners gain content knowledge via online coursework and lectures (usually at home), and face-to-face time is used for teacher-guided projects. Focus is equally on the online component and face-to-face time.
- **Flex**—Learners move through learning activities according to their specific needs. Learners have a high level of control over their learning, and the focus is on the online component. The flex model typically supports personalized instruction.
- **À la carte**—Learners are in a traditional face-to-face learning environment but may take fully online courses in addition to their face-to-face courses. The online focus depends on how many online courses the learner is completing.
- **Enriched virtual**—Learners complete most coursework online outside of a physical school building but also have supplemental face-to-face learning sessions with a teacher. The focus is on online learning. This model supports individualized or personalized learning.

---

5   "Blended Learning Models," Clayton Christensen Institute, accessed November 18, 2020, https://www.blendedlearning.org/models.

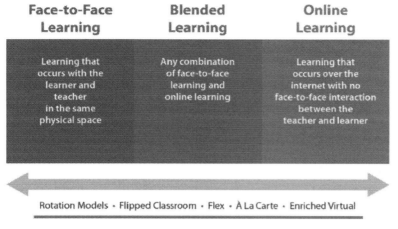

Face-to-Face Learning	Blended Learning	Online Learning
Learning that occurs with the learner and teacher in the same physical space	Any combination of face-to-face learning and online learning	Learning that occurs over the internet with no face-to-face interaction between the teacher and learner

Rotation Models · Flipped Classroom · Flex · À La Carte · Enriched Virtual

Figure 4.4: Blended Learning Models on the Learning Continuum

Keep in mind that these models are not the be-all and end-all of what blended learning can look like. In fact, some learning institutions that utilize blended learning use a mix of these models (yes, a blended, blended model)! Also notice that several of the blended models assume students are in a physical school building for most or all of the learning time. This is where the water becomes murky. Students are experiencing an online component but in a physical school building.

Now that you understand the seven blended models, let's place them on our learning continuum from those that focus more on face-to-face learning to those that focus more on online learning, as shown in **Figure 4.4**.

Now, there could be a lot of debate here. For example, I lumped the rotation models together, but one could argue that the individual rotation model is more online-focused than the flipped classroom model. However, this is really not the point. The point is to show that blended models have varying focuses on face-to-face and online learning, with the rotation models having the most focus on the face-to-face learning component and the enriched virtual model having the most focus on the online learning component.

 Why did we take this small detour into the world of blended learning? By understanding that all blended learning has an online component, you can apply many of the strategies shared in this book to the online component of a blended course. For example, an enriched virtual blended model will use many of the strategies in this book since its focus is on the online component.

Therefore, even though this book focuses on online learning, keep in mind that many of these strategies can be used at different points on the learning continuum either as is or with slight adjustments.

By learning new teaching strategies, you are always investing in your professional self.

How Does Learning Change across the Continuum?

As you begin your journey into online teaching, it is important to focus on the big picture when thinking about how the teaching and learning process changes. **One thing is clear:**

> ## Do not replicate face-to-face instruction in an online environment.

You cannot shift from face-to-face to online learning without changing elements of the learning experience. If your online course is a clone of your face-to-face course, you and your students will not enjoy online learning! The learning process is not something that can simply slide from face-to-face to online without transforming in some way. Gurley states, "Teaching in blended and online learning environments requires different pedagogical approaches than teaching in face-to-face learning environments."[6] If you currently teach a face-to-face course, that course will have to be reimagined in order for it to be a successful online course. If this makes you feel at a bit of a loss, fret not! That is what this book is for.

I find it helpful to think about what elements of the learning experience need to be changed for different learning environments. Analyzing the elements of instructional tools, instructional strategies, and the pillars of teaching helps me design learning experiences across the continuum.

➡ *Instructional Tools and Strategies*

No matter the learning model followed (face-to-face, online, or blended), the digital instructional tools used remain mostly the same across the learning continuum. If you were one of the lucky teachers in 2020 that had to convert your course from face-to-face to online overnight, you may be thinking, "That can't be true, because I had to learn new tools in order to teach online!" That is why I say *mostly*. This depends on factors such as how your personal face-to-face learning looks. For example, a teacher that rarely uses digital tools in face-to-face learning will have to master new tools to teach online. However, once that teacher integrates digital instructional tools into online learning, I guarantee that teacher will start integrating the same digital tools into their face-to-face learning.

---

6   Lisa E. Gurley, "Educators' Preparation to Teach, Perceived Teaching Presence, and Perceived Teaching Presence Behaviors in Blended and Online Learning Environments," *Online Learning* 22, no. 2 (June 2018): 197–220, https://doi.org/10.24059/olj.v22i2.1255.

Face-to-Face Learning	Blended Learning	Online Learning
Learning that occurs with the learner and teacher in the same physical space	Any combination of face-to-face learning and online learning	Learning that occurs over the internet with no face-to-face interaction between the teacher and learner

Digital Instructional Tools = Same   Strategy = Different

Figure 4.5: What Changes as Learning Moves along the Continuum?

Face-to-Face Learning	Blended Learning	Online Learning
Learning that occurs with the learner and teacher in the same physical space	Any combination of face-to-face learning and online learning	Learning that occurs over the internet with no face-to-face interaction between the teacher and learner

Harder →

← **Easier**

Figure 4.6: Adjusting Strategies along the Learning Continuum

In a 2020 survey conducted by the Christensen Institute, 79 percent of teachers indicated that they had discovered new resources during the COVID-19 school closures and planned to continue using those resources post-pandemic.[7]

What really changes as we move along the learning continuum is the *strategy*, as shown in **Figure 4.5**. Remember that the effect size of online learning is 0.14, and as Fisher, Frey, and Hattie explain, "What is far more important are the methods of teaching that spark learning, not the medium."[8]

Many of the instructional strategies used in face-to-face learning must morph as a course moves toward the online learning end of the continuum. I find that it is easier to move right to left as opposed to left to right across the continuum, as illustrated in **Figure 4.6**.

Many online learning strategies can work in a face-to-face environment, but many face-to-face strategies will fall flat in an online environment.

7   Thomas Arnett, "In 2021, Teachers Hold a Key to Transforming Conventional Instruction," *Clayton Christensen Institute* (blog), accessed February 10, 2021, https://www.christenseninstitute.org/blog/in-2021-teachers-hold-a-key-to-transforming-conventional-instruction/.

8   Fisher, Frey, and Hattie, *The Distance Learning Playbook*, 5.

Pillars of Teaching

If you were to write down every instruction-related task a teacher performs over the course of a normal day and then organize those tasks into groups, you might come up with these four categories: content delivery, assessment, feedback, and social-emotional learning (SEL). It helps me to think of these four categories as the "pillars of teaching," as illustrated in *Figure 4.7*.

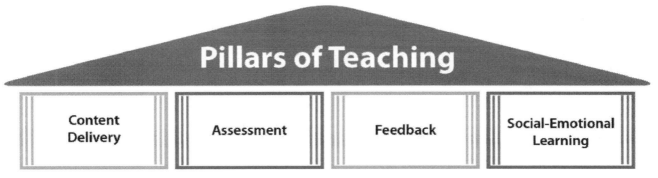

Figure 4.7: Pillars of Teaching

Guess what? These pillars of teaching do not change as learning moves across the learning continuum. If I am a teacher, it doesn't matter if I am teaching in a face-to-face, online, or blended model: I am still spending my instructional time on content delivery, assessment, feedback, and SEL.

Let's add the pillars of teaching to the "What Changes as Learning Moves along the Continuum?" graphic, as illustrated in *Figure 4.8*.

The digital instructional tools and the pillars of teaching remain the same across the learning continuum. The instructional strategies change at different points on the continuum. This means that in order to shift from teaching face-to-face to teaching online, you need to learn some new instructional strategies. That just so happens to be a large focus of this book.

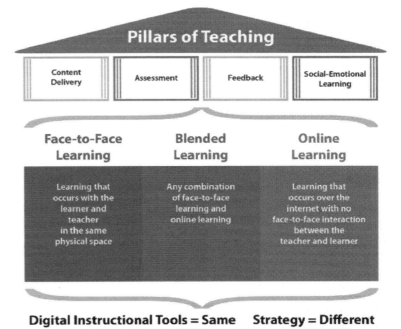

Figure 4.8: Part 2—What Changes as Learning Moves along the Continuum?

Summary

This section outlines the most important parts from the chapter:

- Face-to-face learning is learning that occurs with the learner and teacher in the same physical space. Online learning is learning that occurs over the internet with no face-to-face interaction between the teacher and learner. Blended or hybrid learning is any combination of face-to-face learning and online learning. These three learning environments make up the learning continuum.

- By understanding that all blended learning has an online component, you can apply many of the strategies shared in this book to the online component of a blended course.

- You cannot shift from face-to-face to online learning without changing elements of the learning experience.

- Analyzing the elements of instructional tools, instructional strategies, and the pillars of teaching helps determine what elements of the learning experience need to be changed for different learning environments.

- Digital instructional tools remain mostly the same across the learning continuum. What really changes is the *strategy*.

- There are four pillars of teaching: content delivery, assessment, feedback, and social-emotional learning (SEL). These pillars do not change as learning moves across the learning continuum.

- Many online learning strategies can work in a face-to-face environment, but many face-to-face strategies will fall flat in an online environment.

- By learning new teaching strategies, you are always investing in your professional self.

Reflection

After reading "Chapter 4: The Learning Continuum," reflect on how the content can be applied to your unique learning environment.

Share your reflections online using the **hashtag #TeachersGuideToOnline**. A hashtag is a word or phrase preceded by a hash sign (#) to identify digital content on a specific topic.

What terminology is your educational institution using to describe your learning environment?

Do you have any digital tools that you utilize for face-to-face learning that you could potentially use in your online courses as well?

What is getting in the way of personalized or individualized learning in your course(s)?

Chapter 5: Key Takeaways

As 2020 crept along at turtle speed, I spent the majority of my time helping teachers make sense of online learning. I found myself repeating similar statements over and over again, and these statements became the key takeaways of online learning. The key takeaways are the essence of online learning design. In fact, they are so important that I already introduced the first one in "Chapter 4: The Learning Continuum"! I will introduce and explain each throughout the book. The key takeaways are listed below and displayed in **Figure 5.1**:

- Do not replicate face-to-face instruction in an online environment.

- Understanding when to use synchronous learning and when to use asynchronous learning is key to designing successful online learning.

- Every student does not have to do the exact same thing at the exact same time.

- Within the same time period, you cannot cover as much in online learning as you can in face-to-face. You must whittle your curriculum down to the most essential learning objectives.

- In online learning environments, proximity is not in your favor. You cannot stand over a learner's shoulder and ensure a task is accomplished.

- Face-to-face learning is more forgiving than online learning. Therefore, you have to be more strategic with online learning.

- Your personality is one of your strengths as a teacher—find ways to let it shine in a digital environment!

- Organization and consistency are critical to online learning.

- Maslow before you Bloom! You must focus on the social-emotional side of learning.

- Relationship building does not come naturally in online learning as it does in face-to-face. Therefore, you have to be intentional about consistently embedding relationship building activities into online learning.

- Use technology to duplicate yourself to all learners regardless of when and where they are learning.

- You must maintain regular contact with learners.

- In order for online learning to be successful, you must shift control from teacher to student.

Reflection

After reading "Chapter 5: Key Takeaways," reflect on how the content can be applied to your unique learning environment.

Share your reflections online using the hashtag **#TeachersGuideToOnline**.

(?) **What is your initial reaction to the key takeaways?**

(?) **What do you think is meant by "proximity is not in your favor" when it comes to online learning?**

(?) **How could you use technology to duplicate yourself to all learners regardless of when and where they are learning?**

KEY TAKEAWAYS

Do not replicate face-to-face instruction in an online environment.

Understanding when to use synchronous learning and when to use asynchronous learning is key to designing successful online learning.

Every student does not have to do the exact same thing at the exact same time.

Within the same time period, you cannot cover as much in online learning as you can in face-to-face. You must whittle your curriculum down to the most essential learning objectives.

In online learning environments, proximity is not in your favor. You cannot stand over a learner's shoulder and ensure a task is accomplished.

Face-to-face learning is more forgiving than online learning. Therefore, you have to be more strategic with online learning.

Your personality is one of your strengths as a teacher - find ways to let it shine in a digital environment!

Organization and consistency are critical to online learning.

Maslow before you Bloom! You must focus on the social-emotional side of learning.

Relationship building does not come naturally in online learning as it does in face-to-face. Therefore, you have to be intentional about consistently embedding relationship building activities into online learning.

Use technology to duplicate yourself to all learners regardless of when and where they are learning.

You must maintain regular contact with learners.

In order for online learning to be successful, you must shift control from teacher to student.

Figure 5.1: Key Takeaways

Chapter 6: The Learner Perspective

A book about how to teach online wouldn't be complete without sharing the perspective of the student. After all, learners are the most important stakeholders in online learning. The goal of this chapter is to keep the student perspective at the forefront of your mind as you read this book and as you design your online courses.

To gather the perspectives of online learners, I conducted an anonymous survey of students aged 5–18. I wanted to know what students think about online learning. What do they enjoy? What do they not enjoy? Below is each survey question followed by a summary of the answers received.

→ *What Is Your Age in Years?*

Respondents' ages ranged from 5–18. For those who were too young to type their own answers, an adult caregiver transcribed their answers.

→ *Briefly Explain Your Experiences with Online/Remote Learning.*

Most respondents had their first experience with online learning in early 2020. Of these, about half were still in full online learning.

A handful of students had experienced online learning prior to the forced school closures of early 2020.

→ *What Did You Like about Online/Remote Learning?*

The answers to this question were clearly divided into three camps:

1. Some could be summarized as relating to either "fun activities" or "projects." For example, "doing fun activities like making arts and crafts" or "we did the egg drop project and that was fun."

2. Some responded along the lines of enjoying the time, freedom, and comfort that come with online learning, such as being able to complete their schoolwork when they wanted, at their own pace, or from the comfort of home. For example, "I liked how I could just finish all my lessons at the time I chose rather than having to wait an entire day," and "I liked sleeping in and being done early."

3. Some said they liked "nothing" or "none of it" when referring to their experiences with online learning.

What Did You Not Like about Online/Remote Learning?

Many responses were related to "too many assignments" or "it was harder." There were references to having to "even work on weekends" in order to get all the assignments done. For example:

- "I did not like how it was not interactive with me, and it was a little harder to learn."

- "I had a hard time focusing."

There were a few responses that mentioned disliking "packets." For example:

- "They just sent packets home. We didn't even have a computer. It would have been better if I would have had a computer, because my teacher could have talked to me on ClassDojo or we could have used Google Classroom. We can talk to each other on that too. We didn't use anything like that."

A few respondents said they disliked that certain classes did not continue online:

- "All they gave us was math and reading. I wish we would have still had other subjects like art and music and PE."

- "I did not like that extracurricular activities were canceled."

Other responses included:

- "I am not good at learning by just reading and that is all my teacher gave."

- "My school was new at teaching online, and they didn't make it fun."

- "No video calls."

- "I do not enjoy sharing my camera. I understand that the teachers feel weird without the other face online, but has it ever occurred to them that I might feel weird sharing my face?"

What Would Have Made It a Better Experience?

Many of the responses mentioned "less assignments" or "not so many assignments."

> Within the same time period, you cannot cover as much in online learning as you can in face-to-face. You must whittle your curriculum down to the most essential learning objectives.

Several respondents expressed the desire for more interaction. For example:

- "If some activities were more fun and exciting and if the teacher was more interactive."

- "More interaction with my teachers."

- "Live lessons with my teachers."

Other responses included:

- "My teacher didn't do any Zoom calls. It would have been better if she would have done Zoom calls and taught us and explained the lesson in the Zoom call. Then, when the Zoom call is over, we could do our assignment."

- "My teacher just did videos of someone else explaining what you were supposed to learn. It would have been better if my teacher had made the videos."

- "Sending home our Chromebooks that we have when we are at school."

- "Many of the assignments were easier to do on paper than trying to do them on my tablet."

- "If our work would have been related to something real like we use [sic] to do every day at school."

For the Things You Did Not Like, Could Your Teacher(s) Have Done Anything Different to Make It Better?

Several of the responses related to explaining concepts. For example:

- "Explain things to me more than just give me work."

- "Video chatting and talking about the subject."

Several responses related to completing projects. For example:

- "Instead of just reading and stuff if we did more projects [*sic*]."

- "If she just gave us instructions and what we needed, we could have done projects. For example, we did the egg drop project. I want more of those types of projects."

Other responses expressed frustration at not being able to talk to their teacher or classmates. For example:

- "I didn't even get to talk to my teacher. My teacher only messaged my parents. It would have been better if I would have been able to talk to my teacher."

- "I didn't get to talk to my classmates, that would have made it better."

There were also several responses acknowledging that teachers were doing their best and needed more time.

What Was Your Favorite Learning Activity, If Any?

The answers here were all over the place but mostly focused on hands-on, interactive, and fun activities. A few examples:

- "Mystery Doug videos because it tells [*sic*] you about things like how does hair grow and why are people so scared of bugs and a bunch of other videos like that. It tells me new information I didn't know like how to tell if plants are poisonous. That can really help because you can miss out on some really good berries if you don't know how to tell if a plant is poisonous."

- "I really liked the social studies activities, because I like to write the information on the Google Slides because it's a little easier with the platform."

- "Going on a treasure hunt online."

- "Nothing because all they gave us was math and reading."

- "Arts and crafts."

- "Anything that was hands-on."

- "Math, I got to do Khan Academy."

- "Probably civics, the teacher makes it easy and fun."

- "I liked that we put on a few SNL shows for my playwriting and theater classes. We were able to plan, write, and even act over [*sic*] our meetings and individual recordings. Nice team effort with a realistic and worthwhile purpose."

What Was Your Least Favorite Learning Activity, If Any?

There were many answers related to reading and math. For example:

- "Too many reading assignments."

- "Reading."

- "Too much reading."

- "I was not as intrigued with math, because I did not really learn many new things."

Other responses included:

- "I had to do spelling tests and minusing [sic] and adding on my tablet, so it was basically like I was doing it on paper but instead I had to do it on my tablet, which was harder."

Was Online/Remote Learning Fun? If So, What Made It Fun? If Not, What Do You Think Would Have Made It Fun?

Overall, this was a resounding "no" or "not really" because "I missed my friends" or "kind of because I got to sleep in." There were a few semi-yes answers, such as "[s]ome classes were fun. It mainly depends on the subject and if I find genuine interest in it. As well as if the teacher is upbeat."

Is There Anything Else You Would Like to Share about Online/Remote Learning?

There were lots of "I don't know" or "not really" responses here, along with a smattering of other responses:

- "Having my Chromebook would have at least been better because then I could have at least typed my answers."

- "The online learning did not challenge me."

What Can We Take from This Survey?

Overall, the majority of responses received were no surprise to me, but there were two things that stood out:

1. The desire for real-time interaction—It was surprising to me that those students who didn't have a real-time, interactive component to their online learning experience craved that attention. I am curious if this is primarily due to the isolation experienced in 2020 or if this is a common desire of online learners. I suspect this perspective may be different in K–12 versus higher education, but that is nothing more than my anecdotal observations. There seems to be little research in this area.

2. The struggle with certain technologies and certain digital learning tasks—I was surprised that several students seemed to make the connection that completing digital tasks that could otherwise be done on paper is cumbersome and unnecessary. Some respondents said some form of "it would have been easier to do on paper." This tells me that merely slotting technology into a task that can be completed non-digitally can be more detrimental to learning than helpful. It was

also interesting that some students made the connection that certain devices don't work well for certain learning tasks. For example, there was a reference to having to use a personal tablet and "just needing a keyboard."

I won't lie, my heart hurt a little when I read the "nothing" responses to the question: "What did you like about online learning?" (By the way, my own nieces were in that camp.) However, when I reflected, I realized that many of those answers were most likely in response to the crisis learning of 2020. I had to remind myself that those students did not experience true online learning. This further motivated me to finish this book.

What was not surprising to me was that students want learning to be "fun," and this doesn't change when moving across the learning continuum. Learners respond to online learning that is hands-on and piques their interest. The best learning happens when the student doesn't realize they are learning.

Summary

This section outlines the most important parts from the chapter:

- Keep the student perspective at the forefront of your mind as you continue through this book and as you design your online courses.

- Merely slotting technology into a task that can be completed non-digitally can be more detrimental to learning than helpful.

- Learners respond to online learning that is hands-on and piques their interest.

Reflection

After reading "Chapter 6: The Learner Perspective," reflect on how the content can be applied to your unique learning environment.

Share your reflections online using the hashtag **#TeachersGuideToOnline**.

How can feedback from online learners guide your online course design?

How could you make your online courses hands-on?

Making decisions regarding the organization of your online course should be among the first steps taken when designing online learning.

Equity means making sure every student has the support they need in order to be successful.

Part 2:
FOUNDATIONS

Chapter 7: Considerations for Learning Design

There are certain factors that drive every decision when it comes to learning design. One important factor is equity. When you add technology to the learning design, student data privacy becomes another overarching consideration. I am beginning this book with a discussion of these two key factors, as they should drive every decision you make with your online course planning. You might be tempted to skip past this section and jump right to the strategies, but please stay with me here!

This information is incredibly important.

Equity

When planning and designing online learning, equity should be at the forefront of all decisions. The definition of **equity**, according to Merriam-Webster, is "justice according to natural law or right."[9] What does that mean in the context of education? Equity means making sure every student has the support they need in order to be successful. It means understanding that individual needs vary from person to person, and systems have to be established that ensure every learner has an opportunity for success.

On one hand, online learning can be very equitable, as it provides access to high-quality learning regardless of time or place. In our modern world, this has mostly benefited postsecondary students, allowing those who live in rural areas or who work full-time jobs to continue their education. The K–12 world has also seen some of these benefits, for example by providing more course options to small schools or allowing youth athletes to continue intensive training.

On the other hand, online learning presents several equity challenges that both educational institutions and teachers need to consider. Some of these factors may be largely out of your control (e.g., access to technology); however, there are aspects of equity where even small tweaks from you as a teacher can make a big difference.

---

9   *Merriam-Webster*, s.v. "equity (*n.*)," accessed November 18, 2020, https://www.merriam-webster.com/dictionary/equity.

Home Environments and Personal Lives

Home environments and personal lives are not equitable. That should be no surprise to anyone. However, what is not always obvious is how large an effect personal lives have on online learning, especially in K–12 environments. With face-to-face learning, students are typically placed in the same physical environment and have a supervising adult to guide the learning process in real time. This isn't the case in online learning.

 As an online teacher, you have to be intentional about designing learning experiences that don't require a specific type of home environment or personal schedule for success.

Access to Technology

This includes access to quality devices as well as the internet. Has your educational institution made plans to ensure all learners have this access?

Devices

Will all students be provided a school-issued device? This is referred to as **one-to-one (1:1)** or a 1:1 model. Will they be required to provide their own device? This is known as **bring your own device (BYOD)** or a BYOD model. BYOD models are not equitable and can be challenging for teachers to manage. In a BYOD environment, students will be using devices with different **operating systems (OS)**. An operating system is the software that supports the basic functions of a device. Operating systems that your students would most likely be using include any of the following:

- Windows OS
- Mac OS
- Chrome OS (Chromebooks)

- iOS (iPads and iPhones)
- Android OS
- Fire OS (Kindle devices; rare but still a possibility)

Some tools are compatible with certain operating systems and not others. For example, there may be a tool that has an iOS app but not an Android app. That means it will work for iOS devices but potentially not for Android devices. Therefore, if your educational institution is not providing devices to your students, consider designing your digital learning opportunities to be **device agnostic**. This simply means the tool is not tied to a particular device and is therefore accessible on any device or operating system.

Looking for web-based tools is a smart strategy for ensuring that a tool is device agnostic. A **web browser**, or browser, provides access to the internet. Examples of web browsers include Google Chrome, Mozilla Firefox, Microsoft Edge, and Apple Safari. A **web-based**

 digital tool works in a web browser and requires no downloads. It's even better if the tool has a mobile app available for the two largest mobile operating systems—iOS and Android OS. Not every household is going to have access to a nonmobile device (Windows OS, Mac OS, or Chrome OS), but the majority of households these days have at least one smartphone. Choosing digital tools that are web-based is a small way you can try to improve equity in BYOD learning environments.

 If you are navigating a BYOD environment, leverage the knowledge of your educational institution's technology team.

In addition to access itself, the quality of the device, such as its processing power and speed, is another consideration whether students are using a personal or school-issued device. This is a common issue for some low-cost devices. The device may not have the processing power to run multiple programs at the same time. For example, imagine you are on a video call with students, and you want students to complete a collaborative activity using another digital tool. Some student devices may not be able to run a video call and the other tool at the same time.

Internet

A very real concern is that not all of your students will have internet access outside of a physical school building. In online learning, it is imperative that students have internet access from home.

This should be one of the first planning steps for online schools. It is also an important question to ask school leadership at an interview if you are applying to online teaching positions.

 Educational institutions are embracing many different solutions for home internet access. Providing students with mobile wireless hotspots to take home was a common solution in 2020. Kajeet (kajeet.net) is a company that has several solutions for wireless internet access for schools, including mobile internet hotspots and SmartBus vehicles. Kajeet's SmartBus is an example of a mobile wireless access point that can be parked in a community location for students to use; the idea has been particularly embraced in urban areas. Schools have also begun to partner with internet providers to offer discounted or free internet to homes with qualifying students. Your educational institution may need to get creative about how to provide internet access to all learners.

In addition to internet access, you also need to think about **internet bandwidth**, which is the maximum amount of data that can be transmitted over an internet connection in a specific amount of time. An internet connection with a higher bandwidth performs better than an internet connection with a lower bandwidth. Some internet activities require more bandwidth than others. For example, streaming video and video calls require a larger amount of bandwidth than browsing the internet does. Why is this important? Consider the following scenarios:

- Your student is one of multiple children at home who are all learning fully online.

- Your student has a parent who works from home.

In these scenarios, each person in the household may be asking a lot of their internet connection. What if you require your students to attend a video call as part of their course grade? What if that student can't connect to the video call due to bandwidth limits at their home?

When equity of internet access is discussed, it is often only discussed in black and white terms—access or no access. As a teacher, you also need to consider the bandwidth requirements of your course and ensure you aren't setting requirements that are out of reach for some learners.

Accessibility of Learning

Is learning accessible to all? Are all provided learning materials accessible to all learners? Accessibility isn't a new topic for educators. However, rethinking accessibility as it relates to online learning may be.

In order to ensure your learning experiences are accessible to all, I highly recommend reviewing the **Universal Design for Learning (UDL)** framework. UDL guides the learning design to ensure accessibility of learning to all. As Pearson and Koppi argue, "the needs of learners with disabilities should be addressed at the design stage rather than attempting to retrofit solutions."[10] This is the exact goal of UDL. Explore the UDL guidelines (udlguidelines.cast.org) for assistance implementing the framework.

UDL Guidelines

---

10   Elaine J. Pearson and Tony Koppi, "Inclusion and Online Learning Opportunities: Designing for Accessibility," *Research in Learning Technology* 10, no. 2 (2002), https://doi.org/10.3402/rlt.v10i2.11398.

In addition to using UDL for learning material design, here are a few quick tips for ensuring learning materials are accessible:

- All videos should have captions. Tips on adding captions will be provided in "Chapter 14: Maslow before You Bloom."

- Ensure you are creating accessible links. When text is linked within digital materials, screen readers identify the link, state "link," and then read whatever text the link is attached to. Therefore, according to WebAIM, links should be understandable when read out of context, be unique to the web page, and inform the user what will appear if the link is clicked.[11] Don't add links to text such as "click here" or "read more." This is uninformative and potentially not unique to the page. At the same time, don't overdescribe the link either. **Figure 7.1** provides an example of accessible link text. Never place a long URL directly into digital materials, as screen readers will read the entire URL—yikes! Also, stick to linking from text and avoid linking from graphics.

Accessible Link Text	*Uninformative Link Text*	*Overly Detailed Link Text*
Explore the UDL guidelines for assistance implementing the framework.	Click here for the UDL guidelines.	Here is the UDL guidelines page with a graphic of the framework guidelines broken into three categories.

Figure 7.1: Accessible Link Text

- All images need to have alternative text or **alt text**, which is text that describes an image. Alt text is read by screen readers in the place of an image. Alt text is usually very easy to add, but exactly how that is done depends on the program you are using. In word processing programs such as Microsoft

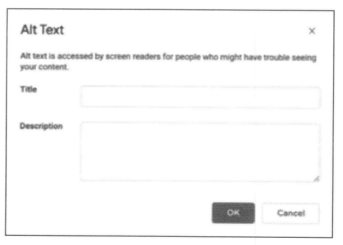

Figure 7.2: Alt Text Menu in Google Docs

---

11   "Links and Hypertext," WebAIM, accessed January 16, 2021, https://webaim.org/techniques /hypertext/.

Word and Google Docs, simply right click on an image and choose "Edit Alt Text" or "Alt Text," respectively. **Figure 7.2** shows the alt text menu in Google Docs. Give the image a title and add a description of what is found in the image.

As you are building and curating learning materials, you can use **accessibility checkers** to ensure the materials are accessible. Accessibility checkers flag common accessibility concerns, such as missing alt text for images. The accessibility checker used depends on several factors:

- For Microsoft Office users: Microsoft Office documents (as well as other tools in the Microsoft 365 suite, such as Sway) have a built-in accessibility checker, usually found under the "Review" tab.

- For Google Workspace users: Grackle Docs (grackledocs.com) is an add-on that can be used in Google Docs, Slides, and Sheets to flag accessibility issues.

- For websites: WebAIM has an accessibility checker for websites titled WAVE (wave.webaim.org).

Remember that throughout this book, specific points related to accessibility will be highlighted with the pink heart icon.

➡ Adult Support

This is a consideration for those teaching in K–12 environments. Is your course designed in a way that learners can complete learning tasks with minimal adult support? The answer to this will vary drastically depending on many factors, such as the age of your learners and if learning tasks are synchronous or asynchronous. As the course designer, you do not want to create a situation where success in your course is dependent on adult support, as many learners may have little to no adult support during their online learning journey.

➡ Access to Learning Materials

Another factor to consider in regard to equity is the access students have to materials needed for learning aside from a device and an internet connection. In online learning, you can't simply hand students needed materials. If your course is particularly hands-on or if you want to assign non-digital tasks, be sure to consider equity. For example, if I am assigning a design challenge, I can't assume that every student will have glue, scissors, and construction paper at their disposal. Below are two ideas for approaching equity in regard to accessing materials:

1. Can you create learning opportunities that use regular household items but don't require anything specific?

2. Can you send home "learning kits" that include items your students could use over and over again or for specific projects?

For option 1, make sure to provide lots of options and flexibility. For example, if I wanted students to cook a meal, I might provide several suggestions but not require a specific recipe that needed specific ingredients.

Option 2 may not be an option for every teacher, but I encourage you to send home learning kits if you can. Below is a sample kit for an elementary-aged student:

- Crayons/markers/colored pencils
- Pencils/pens
- Highlighters
- Construction paper
- Glue
- Play-Doh or other sculpting material

- Maker supplies such as pipe cleaners and rubber bands
- A handheld whiteboard and dry-erase markers
- A coding kit
- Supplies for at-home science experiments

Learning kits are especially important if you teach a class that is particularly hands-on, such as art or career and technical education content. Of course, there are logistics to plan, such as how the kits will get into the hands of students. Mailing and/or providing at-home drop-off are the most equitable options. For example, I facilitated a virtual professional development session on creating e-textiles. We mailed a kit to each participant that included the essential items:

- Sewing needles
- Conductive thread
- Sewable battery packs

- Coin cell batteries
- LED sequins
- Alligator clips

Participants were expected to provide an article of clothing (anything, even a piece of fabric) and scissors. Participants were told ahead of time what materials they would need to provide. This is an example of what a learning kit could look like for high school level courses.

If you are part of an online school initiative, advocate for sending home learning kits as part of the planning and budget. If you are interviewing for an online teaching position, ask if the educational institution sends supplies home to students, and make sure this is included in the budget.

Is It an Engagement Problem or an Equity Problem?

If you have a student that disengages or seems unmotivated, you must analyze if the issue is engagement or equity. Let me provide an example: as an agriculture teacher, I assign all learners to create a visual guide of the plants in their neighborhood. A student doesn't complete the project. I could assume that the student is not motivated to complete her work. However, I instead ask the student how I can help her complete the task. The student explains that she lives in a neighborhood in which she doesn't feel comfortable walking around. Just like that, I have uncovered an equity, not an engagement, issue. I instruct this student to research the plants most likely found in the neighborhood/city/state instead.

These types of equity hurdles can occur in face-to-face learning too, but they seem to be more common in online learning. As an online teacher, keep equity at the forefront of your mind when teaching. The COVID-19 pandemic is shining a light on the issue of equity, and I hope it sparks change. Advocate to your educational institution for equity for all.

Remember that throughout this book, specific points related to equity will be highlighted with the purple circle icon.

Student Data Privacy

Disclaimer: This section is specific to my knowledge of student data privacy issues and concerns in the United States. If you are located in another country, make sure to do research regarding local student data privacy laws.

According to "The ABCs of Student Data Privacy for Administrators," by Andrew Bloom and Linnette Attai, "**Student data privacy** covers the use, collection, handling, and governance of students' personally identifiable information."[12] **Personally identifiable information (PII)** includes any information that can be

---

12   Andrew Bloom and Linnette Attai, *The ABCs of Student Data Privacy for Administrators* (McGraw Hill Education), accessed November 18, 2020, https://cosn.org/sites/default/files/Platform_Student_Privacy_White_Paper.pdf.

used to identify, locate, or contact a student, including name, address, birth date, student ID, academic information, and health records.

Student data privacy is a big deal because there are legal limitations on the handling of student PII. Issues of student data privacy have always been a concern; however, the topic has come to the forefront in recent years as schools use more and more technology and therefore collect more and more information electronically. In addition, many states have passed student data privacy laws.

Any digital tool used in any learning environment should meet federal and state student data privacy laws. Some educational institutions may have their own student data requirements as well. In the United States, there are three main federal laws that govern the regulation of student data:

- Children's Online Privacy Protection Act (COPPA)

- Family Educational Rights and Privacy Act (FERPA)

- Protection of Pupil Rights Amendment (PPRA)

If you work with students under the age of thirteen, COPPA will affect your online course, as it requires parental consent for websites that collect PII from students under the age of thirteen. Most likely your school has this covered already for approved websites, but make sure to consult with your school leaders.

FERPA relates to the access of student records. This shouldn't be an issue that comes up in the planning of an online course, but, again, be sure to consult with your school leaders.

PPRA involves parental review of surveys and evaluations that require the student to reveal sensitive subject matter (e.g., income, religion, political affiliations, etc.). This shouldn't be information collected in online courses and therefore should not be much of a concern.

Disclaimer: I am emphasizing "shouldn't" above, but you really never know. I am not a lawyer, and I am not giving legal advice.

State laws will most likely affect what digital tools you use for learning. Every state is different, so make sure to understand what student data privacy laws are in your state.

Throughout the book, content that could relate to student data privacy and may warrant further discussion with your educational institution will be highlighted by the blue lock icon.

Your educational institution's technology director is a good resource to learn about your state's student data privacy laws.

Even though policy varies from state to state, state laws regarding student data typically have common points:

- Governing the permissible activities of online service providers

- Prohibiting service providers and districts from selling or profiting from student PII

This means that you need to ask the questions below of any digital tool you use:

- Does the digital tool collect student PII? A good rule of thumb to know if student PII is being collected is if students have to create an account to use the tool or if you enter student information into the tool. Even if you determine that a digital tool does not collect student PII, it is still a good idea to review the privacy policy. Any reputable company will have their privacy policy posted on their website.

- If the tool does collect PII, what does the tool's privacy policy say they do with that information? This is the key to knowing whether a digital tool meets student data privacy standards or not. If the tool does not sell or profit from student PII, then that tool will most likely meet student data privacy standards; however, I heavily stress the phrase "most likely." Please do not take this to mean you can automatically use any tool that does not sell or profit from student PII. Please do your due diligence and research student data privacy requirements in your state carefully. It is a very complicated subject.

Many state laws require schools to establish privacy agreements with any digital resource that collects student PII before that tool can be used with students.

If your state is a member of the Student Data Privacy Consortium (SDPC), you can easily search the SDPC website (sdpc.a4l.org) for your state and see which companies have signed your state's standard privacy agreement.

Student Data Privacy Consortium

If you are teaching an online course that has learners in multiple states, make sure you are in compliance with each state's data privacy laws.

In conclusion, you may notice a theme within the information above—consult with your educational institution regarding student data privacy. This is another time to leverage the knowledge of the technology team at your educational institution. The big question to ask:

> ## What digital tools am I allowed and not allowed to use with learners?

There are two parts to educational technology: the technical and the instructional. The technical and instructional teams must collaborate and compromise. The instructional side needs access to the tools that are best for learning, and the technical side needs to ensure those tools are safe and manageable.

Summary

This section outlines the most important parts from the chapter:

- Equity and student data privacy are two factors that drive every decision when it comes to online learning design.

- Equity means making sure every student has the support they need in order to be successful.

- On one hand, online learning can be very equitable, as it provides access to high-quality learning regardless of time or place. On the other hand, online learning presents several equity challenges, such as disparities in home environments, personal lives, access to technology, accessibility of learning, adult support, and access to learning materials.

- If you have a student that disengages or seems unmotivated, you must analyze if the issue is engagement or equity.

- Student data privacy covers the use, collection, handling, and governance of students' personally identifiable information.

- Any digital tool used with students should meet student data privacy laws.

- Consult with your educational institution regarding student data privacy to determine which digital tools you can and cannot use.

Reflection

After reading "Chapter 7: Considerations for Learning Design," reflect on how the content can be applied to your unique learning environment.

Share your reflections online using the hashtag **#TeachersGuideToOnline**.

? **What can you do to ensure your online course is equitable?**

? **What is one strategy you can implement to make your learning materials more accessible?**

? **What student data privacy laws apply to your online course(s)?**

? **Do you know which digital tools you can and cannot use with students?**

? **Is there someone at your educational institution that you can consult regarding student data privacy information?**

Chapter 8:
Course Organization

Making decisions regarding the organization of your online course should be among the first steps taken when designing online learning.

Synchronous or Asynchronous?

There are two types of online learning: synchronous and asynchronous. This is one of the most important things to understand in order to be a successful online teacher, which means it is time for a new key takeaway:

> **Understanding when to use synchronous learning and when to use asynchronous learning is key to designing successful online learning.**

Synchronous learning is learning that happens in real time. Teachers and learners are engaged in learning at the same time in the same virtual learning environment. With synchronous learning, educators set a specific time for learners to meet. Meetings could be with the whole group, in small groups, or individually. Typically, synchronous learning is facilitated through a video conferencing tool, but it could also be conducted via a live chat format. The most common video conferencing tools in education at the time of writing are Google Meet, Microsoft Teams, and Zoom. We will discuss these tools in depth later in the book.

Asynchronous learning is when learners complete work related to the course on their own schedule. Asynchronous learning is harder to describe because it can take many different forms. Typically, educators provide learning materials and assign learning tasks that learners can review and

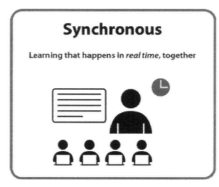
Synchronous
Learning that happens in *real time*, together

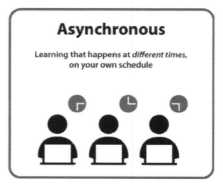
Asynchronous
Learning that happens at *different times*, on your own schedule

Figure 8.1: Synchronous versus Asynchronous

complete at their own pace within a designated time frame (e.g., one week). Throughout this time period, learners may collaborate using digital tools or watch a video and respond to a prompt. *Figure 8.1* illustrates synchronous versus asynchronous online learning.

Online learning does not have to be completely synchronous or completely asynchronous. There are endless options of blending synchronous and asynchronous learning to create an online course that works for you and your learners. For example, the required elements of the course could be asynchronous, with an optional one-hour synchronous all-class meeting every week. Alternately, the optional synchronous component could be virtual office hours where students can seek extra help or ask questions.

There are endless possibilities, but I will say that the most successful online courses I have experienced, both as a learner and as a teacher, are those that focused primarily on asynchronous online learning.

 Asynchronous learning tends to be more equitable. My recommendation to most online teachers is to focus on asynchronous online learning, with teacher office hours and an optional synchronous video call offered at least once per week. In fact, I highly recommend focusing on asynchronous learning whether your learning environment is face-to-face, blended, or fully online. This allows students to work at their own pace, even in face-to-face environments.

Later in the book, we will dive into specific strategies for synchronous and asynchronous online learning, and you will see how the different parts of your course best fit into each category.

Timeline

Consider how you will organize the timeline of your course. This is going to vary for every educational institution and class.

However, one tip for online learning is not to plan for individual days. This can be a challenging shift in mindset for teachers who have taught in traditional face-to-face learning environments. "Teacher Planners" are even divided into five blocks for the five days of the week! One of the chief benefits of online learning is that it allows for learning anytime, anywhere.

However, that very freedom makes balancing a specific daily schedule in online learning challenging for teachers, students, and students' families alike.

The fixed time of a class period or a school day is no longer a factor in online learning. This opens the door for providing lots of choice and flexibility to customize learning for students. Therefore, when planning the timeline of your online course, it is important to consider this key takeaway:

> **Every student does not have to do the exact same thing at the exact same time.**

➔ Timeline for Non-Individualized or Non-Personalized Learning Environments

Let's start by discussing a timeline for the scenario that is most common in education and is easiest for most teachers to envision: a non-individualized or non-personalized learning environment. This means that students are working at the same pace.

Regardless of a synchronous or asynchronous setup, a strong organizational strategy for online learning is to group learning tasks into time chunks (e.g., one or two weeks), set open and closing days, and stick to that schedule for the entire course. This makes managing course deadlines much easier on you and your learners. For example, I found this schedule to work great for my online classes: lesson material is grouped by week, opens for the week on Wednesday morning, and is due Tuesday night . . . and repeat for each week of the course. Why Wednesday/Tuesday and not Monday/Sunday?

I found that if learning tasks were due on Sunday or Monday, I would get a slew of questions via email over the weekend. By changing the due date to Tuesday night, questions come in during my typical workdays. I don't have to answer emails on weekends, nor do my students have to finish their learning tasks then. It is a win-win situation!

No matter what, when considering the timeline for online courses, group tasks in a way that allows maximum flexibility for learners to complete the tasks on their own time schedules. Below are questions to consider as you plan the timeline of your course:

- When will you open course content?

- Will you open all course content at once or have a staggered rollout?

- When will learning tasks be due?

- If facilitating synchronous learning, how often will you meet?

Individualized or Personalized Learning Environments

In the case of an individualized or personalized learning environment, the discussion of timeline is in some ways a moot point because each learner is working at their own pace. If you are in this type of learning environment, chances are you have had a plethora of training on how to make this work, and I am confident you can apply the strategies in this book to a flexible timeline. In fact, you can most likely apply the weekly grouping strategy to student goals in individualized and personalized learning environments.

How Much Is Too Much in Online Learning?

When planning your course timeline, it is essential to understand that online learning takes more time than face-to-face learning does.

> **Within the same time period, you cannot cover as much in online learning as you can in face-to-face. You must whittle your curriculum down to the most essential learning objectives.**

It will take you more time with online learning to get through what you would typically cover in a face-to-face course of the same duration. This is the nature of online learning. Studies of online learning in higher education have indicated that students feel a heavier workload in the online medium than they do in face-to-face environments.[13] The K–12 space is much different than higher education, but an increased workload will most likely lead to student disengagement. Therefore, you must whittle your curriculum down to the most essential learning objectives. I know this is difficult, but it will make you a better teacher in the end. Once you weed a garden, it is beautiful and healthy. Your course will be beautiful and healthy when you don't get stuck in the weeds!

I know, I know. You already don't have time to teach everything! This is why you have to become a master of using pre-assessments and responsive feedback to ensure you are not teaching students what they already know.[14] You must use your time wisely and efficiently. Effective online learning requires a significant amount of instructional design and planning.

---

13   Virginia Roach and Linda Lemasters, "Satisfaction with Online Learning: A Comparative Descriptive Study," *Journal of Interactive Online Learning* 5, no. 3 (2006), https://www.ncolr.org/issues/jiol/v5/n3/satisfaction-with-online-learning-a-comparative-descriptive-study.html.

14   Fisher, Frey, and Hattie, *The Distance Learning Playbook*, 5.

Summary

This section outlines the most important parts from the chapter:

- Synchronous learning is learning that happens in real time, together. Asynchronous learning is learning that happens at different times, on your own schedule.

- Understanding when to use synchronous learning and when to use asynchronous learning is key to designing successful online learning.

- Online learning does not have to be completely synchronous or completely asynchronous.

- Asynchronous online learning tends to be more equitable.

- In online learning, do not plan for individual days, because balancing a specific daily schedule is challenging for teachers, students, and students' families alike.

- In online learning, the fixed time of a class period or a school day is no longer a constraint, so you can provide lots of choice and flexibility to customize learning for students.

- A strong organizational strategy for online learning is to group learning tasks into time chunks, set open and closing days, and stick to that schedule for the entire course.

- It will take you more time with online learning to get through what you would typically cover in a face-to-face course of the same duration.

- Effective online learning requires a significant amount of instructional design and planning.

Reflection

After reading "Chapter 8: Course Organization," reflect on how the content can be applied to your unique learning environment. Share your reflections online using the hashtag **#TeachersGuideToOnline**.

 Will your online course(s) be synchronous, asynchronous, or a blend of both?

 How will your online course be organized?

Chapter 9:
Digital Course Homebase

Figure 9.1:
Digital Course Homebase

You absolutely must have a **digital course homebase**. This, also known simply as a digital homebase, is the digital location where all communication for learning flows in and out as illustrated in Figure 9.1. Think of it as a digital hub where learners go to access all information for your course. It is the one-stop shop for everything relating to a particular course.

A digital homebase is necessary for every teacher regardless of where your course lies on the learning continuum. A digital homebase is essential to online and blended learning and can make face-to-face learning environments more efficient and self-paced.

Learning Management System

Many educational institutions use a **learning management system (LMS)** as a digital course homebase. A learning management system is, as it sounds, software designed to help you manage learning. The goal of an LMS is to have most of the learning happen within the ecosystem of the LMS using built-in tools such as discussions and quizzes.

You may also hear the term **course management system (CMS)**. A CMS is very similar to an LMS. In fact, the two terms have been used interchangeably over the last ten to twenty years, and it is almost impossible to distinguish the differences between them now. Whether it is called an LMS or a CMS, the goal is to have a digital tool that creates a single online environment for teaching and learning. The major players under the LMS/CMS umbrella have embraced the term LMS; therefore, that is the term we will stick with for the remainder of this book.

There are many different LMSs. Some, such as Instructure's Canvas (instructure.com) and PowerSchool's Schoology (schoology.com), are more popular in the K–12 learning space. Others, such as Blackboard Learn (blackboard.com) and D2L's Brightspace (d2l.com), are more widely used in higher education. These are only four examples out of hundreds of LMSs.

Most LMSs will come with a hefty price tag. Some offer what is known as a **freemium** model, which is a digital tool that offers certain features for free and charges for premium features.

Other Digital Homebase Options

A new category of homebase tools that don't necessarily fit under the LMS umbrella has emerged in the last several years. The big players in this category are Google Classroom (bit.ly/aboutgoogleclassroom), Microsoft Teams (bit.ly/whatismicrosoftteams), and Seesaw (web.seesaw.me).

Google Classroom

Microsoft Teams

Seesaw

There are a lot of strong feelings in the educational field regarding whether these tools are LMSs or not. Some will argue that they represent a new type of LMS; others say they are "limited" LMSs, while still others say they are in a category of their own. I don't think the distinction really matters as long as you understand that the purpose of these tools is to provide a "one-stop shop" for learning.

Both Google Classroom and Microsoft Teams are free to educational institutions, but they do require set up of Google's or Microsoft's **cloud-based** solutions. Cloud-based software stores data online (or "in the cloud") instead of locally, such as on a local server or hard drive. To use Google Classroom, an educational institution needs to set up **Google Workspace for Education** (bit.ly/googleworkspaceedu). To use Microsoft Teams, an educational institution has to set up **Microsoft 365 Education** (bit.ly/microsoft365edu). It is worth setting up both Google Workspace for Education and Microsoft 365 Education, as a host of other digital tools come along with both platforms. Some educational institutions stick to one platform or the other, while others use both.

Google Workspace for Education

Microsoft 365 Education

I could go on and on about the technical side of Google Workspace for Education and Microsoft 365 Education. For the sake of this book, understand that if you want to use either Google Classroom or Microsoft 365 Education as a digital homebase, your educational institution needs to set up either Google Workspace for Education or Microsoft 365 Education.

You can use Google Classroom as part of a personal Google account. However, I do not recommend using your personal account with students. Stick to accounts issued by your educational institution.

For training on Google Classroom, visit the Google for Education Teacher Center (edu.google.com/teacher-center). For training on Microsoft Teams, visit the Microsoft Educator Center (education.microsoft.com).

Google for Education Teacher Center

Microsoft Educator Center

Seesaw has made major headway in K–8 education over the last several years. If you work with elementary-aged learners, Seesaw may be a great digital homebase option for you, as it is designed for younger learners and has a solid caregiver sharing feature. Seesaw is a freemium tool, and you can create a free account with your school-issued email. Seesaw has an entire section of their website for Training and Professional Development (web.seesaw.me/training-and-pd) resources.

Seesaw Training and Professional Development

What Features Does a Digital Course Homebase Need?

Regardless of what tool you use, your digital course homebase should include at minimum the following features.

Individual Course Space

The tool needs to have the ability for you to create a different digital "space" or class for each course you teach. If you teach multiple sections of the same course, you will have to decide if you would like a separate space for each or would prefer to put all sections into one space. This depends on size of the class, personal preference, and features of the digital homebase tool you choose.

Easy Learner Communication and Organization

Perhaps one of the most important features is the learner side of the tool. I find that critically evaluating the learner side is often missing or lacking when it comes to choosing a homebase tool, yet this can completely make or break successful online learning with elementary-aged and secondary-aged learners.

As educators express challenges with online learning, similar themes tend to emerge:

- Students (and their caregivers) struggle to understand what needs to be done and when.

- Students are disengaged with learning and either submit learning tasks below their normal quality or do not submit any learning tasks at all.

To help with these two challenges, the digital homebase must help students organize their online learning tasks in an easy-to-understand, straightforward way. If students become frustrated trying to determine what learning tasks they are going to do and when, they will disengage. We will discuss this in more detail in upcoming chapters. For now, consider the points below when choosing your digital homebase tool:

- Does the tool allow you to organize course content in a way that will be both clear and engaging to your learners? What is clear and engaging to your learners will depend on their age. For example, there are certain LMSs that I would not use with elementary-aged learners.

- Does the tool have a place to post announcements and other course communication for learners?

- Are communications from you obvious and easy to access from the learner perspective?

- Does the tool provide a way for students to easily organize and manage their work? If your course is designed around specific due dates, does the tool have a way for students to create a to-do list organized by due date?

- Most students live on their mobile devices. Does the tool offer a mobile app that helps students organize their coursework?

The element of learner organization is so important that companies have started to design tools for this exact purpose. For example, Hāpara (hapara.com) created Student Dashboard to help students organize themselves by aggregating information from Google Classroom, Google Drive (drive.google.com), and Gmail (mail.google.com) into one to-do list view.

Calendar

The calendar may be part of the learner communication and organization but should include, at minimum, major course dates. Preferably, the calendar should link to the learning task submission location for easy management of course due dates by teacher and students.

Easy Family Communication

Family communication is a particular consideration for K–12 environments, where family members and other caregivers must be informed of their child's progress. For online learning, it is a necessity that this be as seamless as possible for all stakeholders. Some LMSs and other digital homebase tools, such as Seesaw, have begun to integrate a portfolio feature as a convenient solution to family communication.

Learning Task Submission Location

How will learners submit their learning tasks to you? The tool needs to have a "learning task submission location" (like a drop box for learning tasks) where students can submit their work and you can easily provide feedback and either return for revision or return as complete. This feature is typically called "Assignments" in LMSs.

This feature is critical for all modes of learning across the learning continuum, whether online, blended, or face-to-face. The feature must make it easy for you as the teacher to see what tasks need feedback and/or scoring, how many tasks have/have not been submitted, and which students have submitted/not submitted each learning task. A preferable feature is the ability to return tasks for a revisit and track when the task is resubmitted. Most importantly, the feature needs to be easy for learners to use.

This feature must include a way for the teacher to provide feedback to learners and for learners to easily review and respond to this feedback.

 It is a bonus if feedback can be given in multiple formats—written, audio, video, and images. There should also be a way for you to score learning tasks, whether through a pass/fail, point-based, standards-based, competency-based, or other system. **Standards-based** systems measure student proficiency of course objectives. **Competency-based** systems allow students to advance based on their ability to meet proficiency or master a skill.

Easy Sharing of Learning Content

Sharing of learning content goes both ways—teacher to student and student to teacher. Consider the following questions when it comes to sharing learning content:

- Does the tool allow easy formatting of text?

- Does the tool allow easy linking and/or embedding of websites, videos, and other multimedia content?

- Is multimedia functionality, such as a video recorder, camera, or annotation tools, built within the tool?

Let's elaborate on that last point. It is a big bonus for you and your students if functionality, such as a camera, is integrated. For example, can a student click a button and record their learning via audio and/or video within the tool? Can students press a camera button and take a picture of their non-digital work to add to their assignment? Or do they have to navigate away from the tool to perform these actions?

Having integrated multimedia is not necessary but extremely helpful. It can be the difference between leveraging technology for transformational learning and time wasted trying to get technology to work for learning.

Optional Features

Below are optional features that aren't required but that can be a helpful part of a digital course homebase.

Device Agnostic

 If your learners are using a variety of device types, the homebase needs to be device agnostic. Remember to check if the tool is web-based. We live in a mobile world, so in addition to being web-based, I would also recommend a tool that is mobile friendly. Preferably, the tool should have a mobile app available for the major mobile players—iOS and Android OS. Even if your educational institution provides a device to all students, those students with smartphones will likely want to access course information from their smartphone as well. This also increases engagement in the course.

Reports and Analytics

Being able to quickly download reports and other analytics from your digital homebase tool can help you make important decisions regarding your course as a whole as well as track the progress of individual learners. There are many reports that can help facilitate online learning:

- Learner progress and activity

- Learner completion rates

- Assessment results

- Learner participation

- Standards or learning objectives that have and have not met proficiency (if you teach in a standards-based or competency-based environment, this will be a requirement)

Support and Training

Is there a way to get technical support regarding the tool, if needed? Does the tool provide training on how to utilize it effectively for delivering online learning? If not, is training content available from other sources?

Integration with Student Information System (SIS)

Most educational institutions use a **student information system (SIS)**. A student information system is a tool that manages all student information and records. A SIS is often referred to as a gradebook, and examples include Infinite Campus (infinitecampus.com), PowerSchool SIS (powerschool.com), and Skyward SIS (skyward.com).

When choosing your digital course homebase, you may want to consider a tool that integrates with your educational institution's SIS. Integration of your digital homebase and SIS may mean that grades automatically transfer, students are automatically added to the correct courses in the homebase, and so on.

➔ *Grading Options*

As mentioned earlier, there should be a way for you to score learning tasks in a variety of methods, whether pass/fail, point-based, standards-based, or competency-based methods.

Choosing Your Digital Course Homebase

For most of you, your educational institution has likely designated a tool to use as a digital homebase. If your educational institution does not have a designated tool, Canvas and Seesaw are both freemium tools that allow you to sign up with your school email address.

I have taught many online courses (and a few blended courses) through Canvas, and as a bonus, Canvas has Microsoft's **Immersive Reader** built into it. Immersive Reader is an accessibility tool that customizes the reading experience for the user.

Seesaw is an amazing digital homebase for elementary classrooms and will be discussed in more detail in "Chapter 21: Online Learning with Littles."

No matter what tool you choose, ensure the tool meets your local student data privacy laws.

Summary

This section outlines the most important parts from the chapter:

- A digital course homebase is the digital location where all communication for learning flows in and out.

- A digital homebase is essential to online and blended learning and can make face-to-face learning environments more efficient and self-paced.

- Many educational institutions use a learning management system (LMS) as a digital course homebase, but other options include Google Classroom, Microsoft Teams, and Seesaw.

Reflection

After reading "Chapter 9: Digital Course Homebase," reflect on how the content can be applied to your unique learning environment.

Share your reflections online using the hashtag **#TeachersGuideToOnline**.

What digital course homebase tool will you use?

What features of a digital course homebase are the most important to you and your online course(s)?

Chapter 10:
Essential Instructional Tools

As an instructional technologist, I always stress that the focus should not be on the tool but instead on the ultimate learning goal. Thus, the learning goal should always be the first consideration in instructional design, and tools should be chosen that help reach that learning goal. In fact, based on John Hattie's studies, when it comes to digital tools, the effect size of adding technology to the learning process is low.[15] Again, it is the strategy used that has the most positive effect on learning.

With these thoughts in mind, I originally had this chapter toward the end of the book. However, as I wrote, I found myself mentioning these digital instructional tools over and over again. Therefore, I decided to place this chapter toward the beginning of the book to provide context throughout for the reader.

The fact of the matter is, to be a successful online teacher you must have a handful of digital instructional tools that you can choose from in order to meet learning goals. Note that I say a "handful." You do not need to master fifty different digital tools.

In fact, the key to keeping your head above water as a first-time online course instructor is to focus on a few tools that can accomplish many things; these can serve as your essential instructional tools.

So what exactly are the essential instructional tools? Every teacher is going to have their own preferences. I want to explain how I came up with my own list that will be shared in this chapter.

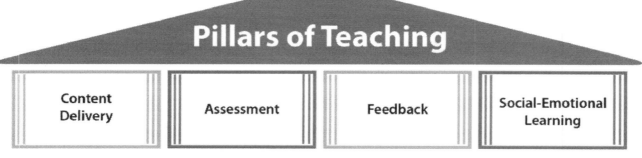

Figure 10.1: Pillars of Teaching

---

15   Fisher, Frey, and Hattie, *The Distance Learning Playbook*, 5.

I used the pillars of teaching (**Figure 10.1**) to guide my essential tool list. I made a list with a category for each pillar. Then, I added the tools that I use to accomplish the goals of each pillar to each category. I circled the tools that appeared under all four pillars. This narrowed down my list of instructional tools to the ones that give me the most bang for my buck because they can be used to assist with each pillar of teaching.

Once the tools were narrowed down to those that can be used in each of the four pillars of teaching, I was able to see common types of tools appear:

- Forms
- Slides
- Easy collaboration
- Video conferencing
- Screencast video creation

Before we dive into the details of these categories, let me point out that these tools are used in addition to the digital course homebase. These are the tools that link from the homebase and allow students to accomplish learning tasks of many different varieties, as illustrated in **Figure 10.2**. This is perhaps one of the most important things to understand about building an online learning course. No matter what digital homebase you use, you should link learning tasks from the homebase using digital tools. Some LMSs will have tools built into the system that may accomplish similar tasks as the essential instructional tools.

Figure 10.2: Digital Course Homebase Plus Digital Tools

Don't forget to make sure that any digital tools you use meet student data privacy laws applicable to your learning situation.

Forms

Forms are survey tools that allow you to set up questions that others can answer. *Figure 10.3* shows the beginning of a form created in Google Forms. Forms can be used for all four pillars of teaching: content delivery, assessment, feedback, and social-emotional learning.

Forms are great for gathering data, and in online learning, you gather a lot of data. Think of all the times you ask your students to raise their hands to gather a quick poll, and remember that you can't do that in an asynchronous online environment.

There are many form creation tools, but Google Forms (forms.google. com—as it is built into Google Workspace for Education) and Microsoft Forms (forms.microsoft. com—as it is built into Microsoft 365 Education) are the two most popular form creation tools in education. Both options are free to educators and device agnostic.

 Immersive Reader is also embedded within Microsoft Forms.

Figure 10.3: Form Example
Online Learning Daily Check-In
(found at intechgratedpd.org/vip)

Google Forms

Microsoft Forms

Forms will be mentioned throughout the book in the context of specific strategies. For quick reference, below are a few ideas for using forms in online learning, several of which will be elaborated upon throughout the book:

- Course roster

- Check-ins

- Formative assessments, such as exit tickets

- Pre- and post-assessments

- Content delivery

- Gathering course feedback—What is going well? What is challenging?

- Sign-ins or sign-ups

- Learning logs

Slides

Slides are a teacher's best friend, as you can use them for so much more than slideshows. **Figure 10.4** shows an example of a getting-to-know-you activity using Google Slides, which is the most common slide creation tool alongside Microsoft PowerPoint. Google Slides

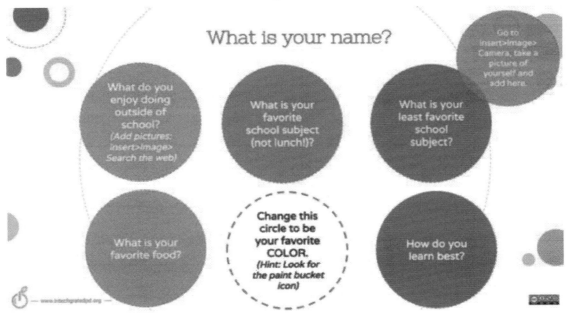

Figure 10.4: Example Slide Activity

and PowerPoint are both mobile friendly with iOS and Android apps. Google Slides as well as PowerPoint Online are web-based. Slides can be used for all four pillars of teaching: content delivery, assessment, feedback, and social-emotional learning.

Why do I consider slides an essential digital tool? Let me count the ways:

- Numbered slides—Numbered slides create organized "learning spaces." The numbers make it easy to refer learners to a specific spot—for example, "Click on slide 2, and complete the instructions." This is easier and more convenient than pages in a word processing program such as Microsoft Word or Google Docs.

- Easier to **format**—Format refers to layout, design, or appearance. Editing the format, otherwise known as formatting, is a lot easier in slides than it is in a word processing program. In slides, it is easy to add images, move text around, and so on, which means it is easier to create interactive learning activities—for example, "Drag all examples of nouns to the nouns section of the slide." These interactive features are important in online learning.

- Collaborative—Both Google Slides and PowerPoint Online are real-time collaborative tools, which means you can have more than one learner working in the same slide file at a time. This is great for small-group work or full-class collaborative activities. This will be discussed in detail in "Chapter 17: Asynchronous Online Learning."

Slides will be mentioned throughout the book in the context of specific strategies. For quick reference, below are a few ideas for using slides in online learning, several of which will be elaborated upon throughout the book:

- Introduction activities
- Reflections—individual or collaborative
- Learning journals
- Presentations
- Animated videos
- Stop-motion videos
- Choose-your-own-adventure learning activities

- Digital storytelling or story books
- Poems
- Digital portfolios
- Hyperdocs (hyperdocs.co)
- Certificates or badges
- Digital notecards or flashcards
- Comic strips

I usually start with a slide template when building learning activities. The resources below include great slide templates for both Google Slides and Microsoft PowerPoint:

- SlidesMania (slidesmania.com)—includes a section specific to education, including notebooks, art galleries, choice boards, and more

- SlidesCarnival (slidescarnival.com)

- Slidesgo (slidesgo.com)

SlidesMania

SlidesCarnival

Slidesgo

Easy Collaboration

There is an entire section later in the book about asynchronous collaboration. For now, let's simply introduce two tools that can be used for easy collaboration: Padlet (padlet.com) and Flipgrid (flipgrid.com). Both tools may be used for content delivery, assessment, feedback, and social-emotional learning. Also, it is important to note that these tools do not have to be used collaboratively; they can be used for individual learning tasks as well.

 Flipgrid

Flipgrid

Flipgrid is a great tool to be able to "see" others asynchronously in an online course. Short videos are recorded on a shared board. Students can then record a response to the board complete with **emojis** and props to make the video creation process equitable and fun. Emojis are images used to express ideas and emotions.

Emojis and props are not only engaging, but students can also use them to hide faces and unwanted backgrounds. The creator of the Flipgrid can set a time limit for the video recording as well.

Check out the A Teacher's Guide to Online Learning Flipgrid (bit.ly/teachersguidetoonlineflipgrid) and add a video of your own!

I can't tell you how great a tool Flipgrid is, especially for the asynchronous online component. Flipgrid helps with relationship development between teacher and student as well as student to student. Flipgrid is available on the web and has an iOS and Android app. It is also free to all.

A Teacher's Guide to Online Learning Flipgrid

 As an extra bonus, Flipgrid includes Immersive Reader.

➡ *Padlet*

Padlet is a web-based tool that is similar to a digital sticky board wall, as shown in **Figure 10.5**. Navigate to the "What Is Your Top Takeaway from the Book?" Padlet board (bit.ly/samplepadletboard) and add your top takeaway so far.

Padlet

♡ ⇄ REMAKE ↗ SHARE ⚙ … 👤

padlet

👤 Lindy Hockenbary + 1 ⚡ 1m
What is your top takeaway so far from the book, "A Teacher's Guide to Online Learning"?
Sample Padlet board

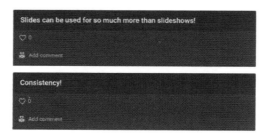

"*What Is Your Top Takeaway from the Book" Padlet board*

Figure 10.5: Sample Padlet Board

When you create a Padlet wall, the first choice you make is what type of wall to create:

- Stream wall—**Figure 10.5** above is an example of a stream wall, which organizes the posts in chronological order.

- Canvas wall—This wall is the most unstructured, free-flowing wall type. The canvas wall really looks like a sticky note board.

- Wall and grid wall—This wall provides more structure and organization to the posts.

- Shelf wall—This wall organizes content into columns. This is an effective option if students are responding to more than one prompt.

- Backchannel wall—This wall is more of a chat feature and is a great option for synchronous collaboration.

- Map wall—This wall is a fun option for anything relating to geography. For example, I helped conduct a *Minecraft: Education Edition* build challenge where students across the country built local landmarks in *Minecraft* and then added pictures of their builds to the actual location of that landmark using the Padlet map feature.

- Timeline wall—Of course, this wall is a favorite of social studies teachers.

No matter what type of wall you choose, Padlet allows for the addition of many types of media, including text, images, videos, and GIFs. Several of these media types are integrated features. Padlet is a freemium tool. Users need a Padlet account in order to make a Padlet wall but not to post to one. However, if you post to a Padlet wall without being logged into an account, the post will show as anonymous.

The user who creates the Padlet wall has complete control of the settings for that wall, including who can post, whether the wall is private or unlisted, whether the creator has to approve posts before they show on the wall, and so on. Padlet has a lot of useful settings, including a profanity filter and options for responding to posts, such as comments, star ratings, and thumbs up/down.

Collaboration tools such as Flipgrid and Padlet will be mentioned throughout the book in the context of specific strategies.

For quick reference, below are a few ideas for using collaborative tools in online learning, several of which will be elaborated upon throughout the book:

- Reflections
- Responding to anticipatory set prompts
- Introductions
- Relationship development
- Small-group collaborative work

- Peer reviews
- Feedback
- Formative assessment
- Teaching a concept

Video Conferencing Tools

A **video conferencing tool**, or video call tool, allows two or more people to communicate via video using the internet. Mastering a video conferencing tool is an absolute must for online learning. There are many video conferencing tools, but the three most commonly used in education are Google Meet (meet.google.com), Microsoft Teams (bit.ly/whatismicrosoftteams), and Zoom (zoom.us).

Google Meet

Microsoft Teams

Zoom

If your school uses Google Workspace for Education, Google Meet will likely be the video conferencing tool used. Google Meet is great for Google users, as it integrates with other tools in the Google ecosystem such as Calendar, Classroom, Gmail, and Jamboard.

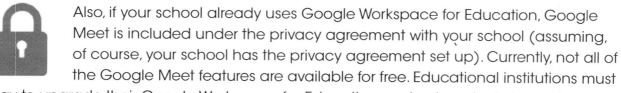 Also, if your school already uses Google Workspace for Education, Google Meet is included under the privacy agreement with your school (assuming, of course, your school has the privacy agreement set up). Currently, not all of the Google Meet features are available for free. Educational institutions must pay to upgrade their Google Workspace for Education version in order to have access to additional Google Meet features, including recording and breakout rooms.

If your school uses Microsoft 365 Education, Teams meetings may be the video call tool for you. Microsoft Teams performs many functions but has Teams meetings built into it.

If your school already uses Microsoft 365 Education, Teams is included under the privacy agreement with your school (of course, assuming your school has the privacy agreement set up). Microsoft Teams meetings integrate with Microsoft Whiteboard to provide an annotation/whiteboard feature. They also integrate with several LMSs, such as Canvas, Schoology, and Brightspace. Currently, Microsoft Teams is free to educational institutions, and the free version includes almost all Teams meetings features.

In the year 2020, Zoom was the leading video conferencing tool in the world. Because of this, your educational institution may choose to utilize it. Currently, the free version of Zoom limits the length of video sessions. Therefore, if you are using Zoom, you will most likely have to pay to upgrade to a licensed version.

Most likely your educational institution has selected one of these video call tools for you to use and has vetted it for safety and privacy. If your educational institution has not specified a video conferencing tool, I recommend having a discussion with your school technology director to ensure the tool you use meets student data privacy laws in your area. Audio containing a person's voice and video containing a person's likeness are both considered PII and must be protected under United States law. If you are in another country, make sure to do your research regarding student data privacy and video conferencing tools.

Video conferencing tools will be mentioned throughout the book. Below are a few ideas for how video conferencing tools may be used in online learning:

- Synchronous group or whole-class sessions

- One-on-one meetings with students

- Office hours

- Small-group work

During the COVID-19 pandemic, video call hijackers or "bombers" came out in full force. This became known as **zoombombing**: disruptive intrusion into a video call by unwanted and uninvited guests. It became clear very quickly that the security of video calls must be paramount. The settings you need to establish for video call security will vary a bit between tools but will most likely include either requiring users to enter a password to join or putting the onus of admitting participants on the host(s). Your educational institution may have default security settings for your video conferencing tool, such as not allowing anyone without a school account to join.

No matter which video conferencing tool you end up choosing, you will create a call as well as a link that allows others to join the call. Share that join link with your students in your digital homebase—perhaps in the calendar.

 Never post this link publicly, especially on social media; make sure the link is only available to your students and any other necessary school staff, if applicable. If you can, create one link and use it for the entire duration of the course; this will save you time. Some digital homebase tools now make this really easy. For example, Google Classroom has Google Meet integration, and each class has its own Meet link that can be used over and over again.

If you plan to record any video call sessions, make sure you are permitted to do so. Also, clarify with your educational institution where you should save these recordings to ensure privacy of student data. Also, never share a recording with anyone outside of your educational institution. Remember that parents, guardians, or other adults supporting learners at home should not be allowed on a video call with other students in the class.

Something you never want to think about, and hope you never have to implement, is a plan for what to do if you witness something concerning while on a video call with a student(s). Make sure your educational institution has a protocol in place for how to handle this situation.

If you have students with internet speeds that won't support video calls, most video tools will allow you to create a "call-in" number that students can dial into with a phone line to join the meeting. Keep in mind that students will only have audio and will not be able to view webcams or shared content.

 Finally, remember that when you are in a video call with a student, you are a guest in their home. Never require students to turn on their webcam in a video call. I will discuss this in detail in "Chapter 16: Synchronous Online Learning." In short, it is an equity issue.

Screencast Video Creation

A **screencast video** is a video recording of your computer screen that usually includes audio narration. If you have ever seen a how-to video for a website, software, or something similar, it was most likely a screencast video. Screencasting can be used for content delivery, assessment, feedback, and social-emotional learning.

Screencasting is a great way to quickly share information with your learners in an online setting. Think of all the times you show your computer screen on your projector or other external display in your classroom. Now think of screencasting as the same thing for online learning.

There are many screencasting tools available. For quick, simple videos, reference my go-to screencast tools below:

- Screencastify (screencastify.com)—If you are a Google user, Screencastify might be the screencasting tool for you. Screencastify is a Google Chrome extension. Videos automatically save to Google Drive and integrate with YouTube (youtube.com) and Google Classroom. Screencastify is a freemium tool.

Screencastify

- Loom (loom.com)—Loom has both a desktop app and a Google Chrome extension. Loom is a freemium tool as well. Loom has a video sharing library feature, which allows you to copy a sharable link directly to the video within Loom. This is a useful feature if you don't want to have to worry about exporting, saving, or hosting your videos in another location.

Loom

- Screencast-o-matic (screencast-o-matic.com)— Screencast-o-matic is a website that includes a free screen recorder download. Videos save as a video file and can upload directly to YouTube. Screencast-o-matic is a freemium tool.

- Flipgrid—If you are already a Flipgrid user, Flipgrid has a built-in screen recording feature that you can use to create screencast videos.

All of the above examples are web-based tools. There are other screencasting tools for specific scenarios that you may find fit your unique situation:

- If you are comfortable using a video conferencing tool such as Zoom, Google Meet, or Teams meetings, start a video conferencing session and don't invite anyone. Click record and ta-da! You have a screencast video!

- If your school has Microsoft 365 Education, Stream (bit.ly/microsoftstream) has a built-in screen recorder.

- If you are a Mac OS user, selecting "shift + command + 5" at the same time brings up a built-in screen capture tool.

- In March 2021, Chrome OS added a built-in screen capture tool.

- If you are ready to take your videos to the next level, I would recommend Snagit or Camtasia. These are both software products made by the company TechSmith (techsmith.com). Both products must be purchased but are worth every penny if you are going to be doing higher-level screencast video creation.

Screencasting will be mentioned often throughout the book. Below are a few ideas for using screencast videos in online learning:

- How-to videos/tutorials

- Providing instructions

- Instructional videos including content

- Virtual tours

- Course updates

- Answering a question (this can save time versus typing an email)

- Learner feedback

- Demonstrating how to use a digital tool, website, or software

- Student-created videos to explain their learning

Introducing Digital Tools to Learners

Have a practice before the big game.

I use this analogy when introducing new digital tools to learners. In other words, in sports you would never go straight to a game without first holding structured practices. The process of learning should be no different. Give students a chance to use new digital tools in low-stakes ways first. Then, move to uses with higher stakes, such as assessments. Below is a step-by-step breakdown of how this process would look, using Google Slides as an example:

1. While in an all-class video call, students are asked to create a new Google Slide. The teacher sets a ten-minute timer and instructs students to explore the tool. During this exploration time, no specific tasks are assigned.

2. At the end of the ten-minute time period, the teacher asks for volunteers to share one feature of the tool they discovered and how they think that feature could be used for learning.

3. Students are given an asynchronous assignment to create a Google Slide that illustrates their favorite hobby. The slide must contain at least one image.

4. If students are successful in the above task, the teacher uses Google Slides in a formative assessment task.

5. As slide skills progress, slides can be offered as a format for an assessment choice.

6. As slide skills become more advanced, a learning task explores using slides for more complex creation, such as stop-motion videos.

Other Instructional Tools to Enhance Online Learning

If you are ready for next steps and are craving more digital tools for your instructional toolkit, below is a list of some favorites organized by type. If you are feeling overwhelmed, skip past this section and keep your focus on the essential digital tools.

You may want to eventually master one tool under several of these categories. Mastering productivity suite, interactive lesson, and multimedia tools should be at the top of your list after the essential tools. Multimedia tools are particularly useful: studies have shown that the use of multimedia in online learning increases student learning.[16]

---

16   Kimber Underdown and Jeff Martin, "Engaging the Online Student: Instructor Created Video Content for the Online Classroom," *Journal of Instructional Research* 5 (2016): 8–12.

The specific tool you choose from each category will depend on many factors, including the type of device you use. Many of these tools will be mentioned in the context of specific strategies throughout the book.

3D

Adding 3D elements to digital materials can bring concepts to life in a virtual classroom. There are a vast number of 3D tools available for consumer use, and this number grows every day. The 3D tools you are able to use will depend on the device(s) available, so I am providing a variety of options below:

Paint 3D

- Paint 3D (bit.ly/microsoftpaint3D) is a software for Windows 10 OS that has a library full of 3D models, such as plant cells, DNA strands, animals, and sculptures. In addition, users can draw in 3D and paint over 3D objects.

- Microsoft PowerPoint also includes a 3D model library. Insert 3D models into a slide and add animations to bring the model to life.

Sketchfab

- The Google search engine includes a view in 3D feature. Using an Android OS or iOS mobile device, conduct a Google search for terms such as lion, skeletal system, cell wall, organic chemistry, solenoid, Chichén Itzá, or Apollo 11. Look for the "View in 3D" option as shown in **Figure 10.6**. This opens a 3D model that can be manipulated as shown in **Figure 10.7**. There is also a "View in your space" **augmented reality (AR)** feature. AR is a technology that renders a digital image onto a user's view of the real world. Imagine placing a model of the skeletal system over an actual human body!

Tinkercad

- Sketchfab (sketchfab.com) is a web-based 3D model hosting site. Users upload 3D files, which creates a large 3D model gallery. Sketchfab is a freemium product.

- Qlone (qlone.pro) turns iOS and Android OS devices into 3D scanners. Scan a physical model and upload to Sketchfab to share the digital 3D version with students. Qlone is a freemium product.

Minecraft: Education Edition

- Tinkercad (tinkercad.com) is a free, web-based 3D design tool that enables users to create 3D models from basic shapes.

- Leopoly (makers.leopoly.com) is a free, web-based digital sculpting tool. Imagine creating with digital clay or Play-Doh.
- *Minecraft: Education Edition* (education.minecraft.net) is a digital world and game made of blocks. Imagine digital Legos that allow you to build just about anything in 3D. *Minecraft: Education Edition* requires Microsoft 365 Education and licensing is tied to your educational institution's Microsoft license agreement. Compatible devices include Windows OS, Mac OS, Chrome OS, and iPad.

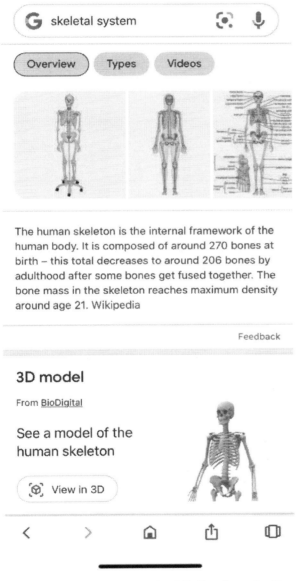

Figure 10.6: View in 3D Feature in the Google Search Engine

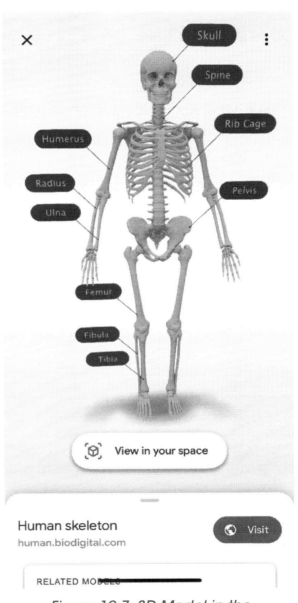

Figure 10.7: 3D Model in the Google Search Engine

Annotation

Annotation tools make it easy to highlight, drag, write, draw, and more. For example, the teacher adds a picture of a Van Gogh painting. Students are tasked with identifying some of the common traits of Van Gogh's artwork by labeling the painting.

Annotation tools are also handy for synchronous online learning if you need to explain a concept visually. Most video conferencing tools have a built-in or integrated annotation tool.

Google Jamboard

- Google Jamboard (jamboard.google.com) is web-based and has Chrome, Android, and iOS apps. Jamboard integrates with Google Docs tools as well as Google Meet. Jamboard requires a Google account.

- Microsoft Whiteboard (bit.ly/trymicrosoftwhiteboard) is web-based and has Windows and iOS apps. Whiteboard integrates with Microsoft Teams meetings. Whiteboard requires a Microsoft or Microsoft 365 account.

Microsoft Whiteboard

Both Google Jamboard and Microsoft Whiteboard can be used individually or collaboratively. Using the Van Gogh example, either tool could be used collaboratively where students work together to identify the common traits of Van Gogh's artwork either synchronously or asynchronously.

Audio Recording

The process of recording audio has come a long way with web-based tools. Audio recording tools can be used to record directions, create podcasts, or record students reading aloud. If a student does not feel comfortable being on camera, audio recording is a great alternative to video.

- Soundtrap (soundtrap.com) is web-based and has iOS and Android apps. It is a freemium tool that has specific subscriptions for education, and an account is required.

- Vocaroo (vocaroo.com) is web-based and as simple as you can get. There is no logging in to access past recordings, so it is best used for quick, one-off projects, such as recording directions. Be aware that the playback page does have ads.

Design

Design tools are used to create images, posters, social media graphics, graphic organizers, infographics, and more.

- Canva (canva.com) is web-based and has iOS and Android apps. With its large library of templates and built-in design elements, Canva makes it easy to create professional-looking designs. An account is required. It is a freemium tool, but educators can get an upgraded version (Canva for Education [canva.com/education]) for free.

Canva

- Google Drawing (docs.google.com/drawing) is integrated into Google Workspace for Education as one of the platform's free tools. It is web-based and can be used individually or collaboratively. If you are already familiar with other Google Docs tools, Google Drawing will be easy to learn.

 Even though Google Drawing is built for design work, Google Slides can be used in the same way.

Discussion

Discussion tools are slightly different than collaboration tools. You can accomplish many different tasks with collaboration tools, but as the name suggests, discussion tools are built specifically to facilitate online discussions. LMSs almost always have a built-in discussion tool.

Parlay

- Parlay (parlayideas.com) is web-based. It adds several features to typical discussion boards that help students facilitate meaningful online discussions. It is a freemium tool, and an account is required.

Interactive Formative Assessments

There are many digital tools that create interactive formative assessments or quizzes. Depending on the exact tool used, these formative assessments can be used individually or as a group. They can also be self-guided or teacher-guided.

- Quizizz (quizizz.com) and Kahoot! (kahoot.com) are web-based and have iOS and Android apps. Both create gamified, interactive quizzes. An account is required to create a quiz but not to complete one. Both are freemium tools.

- Others tools to try out include Quizalize (quizalize.com), Gimkit (gimkit.com), formative (goformative.com), and Blooket (blooket.com).

Quizizz

Kahoot

Interactive Lessons

This is a broad category that includes tools that enable teachers to create lessons that students interact with in some way—answering questions, drawing, and so on. Consider adding one or two of these tools to your instructional tool kit:

- Nearpod (nearpod.com) and Pear Deck (peardeck.com) are similar tools that create interactive slideshow-type lessons. Both are web-based and freemium tools. Nearpod also has Android and iOS apps. An account is required to create but not complete.

 Both tools include Immersive Reader.

- Edpuzzle (edpuzzle.com) is a little different, as it creates interactive videos. Add a video to Edpuzzle and then add reflection points within that video. It is a web-based, freemium tool. An account is required.

- Microsoft Stream will be a valuable tool if you are a Microsoft 365 Education user, as you can embed Microsoft Forms within Stream videos.

Nearpod

Pear Deck

Edpuzzle

Multimedia-Rich Content Creation

This is another broad category that includes many different tools with the commonality of easy multimedia integration. These tools shine when it comes to creation. Using multimedia resources in your online course is essential to online learning.[17]

- Book Creator (bookcreator.com) is a web-based, freemium tool. Don't let the word "book" limit your thinking. This tool includes integrated video, camera, audio, drawings, shapes, emojis, and more. Accounts are required to create.

Book Creator

- Sway (sway.com) is a free web-based Microsoft tool that is integrated into Microsoft 365 Education. It is a multimedia powerhouse that focuses on creating beautiful designs. A Microsoft or Microsoft 365 account is required.

Sway

 Sway has an accessibility view.

- Buncee (buncee.com) is a web-based, freemium tool that also has an iOS app. Buncee is a creation powerhouse that has numerous integrated features, such as video, camera, shapes, text, drawing, animations, emojis, and more. Accounts are required.

 Buncee includes Immersive Reader.

- Thinglink (thinglink.com) is a web-based, freemium tool that also has iOS and Android apps. Accounts are required.

 Thinglink creates interactive images and includes Immersive Reader.

---

17   Swapna Kumar et al., "Award-Winning Faculty Online Teaching Practices: Elements of Award-Winning Courses," *Online Learning* 23, no. 4 (2019), https://doi.org/10.24059/olj.v23i4.2077.

Online Libraries

There are many options for accessing eBooks:

- Epic! (getepic.com) is web-based and has iOS and Android apps. Accounts are required, and access is free for educators.

- OverDrive (overdrive.com) and hoopla (hoopladigital.com) are free resources that connect people with content from local libraries. Accounts are required and must be connected to local libraries.

- Audible (audible.com) includes audiobooks, and while many are for purchase only, you can also find free options. An account is required.

Open-Source Content

Every online teacher needs an open-source content resource. Open-source content can be used to build learning tasks, which will be covered in later chapters.

- CK–12 (ck12.org) is a free, web-based tool with content for almost every grade and subject. Content can be viewed without an account.

CK–12

- Newsela (newsela.com) is a web-based, freemium tool that includes mostly current event articles for about every grade and content area. Articles can be adjusted by Lexile score and translated to Spanish. An account is required.

Newsela

Productivity Suite

- The Google Docs suite of tools includes Google Slides and Google Forms in addition to Google Docs, Sheets, and Drawing. The suite is integrated within Google Workspace for Education as well as free Google accounts. A Google Workspace or Google account is required.

- Microsoft Office includes Microsoft PowerPoint in addition to Microsoft Word, OneNote, and Excel. There are the Office Online tools, which are web-based, as well as Microsoft Office, which are local tools. The Office Online tools are free to teachers and students through Microsoft 365 Education.

Video Creation

This includes video creation tools other than screencasting tools.
These tools can be used for video project creation or instructional
video creation.

WeVideo

- WeVideo (wevideo.com) is a web-based, freemium tool
  with iOS and Android apps. WeVideo is a popular video
  creation app for education. Accounts are required to
  create videos.

- Powtoon (powtoon.com) is a web-based, freemium tool
  that creates animated videos. Accounts are required
  to create videos.

- VideoScribe (videoscribe.co) is a web-based,
  freemium tool that creates whiteboard videos.
  Accounts are required to create videos.

Website Creator

Website creators can be used by both teacher and student alike. A website creator can be
used for portfolios or project showcases. Website creation tools have come a long way in
recent years, and you would be surprised at how easy it is to create a beautiful website.

- Google Sites (bit.ly/seegooglesites) will most likely be your website creator
  of choice if you are a Google Workspace for Education user. Google Sites
  is completely web-based and has a great integration with Google Drive to
  easily embed Google Docs file types. A Google Workspace or Google
  account is required.

- Weebly (weebly.com) is a web-based, freemium tool with drag-and-drop
  website design features. An account is required to create.

***Don't forget to make sure that any digital
tools you use meet student data privacy laws
applicable to your learning situation.***

Summary

This section outlines the most important parts from the chapter:

- The learning goal should always be the first consideration in instructional design, and tools should be chosen that help reach that learning goal.

- To be a successful online teacher, you must have digital instructional tools to use to meet learning goals.

- Focus on a few tools that can accomplish many things; these can serve as your essential instructional tools.

- Use the following categories as the starting point for your essential instructional tools: forms, slides, easy collaboration, video conferencing, and screencast video creation.

- No matter what digital homebase you use, link learning tasks from the homebase using digital tools.

- Give students a chance to use new digital tools in low-stakes ways first. Then, move to uses with higher stakes, such as assessments.

Reflection

After reading "Chapter 10: Essential Instructional Tools," reflect on how the content can be applied to your unique learning environment.

Share your reflections online using the hashtag **#TeachersGuideToOnline**.

What digital tools do you have access to at your educational institution?

Which of the tools shared in this chapter are you most interested in exploring for your online course(s)?

What is one goal you can set for yourself to add a digital instructional tool to your teacher toolbox?

Chapter 11: The First Hurdle—Get to Homebase!

Let's imagine that online learning is a race. The start date of the course is here. Your students line up and get situated on their starting blocks. They take off! However, students only make it about one step along the track before they reach the first hurdle. That hurdle is logging into the digital course homebase. In online learning, students won't get very far, if anywhere, unless they open the homebase, as it is the one-stop shop for everything regarding the course. This brings us to an important truth and key takeaway regarding online learning:

> **In online learning environments, proximity is not in your favor. You cannot stand over a learner's shoulder and ensure a task is accomplished.**

This means that you could have designed the best online learning ever; however, if learners never get into the homebase, your amazing learning experience never gets touched. In online learning, getting learners to open the digital homebase is half the battle. This is what the title of this chapter is alluding to—just get students to the homebase!

How do you help students over this first hurdle? How do you get students to pick up their device and log into the digital course homebase? Remember one of the key takeaways:

> **Face-to-face learning is more forgiving than online learning. Therefore, you have to be more strategic with online learning.**

This is a great example of when you have to be more strategic. In online learning, it is not as simple as physically handing a learning task to each student, which ensures their nonverbal acknowledgment that they at least received it. You have to think bigger.

Ask yourself—
What will make learners want to check the homebase?

For me, it comes down to three things:

Get Creative   **Have Fun**   **Incentivize**

How could you make learning fun so students choose learning over other things they could be doing with their time? How can you encourage your students to choose learning?

Embed Fun Activities

Embed fun activities into your course homebase:

- Host a virtual talent show using a tool such as Flipgrid.

- Host a virtual show-and-tell during synchronous online time or using a tool such as Flipgrid.

- Use BreakoutEDU Digital (breakoutedu.com/digital)—BreakoutEDUs are like escape rooms where students solve puzzles. You can even integrate this into your content area. The BreakoutEDU site has tons of fully digital BreakoutEDUs and ideas for integrating this strategy into different content areas.

BreakoutEDU Digital

- Create a scavenger hunt and sneakily integrate the items into your content area. What everyday items relating to your content area could students find around their homes? Be sure to keep equity in mind. GooseChase (goosechase.com/edu) is a digital tool that makes creating scavenger hunts easy.

- Initiate a TikTok (tiktok.com) dance challenge during synchronous online time or using a tool such as Flipgrid.

- Introduce a challenge to the class—but students have to find the challenge in the homebase to know what it is! Challenges could be something silly, such as "Add a picture of your funniest face," or related to your content area.

For example, if you teach health enhancement, a challenge could be to video yourself doing as many push-ups as you can without stopping. Primary teachers could challenge students to post a picture of an item that starts with the letter "J."

- Latch on to the current pop culture trends. As I write this, the game *Among Us* is the current kid obsession. I have to admit it is quite fun! By the time you read this, a new game will have probably emerged as the favorite. Whatever game is the current flavor of the day, use this to your advantage! Could you make your course *Among Us* themed? Could students design a digital avatar based on a popular game? Is there a popular movie that you could utilize?

Share about Your Life

> Your personality is one of your strengths as a teacher - find ways to let it shine in a digital environment!

Your students need to get to know you. Do you have a hobby that you can talk about? Could you share about your kids, grandkids, and/or pets? I have dogs, so my students get to hear about the love story between my Boston terrier, Dublin, and his girlfriend at doggie daycare. I have discovered that I can't seem to keep succulents alive, so recently, everyone got a play-by-play of my half-dead plant's battle for survival. In this gripping cliffhanger story of love and loss, we did not know if tomorrow the plant would be completely dead or if the half that wanted to live would pull through. Spoiler alert—the succulent did not make it! Really, it is the little things that count.

Bitmojis, Bitmojis, Bitmojis

One way to show your personality in a digital environment is by using **Bitmojis**. A Bitmoji is a personal avatar that you can create to look like you. The Bitmoji website (bitmoji.com) will provide you with more information. You will need to create your Bitmoji from an Android or iOS device using the Bitmoji app.

Bitmoji

Figure 11.1: Bitmoji Chrome Extension Custom Text

If you want to use your Bitmoji on a Windows, Mac, or Chrome device, there is a Bitmoji extension for the Google Chrome browser that allows you to quickly copy and paste Bitmojis into your learning content. The Chrome Bitmoji extension (bit.ly/bitmojichromeextension) also allows you to customize the text of your Bitmojis. This is a great way to create custom stickers for feedback. To add custom text, you simply type the text in the search bar of the Chrome extension as shown in *Figure 11.1*.

Another idea for making connections with Bitmojis is to create virtual classrooms that you can integrate throughout your digital homebase. These are fun and easy to create. The Bitmoj for Educators Facebook group (bit.ly/bitmojifacebookgroup) includes many great templates that you can copy and use.

There is also a Bitmoji add-in for Gmail (bit.ly/bitmojichromeextension), so you can use Bitmojis in emails to learners. I use this a lot—even with colleagues!

I don't suggest having students create Bitmojis themselves, because while most are completely fine, there are some that would be deemed inappropriate for a learning setting. Be aware of this when choosing your Bitmojis to use in your class, too.

Initiate Sharing Activities

Remember that online learners don't have halls and lunchrooms to socialize and conversate, so give them (appropriate) topics of discussion in the course homebase. I like to choose topics that the majority of people relate to and enjoy (e.g., food, pets, music):

- Share a picture of your pet. If you don't have a pet, what is your dream pet?

- Describe yourself using one ice cream flavor.

- What is your favorite snack food and why?

- I like to prompt questions with yes/no answers. For example, pineapple on pizza? Pistachio ice cream? Salt on watermelon?

- Prompts involving food, specifically polarizing food topics, are always popular! Cilantro—yummy or soapy? Chunky or creamy nut butter? Coffee or tea? Deep-dish or thin-crust pizza? Ketchup, mustard, both, or neither?

- "Would you rather . . . ?" questions are also popular. Would you rather eat cake or cupcakes? Would you rather play *Among Us* or *Roblox*?

- How do you pronounce caramel? Tomato? Espresso? Pecan?

- What song best describes you?

- What is your favorite song?

- What would be the name of your band and why?

- What would the soundtrack of your life/personality be called?

Gamify the Learning Experience

Gamification means you are adding game elements, such as points and leaderboards, to the learning experience. Gamification increases course interaction and makes the learning experience more enjoyable.[18] In addition, a 2020 study on learner needs in online learning environments states that "learners want a competitive environment with gamification elements such as leaderboards, badges, and notifications."[19]

 Note that gamification is very different than **game-based learning**, which means learning from or through a game.

There are many different ways to gamify the learning experience in order to motivate and engage learners. Some educators will create their own point system and leaderboards using spreadsheets. If this idea excites you, go for it! However, if the idea of creating your own gamification experience seems daunting, luckily there's a tool for that!

---

18   Prajakta Diwanji et al., "Success Factors of Online Learning Videos," in *2014 International Conference on Interactive Mobile Communication Technologies and Learning* (IEEE, 2014), 125–32, https://doi.org/10.1109/IMCTL.2014.7011119.

19   Muhittin Şahin and Halil Yurdugül, "Learners' Needs in Online Learning Environments and Third Generation Learning Management Systems (LMS 3.0)," *Technology, Knowledge, and Learning* (2020), https://doi.org/10.1007/s10758-020-09479-x.

For elementary teachers, try ClassDojo (classdojo.com). Secondary teachers should try Classcraft (classcraft.com).

 If gamification is a strategy that piques your interest, educator Tom Lademann recommends starting small. Don't try to gamify your entire course overnight. Start small by picking a lesson, week, or unit. Then, figure out what works best and expand.

ClassDojo

Other Ideas

Classcraft

- Place an **Easter egg** somewhere within the homebase or a learning task. An Easter egg in terms of technology is a secret or hidden item or message. For example, navigate to Google.com and search for "askew" or "do a barrel roll." These are both examples of Easter eggs hidden within the Google search engine. Embedding Easter eggs into your online learning materials can be a fun way to encourage learners to engage with course content.

- Add jokes, riddles, or random facts to the course homebase.

- If your homebase tool has a banner or header image feature, change the banner image every now and then with something fun. For example, if you use Google Classroom, there are tons of Bitmoji classroom banners that you can copy, customize, and use as your Google Classroom banner.

- PBIS Rewards (bit.ly/pbisincentivesonlinelearning) has a long list of incentives for online learning that can be filtered by grade.

Many of the ideas in this chapter can achieve more than one objective by embedding learning content and helping you get to know your students (we will discuss the importance of this in "Chapter 14: Maslow before You Bloom"), in addition to enticing students to interact with the course.

Ask yourself—
What interests my students?

Take the answer to that question and run with it. For example, my nieces are currently obsessed with *Roblox*. If I were designing learning for them, I would add a *Roblox* theme of sorts to the homebase and learning materials. No one knows your students better than you do, so I am sure you can think of lots of fun things to entice your learners to open that homebase.

Part of getting students to the homebase also includes creating a routine. Teach students that they start in the homebase for everything, no matter what.

Summary

This section outlines the most important parts from the chapter:

- In online learning, getting learners to open the digital course homebase is half the battle.
- In online learning, you can't simply hand a learning task to each student, which ensures their nonverbal acknowledgment that they at least received it. You have to be more strategic.
- Add elements to your course that will entice students to check the digital course homebase.

Reflection

After reading "Chapter 11: The First Hurdle—Get to Homebase!," reflect on how the content can be applied to your unique learning environment. Share your reflections online using the hashtag **#TeachersGuideToOnline**.

What will make your students want to check the homebase for your online course?

What can you do to engage learners with your online course?

Chapter 12: The Second Hurdle—I Can't Find . . .

We're back to our online learning race. Students have cleared the first hurdle and are finally moving down the track. They don't make it very far, though, before reaching a second hurdle. What is this hurdle, you might ask?

"I can't find what I am supposed to do."

"I can't find my assignment for today."

"What am I supposed to be working on?"

"Where is the weekly reflection for this week?"

> In online learning environments, proximity is not in your favor. You cannot stand over a learner's shoulder and ensure a task is accomplished.

Earlier in the book, I mentioned that one of the most common challenges facing online educators is that students (and their caregivers) struggle to organize what needs to be done when. Added to this is another challenge where learners struggle just to find learning tasks. As Gurley states, "Blended and online learning environments differ from the face-to-face classroom, as educators must effectively communicate when separated from students by time and place."[20] This leads to another key takeaway:

> Organization and consistency are critical to online learning.

There is a significant amount of research that supports the importance of organization, consistency, and clarity in online learning. In "Two Meta-Analyses Exploring the Relationship between Teacher Clarity and Student Learning," it is stated that "higher levels of clarity are associated with higher levels of student learning."[21] With online learning, it is absolutely critical that you make all learning tasks and communication for your course as easy to find as possible. Remember, you can't stand over your students' shoulders and guide them

---

20 Gurley, "Educators' Preparation to Teach."

21 Scott Titsworth et al., "Two Meta-Analyses Exploring the Relationship between Teacher Clarity and Student Learning," *Communication Education* 64, no. 4 (2015): 385–418, https://doi.org/10.1080/03634523.2015.1041998.

where to go or ensure they are accomplishing a task. As stated in *The Distance Learning Playbook*, "Teacher clarity matters more when students are not in front of you to correct, cajole, and to give instant feedback. You cannot immediately evaluate progress as you do in the physical classroom."[22]

In "Assessing Teacher Presence in a Computer Conferencing Context," the authors explain that designing an online course "forces teachers to think through the process, structure, evaluation, and interaction components of the course."[23] Furthermore, a study on online learning effectiveness found that "[i]n face-to-face classrooms, instructors and students can negotiate meanings in real time. This allows instructors to make goals and expectations clear and to remediate student misconceptions and confusions as they occur. In asynchronous courses, this kind of negotiation of meaning is not possible."[24]

> **Face-to-face learning is more forgiving than online learning. Therefore, you have to be more strategic with online learning.**

It can be hard to motivate learners in online learning. Imagine that you do all the work to get students to the digital homebase. What if, once they get there, students can't find what they need to complete the learning task? You have lost them all over again! With online learning, sometimes the challenge that is perceived as disengagement is actually an issue of learners not being able to find what they are supposed to do. This is especially true for K–12 learners that may have little grown-up support outside the physical school building.

Organization and consistency may seem trivial until you put yourself in the shoes of a student. **Figure 12.1** on the next page outlines the perspective of a middle school student who has seven different classes a day.

You may think this is a gross overexaggeration, but I have seen this exact scenario in a real-life school! This is a lot for a middle school student to manage. This would even be a lot for many high school students to manage! As educators, we have to ask ourselves if our students are developmentally able to handle what we are asking of them.

---

22   Fisher, Frey, and Hattie, *The Distance Learning Playbook*, 5.

23   Terry Anderson et al., "Assessing Teaching Presence in a Computer Conferencing Context," *Journal of the Asynchronous Learning Network* 5, no. 2 (2001), https://auspace.athabascau.ca/handle/2149/725?show=full.

24   Karen Swan, "Learning Effectiveness: What the Research Tells Us," in *Elements of Quality Online Education: Practice and Direction*, ed. John Bourne and Janet C. Moore (Needham, MA: The Sloan Consortium, 2003), 13–45.

There is one more group of stakeholders whose perspective needs to be considered when discussing why organization and consistency are critical to online learning. Those stakeholders are the caregivers helping K–12 students navigate online learning. Imagine taking the sample student schedule in **Figure 12.1** and multiplying it by two or three or more children. A caregiver could be helping their children manage seven, fourteen, twenty-one, or more different classes! That is what caregivers are up against with online learning. This is why it is vital that teachers and schools make things as organized and consistent as possible.

Class 1	This teacher uses Google Classroom and organizes by unit.
Class 2	This teacher thinks Google Classroom is too complicated so uses a Google Doc with a page for each day. The link to the Google Doc is emailed to students.
Class 3	This teacher doesn't like Google stuff so uses a Microsoft Word document in chronological order. This is linked from the teacher's website.
Class 4	This teacher uses a Google Site that was set up pre-Google Classroom. The teacher doesn't see the need to transition to Google Classroom.
Class 5	This teacher uses Google Classroom and organizes it weekly in reverse chronological order.
Class 6	This teacher uses Blogger because of the authentic writing element.
Class 7	This teacher uses Seesaw. His kid's teacher uses it, so it must be a good tool.

Figure 12.1: Sample Student Schedule

Why is consistency so important? Consistency means repetition. Repetition leads to fewer questions, which leads to you being able to spend more time on the things that really matter.

Consistent Course Organization

How do you make a well-organized and consistent online course? I am glad you asked! Let's start with the overall navigation of a course, which is accomplished in the digital course homebase tool. Below are some tips to help with organization of the homebase:

- Place learning tasks in reverse chronological order, so the most current learning task is always at the top. Don't make learners scroll to find what they need to work on.

- Add an emoji or symbol to make the current learning tasks stand out. For example: "⭐ Week 3—Nouns and Verbs."

- Organize content into chunks of time, such as a week. Remember, you can no longer think day to day in an online setting, and I really wouldn't recommend organizing by day. If your course is a typical semester in length this will quickly get overwhelming and messy.

- Include a quick list of tasks for the specified chunk of time, such as a "week at a glance" or "weekly checklist." Imagine this is the overview of your week that you write on the board in your physical classroom. Instead of writing it on the board, put it in the digital homebase for all to see anytime, anywhere.

- Use icons and/or emojis to provide consistent visual cues, emphasize directions, and minimize text. Avoid large blocks of text.

- Choose a set of ten or fewer emojis and create an "emoji key" (**Figure 12.2**) that you use over and over in your homebase to call attention to certain items.

Emoji	Meaning
☆	Current week
📝	Week at a glance
🎥	Synchronous video meeting
🧠	Challenge
👩	Parent corner
👨‍👧	Family activity
👂	Listen
😀	Share
➗	Math

Figure 12.2: Emoji Key

 I use emojis frequently in my digital learning materials to draw attention or provide visual cues. However, for accessibility purposes, I always make sure the emoji is an enhancement, not a requirement, to the instructions.

Most operating systems have built-in emoji keyboards. **Figure 12.3** on the next page shows how to access emoji keyboards for different operating systems. You can even search these keyboards to find emojis that relate to your content.

In addition to using an emoji key for consistency, I also use the "pointing" emojis to direct attention: for example, "See below for the link 👇" or "Find the Google Meet link above 👆" to join our weekly video call." You can also use Bitmojis for this purpose. Search your Bitmoji app for "point" or "pose" and you will find lots of pointing Bitmoji options.

 In addition to using emojis within your homebase and in your digital learning materials, you can use emojis in the subject line of emails. This is a great way to draw students' attention to important emails. Also, incorporate emojis into the feedback you provide learners.

Operating System	Emoji Keyboard
Windows OS	Windows logo key + . (period)
Mac OS	Control + command + space bar
Chrome OS	Enable the on-screen keyboard, which includes an emoji keyboard or Add an emoji keyboard extension from the Chrome Web Store

Figure 12.3: Emoji Keyboards

There are a variety of resources for finding icons to use in your learning materials:

- The Noun Project (thenounproject.com)—Includes add-ons for Google Docs and Google Slides (thenounproject.com/for-google)

- Flaticon (flaticon.com)

- Use Google Autodraw (autodraw.com) to make your own icons if you want to get really fancy!

The Noun Project

Flaticon

➡ Naming Conventions

Using consistent naming conventions for learning tasks is also important for consistency. A **naming convention** is a fancy way of saying an agreed-upon format for naming things. What items need naming conventions in online learning?

The categories for how learning tasks are organized (for example, week, topic, or unit) and the titles of learning tasks. **Figure 12.4** shows two examples of category naming conventions.

Naming Convention	Examples
Week number (specific dates) – topic	Week 3 (August 31-September 4) – Characterization Week 10 (November 11-18) – Plants
Unit number (specific dates) – unit title	Unit 5 (January 13-20) – Volume Unit 8 (May 3-7) – The Civil War period

Figure 12.4: Examples of Naming Conventions

For learning tasks, the naming convention may break down as follows: Week number, day of the week – type of task – title of task. Say what? Let me start by giving three examples and then a more detailed explanation:

- 2W – Learning Journal – Vlog Entry
- 4F – Art in Real Life – Design around You
- 5Th – Lesson – Become the Character

Start by numbering every learning task. I like to organize by week; therefore, every learning task starts with the number of that week. You could also number assignments in the order in which they should be completed.

The W, F, and Th stand for days of the week: in these examples, Wednesday, Friday, and Thursday. This can be a pacing guide indicating a recommended timeline for completion of tasks, or this can indicate the day the task is due.

Next, the naming convention identifies what each task is. If you were to write down all the tasks that you have students complete in your class, you could most likely group these tasks into similar categories, such as learning journal, art in real life, lesson, collaborative activity, check your understanding, and so on. Use these groupings in your naming conventions in order to give learners a peek into what the task is all about without them having to open it.

Finally, the naming convention includes the title of the task or assignment.

Of course, what you choose for naming conventions will vary depending on many factors, and I don't expect this to work for everyone. For example, this is way too much text for primary-aged learners. For kindergartners, I might strip this all the way down to a number and an icon. The bottom line is, whatever you choose, keep it consistent!

Speaking of consistency, I have a large suggestion regarding consistency in online learning.

 Make the organization you choose for your homebase and naming conventions consistent not only within your class but across your entire school. Yes, that means every teacher. Yes, that means collaborating and compromising. Whenever I mention this suggestion to educators, I usually get flabbergasted looks, but trust me. This is possible and necessary. Think back to the example of the student and caregiver trying to manage seven, fourteen, twenty-one, or more classes. If you advocate for consistency across your school, this will make your life so much easier in the long run in the form of less confusion and fewer questions.

Once you have decided upon the organization of your course, you will need to teach the organization to your students. Consider creating a scavenger hunt, BreakoutEDU Digital (breakoutedu.com/digital), or another fun activity as an orientation to navigating your course. Repeat certain things, such as naming conventions, over and over to create that routine and consistency.

Consistent Formatting

In addition to maintaining consistency with the organization and navigation of your online course, you will also want your course to have the same look and feel from unit to unit or week to week. To do this, use consistent formatting. Remember that format refers to layout, design, or appearance. The following are examples of formatting elements to be considered:

- Layout
- Design
- Font
- Graphics
- Colors

In essence, you should create a **style guide** for your digital learning materials. A course style guide basically outlines how the course will look. Some would argue that your educational institution should have a style guide that is followed across all courses in that institution.

One note of caution. As you make your digital learning materials aesthetically pleasing, make sure you are also keeping accessibility at the forefront.

Why Consistent Formatting?

Having consistent formatting creates a better user experience across the learning continuum and provides visual cues. For example, the use of icons in this book is a great example of using consistent formatting to provide visual cues. In online learning, your digital learning materials are basically your classroom. Imagine if you changed your classroom decorations or layout every day during face-to-face learning. Or imagine having students move to a new classroom every day. This is somewhat akin to digital learning materials that are not consistent.

Tips for Consistent Formatting

Use the Same Font

All of your digital learning materials should use the same font. Keep all headings and all content text the same font throughout the entire course.

Choose a **sans serif font**, as it is better for those with dyslexia.[25] Sans serif fonts do not have small lines (serifs) at the ends of characters. **Serif fonts** have small lines at the ends of characters. Arial and Calibri are examples of sans serif fonts. Times New Roman and Garamond are examples of serif fonts.

Use Styles to Format Headings

Word processing tools such as Microsoft Word and Google Docs have built-in styles that allow you to easily make headings and subheadings within a document. There are many

---

25   Luz Rello and Ricardo Baeza-Yates, "Good Fonts for Dyslexia," in *ASSETS '13: The 15th International ACM SIGACCESS Conference on Computers and Accessibility* (Association for Computing Machinery, 2013), Article 14, https://doi.org/10.1145/2513383.2513447.

benefits to using styles to create headings instead of simply changing the size and emphasis of the font; one benefit is that styles will create a table of contents for the document. In fact, I used headings to write this book, and all I had to do to update the table of contents was press the "update table" button.

A table of contents is great for any learner but essential for learners who use a screen reader. Simply changing the font size and emphasis of headings does not allow a screen reader to distinguish between the hierarchy of headings. Having the same formatting for each heading level, such as title, heading 1, heading 2, and so on, also creates consistency throughout the course.

Common Page Structure/Layout

Make sure the pages within your course have the same structure and layout. This is especially important if you are using an LMS that houses much of the course content. Having common page structures could include using headings as explained above.

This could be an argument both for and against using an LMS. In some ways, using Google Classroom as a digital course homebase solves this problem as there are no styling options outside of color, whereas LMSs typically offer many styling options; however, the pro-LMS camp would argue that since Google Classroom offers basically no formatting customization, it makes it difficult to organize learning materials well.

Colors

Choose a color scheme and stick to it throughout the entire course (if applicable). There are lots of color scheme creators on the web. Coolors (coolors.co) allows you to browse random color schemes by clicking your space bar. Adobe Color (color.adobe.com) creates color schemes based on the color wheel. Canva Color (canva.com/colors) includes all of the above plus a color palette generator. For all of these tools, the hex code for each color is provided. Copy that hex code and paste it into the custom color option in the tool that you are using. **Figure 12.5** shows the color picker in the Google Docs tools.

Canva Color

If you don't have the color code for colors that you want to use with your digital materials (e.g., school colors, mascot, or logo), use a color picker tool to grab the color codes. I use a Chrome extension called ColorPick Eyedropper (bit.ly/chromeeyedropper).

ColorPick Eyedropper Chrome Extension

Graphics

There are many different types of graphics, including clipart, photos, icons, and illustrations. Consider using the same types of graphics throughout your materials. For example, if you decide you are going to use clipart for design purposes, stick with that type of image throughout, if possible. You can probably tell that I am a fan of icons; they are easy to add and look professional.

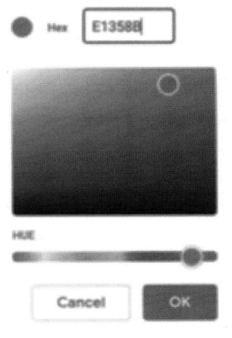

Remember to add alt text to all graphics.

Always ensure you have permission to use the graphics chosen for your learning materials. The last thing you want to do is not model how to follow copyright when it comes to graphics. If you are unfamiliar with Creative Commons, I would recommend visiting the Creative Commons (creativecommons.org) site to begin your copyright learning journey. Remember to teach your students how to follow image copyright too. Below are some tips for finding images.

Figure 12.5: Custom Font Color Using Hex Code

Image Libraries

There are websites that have libraries full of free images. These free images are often referred to as stock photos. Below are some websites for sourcing stock images:

- Pixabay (pixabay.com)—This is my personal favorite because it indicates the exact license, as shown in **Figure 12.6** on the next page.

Creative Commons

- Pexels (pexels.com)

- Unsplash (unsplash.com)

- Pics4Learning (pics4learning.com)—This website is made specifically for graphics used in educational settings.

Pixabay

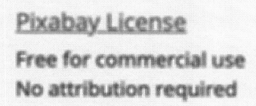

Figure 12.6: Pixabay License

Pexels

 Remember the icon websites shared earlier in the chapter as well.

As mentioned briefly above, consistent formatting is tied to your digital course homebase. No matter what tool you use as your digital homebase, use that tool to drive the consistent formatting you will have throughout the course. Maybe the tool has a color scheme that you can build from or a default font. Whatever the design of your digital homebase, try to bring that "brand" into other digital tools that you link from the homebase (when possible). For example, if I am going to link a Google Doc or Microsoft Word document to an assignment in my homebase, I will ensure I use the same font in the document as I do in the homebase. If you are using an LMS, make sure the content you build in the LMS has consistent formatting. If using slide creation tools, choose one slide template and use it throughout the course. Make it clear to students that when they see that template, they will know they are in your class, just like they instantly know what sportswear store they are standing in front of at the mall when they see the "swoosh" graphic over the door. Remember the slide template tools provided in "Chapter 10: Essential Instructional Tools."

 You can use a font generator such as CoolFont (coolfont.org) to get consistency if you are using a tool that offers little customization of fonts. However, don't choose a "fancy font," as fancy fonts are often not accessible.

Remember that consistency means repetition. Repetition leads to fewer questions. Fewer questions lead to you being able to spend more time on the things that really matter and not on answering endless questions. This applies across the learning continuum, not just to online learning!

Summary

This section outlines the most important parts from the chapter:

- There is a significant amount of research that supports the importance of organization, consistency, and clarity in online learning.

- With online learning, sometimes the challenge that is perceived as disengagement is actually an issue of learners not being able to find what they are supposed to do.

- Ensure the organization and navigation of your course is consistent by utilizing visual cues and naming conventions.

- Use consistent formatting to give your course the same look and feel.

- As you make your digital learning materials aesthetically pleasing, make sure you are also keeping accessibility at the forefront.

Reflection

After reading "Chapter 12: The Second Hurdle—I Can't Find . . .," reflect on how the content can be applied to your unique learning environment.

Share your reflections online using the hashtag **#TeachersGuideToOnline**.

What will you do to ensure organization, consistency, and clarity of your online course?

How will you organize your digital course homebase to ensure consistency and clarity?

What will the style guide for your course include?

Chapter 13:
Supporting Grown-Ups

Elementary and secondary school learners have grown-ups that support them at home. I use the word grown-ups because it is inclusive of all home environments and all caregivers, whether that be a parent, guardian, grandparent, or nanny/babysitter. In online learning, the learning environment and the home environment are one and the same. Therefore, together with this shift in learning environment comes a shift in roles. The grown-ups in your learners' lives move from the role of "homework helper" to "co-teacher." This is often a huge change for many caregivers, who suddenly find themselves taking a very active role in a child's formal learning as opposed to the passive role they have most likely played in the past.

This change in role must not be brushed over or forgotten in the planning of an online course. As an online teacher, you have to be very strategic about supporting these new co-teachers.

Setting elementary- and secondary-aged students up for online learning success includes also setting their grown-ups up for success. The more prepared and knowledgeable caregivers feel about online learning, the more successful their children will be in an online learning environment.

Caregiver success is dependent not only on the decisions you make in your classroom but also on the direction and leadership you receive from your educational institution. Caregiver support and success should be addressed as part of all online learning initiatives.

 If you are a teacher seeking an online teaching position, I urge you to ask about caregiver success plans. Does such a plan exist? If so, what does it entail?

 What has the educational institution done to ensure students are set up for success at home? Does the educational institution have a plan for caregiver communication, training/education, and support?

This chapter will start by sharing caregivers' perspectives of online learning. I am a firm believer that hearing the stories of these at-home "co-teachers" will help you become a better online teacher. Then, Nikki Vradenburg shares her experiences helping teachers and schools create digital communication plans to support parents, guardians, and other caregivers. Nikki is a colleague with many years of experience as an elementary teacher and professional development provider. Throughout the chapter, think about the following key takeaway:

> **Organization and consistency are critical to online learning.**

Caregiver Perspective of Online Learning

To gather information from the caregivers of school-aged kids, I conducted an anonymous survey. The questions and responses are summarized below.

What Age Is Your Child or Children?

Ages of children ranged from 5–22.

Briefly Explain Your Experiences with Online/Remote Learning.

Most caregivers had their first experiences with their children learning online in early 2020. Some had students that were currently back to full face-to-face learning in late 2020, while others had students that were still learning completely online because the school building remained closed due to COVID-19. Some had chosen to opt into full online learning for the 2020 school year due to COVID-19. Some had kids in a blended or hybrid model where learning was half in person and half online.

What Went Well with Online/Remote Learning from Your Perspective?

Several responses focused on learning strategies or student growth:

- "The thing I loved about online learning was that teachers did exactly what I would have done. They used the time they had with students to answer questions and make sure kids were on task/had the skills they needed and then the kids were supposed to work on projects/self-directed learning. Our son wasn't on Zoom all day—just in the morning . . . the learning happened when he was off Zoom."

- "The way my son's learning was handled was great. He was sent work he needed to complete and also had Zoom sessions with his teachers. They also emailed parents, so you knew what assignments were being worked on and when they were due."

- "She is doing well academically. Greater focus and concentration. Growing proficiency with digital skills and tools. Teacher has great class management and sets positive classroom culture."

- "Some teachers, not all, made it a point to include online learners frequently by asking them questions and involving them in the lesson."

A few responses said some version of "nothing."

How Did Your Kids Feel about Learning Online/Remote?

There was almost an exact split between "love it," "hate it," or "didn't mind it but the student misses friends."

For those that loved it:

- "My son was fine with it. He's Generation Z and has grown up in a digital world."

- "He loved it, because he was in charge of his schedule AND he could dive deeper into topics that most interested him. He thought that was great and came to the lunch/dinner table with all this new knowledge he learned while diving deeper into things."

For those that hated it:

- "It was a struggle. She did not enjoy it for the most part."

- "They don't like it. They miss their friends and have a hard time focusing."

For those that didn't mind it but missed friends:

- "She prefers in-person and misses being at school but is motivated to keep her grades up and on top of her work."

- "Misses friends but enjoying the experience. Loves her teachers and the comfort and safety that comes from doing school from home."

How Did You Feel about Your Kids Learning Online/Remote?

The responses seemed to be divided into three camps. The first camp spoke about the need for at least one parent to be available and dedicated to assisting with schoolwork:

- "If I could be there full-time to monitor and supervise, it might not be too bad. However, both parents work full-time, so we could only do the schoolwork at night (no internet access at the childcare provider) or on the weekends. None of us were at our best for learning."

- "I was busy trying to finish my own schooling and am now working full-time, so I struggle when they are remote. I also feel as if they do not absorb and retain as much without a teacher and classroom environment."

The second camp expressed positive feelings:

- "Positive. She is doing quite well. Creates less anxiety for our family."

- "I actually loved it and am hopeful this is the beginning of the changes that need to come to education."

And the third camp expressed negative feelings:

- "I personally think he learns very little."

- "Didn't like it . . . I could see my son becoming withdrawn, skinny, pale . . . not good! Also a hassle with him being marked tardy or absent when he was there."

What Could the School or Teachers Have Done to Make the Experience Better?

Responses to this question centered around three points. The first was regarding communication and consistency:

- "Being consistent. Attendance policies have changed several times (district and state more than school). Sticking with due dates. Have had a few that have changed to either earlier or later without warnings."

- "Communication was lacking—clear concise instructions that matched what was actually posted online, online learning modules were not easily navigable."

> Organization and consistency are critical to online learning.

The second point surrounded the need to build stronger connections and relationships with students:

- "I do think they should have tried to make stronger social/emotional connections. That's where I think my kids felt abandoned."

- "I think 2020 showed that they weren't building those important relationships already."

> Maslow before you Bloom! You must focus on the social-emotional side of learning.

The third point mentioned having too many synchronous video calls:

- "Not require them to stare at a computer monitor from 7:30 a.m. to 2:10 p.m. with the exception of lunch."

- "What WAS disappointing was that in the fall they did a Zoom call for every period every day. So, he was basically sitting on Zoom all day like he would at school. He definitely didn't like that as much, and he certainly didn't learn as much nor deep dive as much."

> Do not replicate face-to-face instruction in an online environment.

→ How Did Your Kids' School(s) Communicate with You as a Parent?

Responses to this question were all over the board, but there were lots of answers that indicated email. A few noted computerized call systems or SISs.

→ What Went Well with Communication?

A few responses indicated positive experiences with school communication:

- "Consistent communication making us feel informed and in the loop has been great. More communication than ever before. School less a mystery."

- "It was clear and straightforward, and I knew when assignments were due so I could give my son a nudge and check he was on track."

- "Weekly newsletter from admin has been nice."

A few responses related to the promptness or availability of school personnel:

- "Prompt response to emails."

- "The teachers being available by email, phone, Zoom, Facebook, etc."

→ Could the School or Teachers Have Done Anything to Make Communication Better?

Responses mostly focused around having a plan for consistent communication:

- "The school could have done a better job of formulating a plan and disseminating that information."

- "Yes. They should have communicated often and in a variety of ways."

Many responses thanked and commended teachers for their hard work. Those in a hybrid model expressed that there didn't seem to be much of an online component:

- "I feel like this hybrid model that our school is using is not much more than partial face-to-face. There doesn't seem like much of an online component."

Enhancing Communication While Learning at Home by Nikki Vradenburg

I never thought I would see the day when I would write a book chapter about supporting parents. When I first started teaching in 2001, communicating with parents terrified me! I had some tough first experiences in my first year of teaching that I carried with me for many years. It was not until I became a parent that I truly understood the importance of a strong connection between home and school. As a new mom, it took every ounce of strength I had to trust a stranger with the care of my infant daughter. In that moment, I realized just how vital it is to develop strong relationships between home and school. I returned to my classroom after maternity leave with a new perspective about parent communication and devoted time to developing strategies that provided the families of my students with an abundance of access to our classroom and to my support without infringing on my personal time. As time went on, I learned that partnering with parents was one of the most effective ways to reach my students.

In 2017, I left the traditional classroom to work with MontanaPBS to implement a grant project devoted to developing professional learning programs for teachers in rural schools by providing support using technology and digital media. I now serve as a digital learning specialist to rural schools and offer one-on-one coaching, small- and large-group learning sessions, and classroom demonstrations. My work with three specific schools allowed me the opportunity to develop strong relationships with administrators and teachers over the course of three school years. Like so many others in my line of work, when the pandemic closed schools in the spring of 2020, I found my email inbox full of requests for help. One of the most common requests I got was from administrators asking for guidance about how teachers could support the parents and caregivers who were assisting students to learn at home. During the school closures, the rural schools I support quickly discovered the holes in their communication strategies and needed help filling those holes. Families with limited or no access to devices or technology were the hardest to engage. There were significant numbers of families who lived in remote areas where there was no internet available, while others had not updated contact information and were unreachable. Teachers found themselves making phone calls, driving to the homes of their students, or meeting families in public locations to deliver instruction. It seemed that every teacher had their own unique communication plan, and some were using multiple tools and strategies. This was overwhelming for families, especially those who had more than one child attending school. It was exhausting for everyone involved and far from sustainable.

When the school year ended, the principal of one school reached out to me for help improving their communication with parents and caregivers. In preparation for a face-to-face training experience with this school, I did some research to help me develop a workshop that would help teachers and administrators build a communication plan that could be implemented when school started back up in the fall. I met with several parents and teachers during and after the home learning experience to gather feedback about using technology and digital tools to support students. Below are the three main pieces of feedback I heard from everyone I visited with:

1. Streamlined communication—School-home communication would have been easier if all teachers/grade levels/schools were using the same platforms and consistency to communicate.

2. Feedback—Students who did not get regular feedback from their teachers struggled to stay motivated while students who did get feedback had an easier time staying engaged.

3. Consistency—Families who had more than one child enrolled in school struggled to manage the variety of teaching styles, communication methods, and digital tools. Even those with just one child engaged in online learning felt frustrated when assignments appeared in an LMS sporadically and did not appear connected to learning goals.

Once these key themes were revealed, I began to think about how I could help teachers provide consistent communication and feedback. I designed a workshop that I facilitated in person and online during the summer of 2020. In this session, I guided teachers and administrators through five steps I developed based on my own past experience as an elementary classroom teacher and the feedback I gathered from my interviews with parents and teachers:

1. *Reflect* on the communication tools and strategies already in place.

2. *Explore* the types of information schools must share with families and the tools that can be used to do this.

3. *Make a plan* for how and when teachers and schools will communicate with families.

4. *Orient* parents and caregivers so they understand the plan and the tools they will need to use.

5. *Provide ongoing support* to families as they develop routines to support home learning.

In the following sections, I will guide you through the exercises and discussions I facilitated with teachers. I invite you to take notes as you read and ponder how to effectively use digital tools to partner with parents.

➡ *Reflect*

Before we can design a strong communication plan, we need to consider what we are already doing and examine whether or not it is working. List the tools and methods you use for communication. Consider the digital and non-digital exchanges you have with families throughout the school year. Think about tools that have multiple functions and how they can be leveraged to make communication easier. Some tools, such as student blogs or portfolio tools, provide students with opportunities to share messages about their progress and the work they are doing. As you build your list, circle or highlight the tools you know you use the most. Consider the questions below as you reflect on your list:

- Which tools and strategies do you use the most?

- How much time do you spend communicating with parents and caregivers?

- How many different digital tools are used to communicate with parents and caregivers?

- What frustrates you about communicating with parents and caregivers?

- What are your strongest communication methods?

- How can students be empowered to help communicate with their caregivers?

- What tools can be adopted that would support student communication with teachers and their families?

Consider the following categories of information shared with families:

- One-on-one parent-teacher conversations
- Announcements
- Assignments
- Reminders
- Recognition
- Learning goals
- Student work samples
- Resources/links
- Grades

Think about how you prefer to share with families. I always recommend teachers choose digital tools that perform multiple functions so that several types of information can be shared using one tool. For example, Seesaw is a student portfolio tool that has a parent communication system built in. Families can see their children's work and have one-on-one texting conversations with the teacher using one application. The paid version of this tool gives schools an option to send schoolwide announcements through the application.

In the reflect stage, I also suggest teachers survey families about their communication preferences. A simple survey can be sent to families about the devices they use at home, the tools they have used in the past with their children, and their preferences. There are people who prefer text messages to phone calls and those who prefer not to read email but love engaging with social media. While it would be impossible to develop a communication plan that meets the preferences of every family, this information can help you meet most parents in their comfort zone. Customizing communication for families is essential for remote learning. Students and their caregivers are more successful if they have direct contact with teachers. Try to keep all surveys short, sweet, and to the point! While open-ended questions provide more details, many parents prefer to answer surveys with more checkboxes and multiple-choice options. The following is a list of questions you might ask on a survey to families:

- What name does your child prefer?
- When is the best time of day to reach you by phone?

- How do you prefer to communicate with the school? With teachers? (e.g., text, email, phone calls, other)

- How often would you like to visit with your child's teacher?

- What kinds of devices do you and your child use at home? (e.g., iPads, Android tablets, smartphones, laptops, etc.)

- What do you want me to know about your child and how they learn?

- What are your hopes and dreams for your child during this new school year?

- Are there specific tools or strategies that you think would work best for your child?

- Are you open to communicating via social media? If so, which platforms do you prefer?

- What questions do you have about our school or classroom?

- How can I best support you and your family during this new school year?

Explore

When I deliver this workshop to teachers, I notice that as they reflect on their communication strategies, they begin to think about what efficient and consistent communication might look like not only in their classroom but also in their school as a whole. The key to a sustainable communication plan is to consistently use a manageable number of digital tools and strategies.

Figure 13.1 on the following pages provides insight into all the types of tools that teachers use on a daily basis to stay in touch with families. Are there tools on this table that were on your list? Are there items you need to add to your list now that you have reviewed this table? Circle or highlight the tools in this table that you are currently using. You can find a Google Doc template with the table in *Figure 13.1* at intechgratedpd.org/vip.

Figure 13.1: Digital Tools for Communication

These tools and platforms are used by teachers to communicate with families. Some tools, such as portfolios and blogs, put the communication in the hands of the students. These tools are marked with an asterisk.

Tool Category	Specific Tools	
Phone/email	Google Groups Individual messages via email or phone Gmail templates	Gmail filters Google Voice Other:
Video conferencing	Google Meet Zoom	Teams Other:
Social media	Facebook Instagram Twitter	Snapchat TikTok Other:
SMS or texting platforms	Remind Bloomz Class Tag ClassDojo	Seesaw* Google Voice Other:
Newsletters	Smore Google Docs Google Drawing Microsoft Word	Microsoft Sway Canva Adobe Spark Seesaw* Other:

Class websites* (Students can create websites using these tools to blog and share work.)	Google Sites Weebly Wix	Adobe Spark Other:
Portfolios and blogs	Seesaw* ClassDojo EduBlogs*	Blogger* Other:
Learning management systems (LMSs)	Google Classroom Canvas Seesaw*	Teams Other:
Student information systems (SISs)	Infinite Campus PowerSchool SIS	Skyward SIS Other:
Other		

As you begin to refine your plans for which tools to use, it is important to look at each tool or platform and consider the type of communication it facilitates. Schools have a variety of messages that need to be shared with households, everything from the yearly calendar to reminders about library books and student progress reports. It is important to match appropriate tools with the message being communicated.

Remember, communications with families can be divided into the categories below:

- One-on-one parent-teacher conversations
- Announcements
- Assignments
- Reminders
- Recognition
- Learning goals
- Student work samples
- Resources/links
- Grades

Figure 13.2 identifies the types of communication that correspond to each tool category. Examine the table and think about all the different information that you send home throughout the year. You may notice how some of the communication methods send the same information. This could provide an opportunity to streamline communication into just two or three methods. For example, many teachers have stopped creating newsletters in favor of keeping a classroom website updated with the same information they used to send home in newsletter format. You can find a Google Doc template with the table in *Figure 13.2* at intechgratedpd.org/vip.

Figure 13.2: Purpose of Communication

Tool Category	Specific Tools	Purpose of Communication
Phone/email	Google Groups Individual messages via email or phone Gmail templates Gmail filters Google Voice Other:	Parent-teacher one-on-one Announcements Recognition Reminders
Video conferencing	Google Meet	Parent-teacher one-on-one

Video conferencing (cont.)	Zoom Teams Other:	Announcements Recognition Reminders
Social media	Facebook Instagram Twitter Snapchat TikTok Other:	Announcements Recognition Reminders Student work samples
SMS or texting platforms	Remind Bloomz Class Tag ClassDojo Seesaw Google Voice Other:	Parent-teacher one-on-one Announcements Reminders Resources
Newsletters	Smore Google Docs Google Drawing Microsoft Word	Announcements Recognition Reminders

Newsletters (cont.)	Microsoft Sway Canva Adobe Spark Seesaw Other:	Learning goals Resources
Class websites	Google Sites Weebly Wix Adobe Spark Other:	Announcements Recognition Reminders Student work samples Learning goals Resources
Portfolios and blogs	Seesaw ClassDojo EduBlogs Blogger Other:	Announcements Recognition Reminders Student work samples Learning goals Resources
Learning management systems (LMSs)	Google Classroom Canvas Seesaw	Assignments Grades Announcements

Learning management systems (LMSs) (cont.)	Teams Other:	Recognition Reminders Student work samples Learning goals Resources
Student information systems (SISs)	Infinite Campus PowerSchool SIS Skyward SIS Other:	Assignments Grades Announcements Reminders Learning goals
Other		

➡ *Make a Plan*

The general reaction that I hear from teachers at this point in our training is that a teacher could spend all day communicating with families. During the school closures in early 2020, that is what some teachers felt like they did! The beauty of digital communication tools is that if they are used strategically, teachers will spend less time sharing information with families and more time planning for and providing instruction to students.

Once you've collected preferences from families, combine that information with your own preferences to create a communication plan. I find when grade-level teams or even the entire school staff engage in this planning together, a uniform plan can be crafted that is easy for families and teachers to follow. Households with more than one child attending school will appreciate having the entire school use the same set of tools and strategies.

I encourage you to complete this exercise with the other teachers at your school using **Figure 13.3**. Have each grade-level team add what tools families will have to interact with if they have a student in that grade. When complete, examine the chart from the perspective of a parent who may have a child across different grade levels. How many tools are parents being asked to manage? You can find a template with the table in **Figure 13.3** at intechgratedpd.org/vip.

I use a digital communication plan template (bit.ly/digitalcommsplan) with teachers in my workshops. You can make a copy of this template to create your own plan. Think about the tools you will use and how often you will use them. Many teachers feel overwhelmed by email and try to find communication methods that keep them away from their email inbox. When I was teaching, I made it a habit to update my classroom website weekly on Thursdays. I emailed parents after each update so they would be sure to check the website. I also included the link to my website in the signature line of my emails so that parents would always be able to find it. I know teachers who send a weekly email to parents with information they will need for the week. Parents will come to expect these emails or website updates on certain days and at certain times.

Grade	Tools Families Will Have to Interact With
K	
1	
2	
3	
4	
5	
6	
7	
8	
9	
10	
11	
12	

Figure 13.3: The Family Perspective

Once created, this plan can be shared with administrators and families. Remember to try and choose the smallest number of tools possible so that communication can be efficient. While communicating is an important part of teaching, it does not have to take the majority of a teacher's time.

➡ *Digital Orientation*

A plan only works if people use it! This is why I recommend that schools make time and space for sharing communication plans and providing training on how to use the digital tools. Caregivers will be more successful communicating with the school if they have the apps downloaded, the passwords saved, and a general knowledge of when to expect certain types of messages as well as where to find information when they need it. Schools I visit have developed creative orientation events for their communities.

Back-to-School Night (In Person or Virtual)

Some schools hold a back-to-school night at the beginning of the school year in person or via video conferencing and make time for the digital tool orientation during that event. Some schools hold a "family boot camp" event where students and their families can engage in some hands-on training to use the digital tools they will need for school. These boot camps can be a series of events over a period of time and can take place in person or online.

Tutorial Videos

Other schools have recorded tutorials about how to use each tool. These tutorials are shared on the school website and social media. Families who need support are encouraged to explore the tutorial videos to troubleshoot if challenges arise.

Initial Contact

For many teachers, the first emails and phone calls they make to families detail their communication plan and how families can expect to hear from teachers during the school year. They also provide information about the tools and applications students will be using for home learning.

→ *Provide Ongoing Support*

As the school year moves along, it is important to stay in touch with families about the communication plan and find out how the digital tools are working for them. Asking for regular feedback and providing opportunities for more training, if needed, are the key to making sure everyone can follow the communication plan.

Dedicated Support Staff

Some schools I work with have identified staff members who can serve as the point of contact for parents who might need help troubleshooting the digital tools students are using. For many families, having a person they can call or email is a tremendous service. These staff members can be teachers, administrators, technology integration specialists, paraprofessionals, or school volunteers. Often, they are paid a stipend for the extra time they may spend supporting families.

Tech Support Website

Other districts I have visited have a designated tech support tab or section to their school website that houses tutorials, troubleshooting tips, and frequently asked questions. When families run into trouble, they can consult the website for help. Teachers are sure to provide the link to this website to families who reach out with problems. It can be more efficient to guide parents and caregivers to find the solutions to their troubles on their own. This is also a tool that can be shared during a family boot camp or back-to-school event for families.

Help Ticket System

Some schools have developed a system for families to ask for help when they need assistance outside of the school day. Families can access a digital form that serves as a "help ticket." These forms are received by IT personnel and administrators who can contact families directly to help solve any technical issues.

Digital Parent Corner

Many teachers I know designate a place on their website or within their learning management system as a "parent corner" where information for parents is shared that may be needed for helping students at home. If these parent corner messages are included in the assignments in Google Classroom, they will also appear in the guardian summaries that are sent via email each week. It can be helpful to use a familiar icon or symbol to identify the parent corner information.

➡ *Pro Tips for Strong School-to-Home Communication*

There is no perfect communication plan, and teachers often find they need to change their plans as the school year progresses based on the needs of their students and families. The best thing teachers can do for families is to consistently reach out with positive messages and support. A little encouragement goes a long way for students and their caregivers. It is important to remember that many adults are new to the world of digital communication and may need more support than their students do in the beginning.

These are my final pro tips for teachers as they begin to build stronger relationships with students and their families through the development of thoughtful communication plans:

- Strong parent-teacher relationships build the foundation for communication between home and school.

- Good communication plans take *time* to implement!

- Feel free to alter the plan if it doesn't work!

- Establish healthy boundaries about communication. It is okay to be unavailable at times!

- Consistency is important, but perfection is not required! Don't be afraid to make mistakes.

Course Communications versus Specific Student Communications

As I was reading Nikki's chapter, it helped me to divide caregiver support in online learning into two parts:

1. Communicating

2. Teaching

As an online teacher, you must support grown-ups by having clear and consistent communications regarding expectations, due dates, and so on.

Organization and consistency are critical to online learning.

However, you must also support grown-ups by teaching them in addition to your students. The grown-ups supporting our students might need assistance with the tasks below:

- How do you organize learning tasks and routines for successful at-home learning?

- How do you use and troubleshoot the digital tools required by online learning? (Remember that many of the tools you will use with students, such as screencasting videos, can be used to create parent resources too.)

- How do you best support online learners? How much is too much or too little student support?

Caregivers also need to understand what online learning is—and is not! You as an online teacher must educate the grown-ups in your students' lives about online learning. Most of these grown-ups have probably never experienced online learning. They must understand that online learning does not mean that the educational institution and/or teacher will keep their child busy all day. They must understand that a day of online learning is most likely going to be shorter than a typical face-to-face school day. Share this information with caregivers. Explain the research behind the challenges and fatigue observed with synchronous learning. They need to understand why you are doing what you are doing with online learning.

In terms of communicating with caregivers, it helps me to think of this in two parts:

1. Communications regarding course information such as announcements, assignments, resources, and so on

2. Communications regarding a specific student

Communications regarding Course Information

I highly recommend connecting this type of communication to the digital homebase, if possible. This is why it is so important to have a homebase tool with solid caregiver communication.

 The reason I recommend connecting to the homebase is because caregiver communication will look similar to, if not the same as, the student view.

It is confusing for caregivers to see a view that is completely different than the student view.

Another tip for grown-up communication is to answer this question in regard to learning tasks: What does "done" look like? One of the most frequent challenges teachers expressed in early 2020 was students not submitting completed work. I would ask, "Did you tell the student (and subsequently the caregiver) what 'done' looks like for that task?" A simple "what does 'done' look like" checklist as shown in **Figure 13.4** empowers caregivers to determine if their student has really completed all learning tasks.

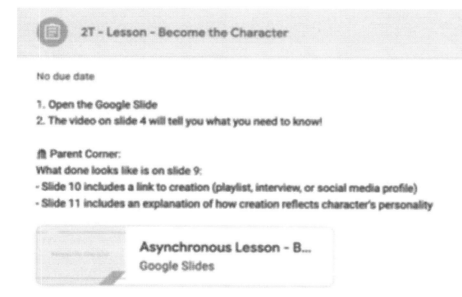

2T - Lesson - Become the Character   Draft

No due date

1. Open the Google Slide
2. The video on slide 4 will tell you what you need to know!

Parent Corner:
What done looks like is on slide 9:
- Slide 10 includes a link to creation (playlist, interview, or social media profile)
- Slide 11 includes an explanation of how creation reflects character's personality

Asynchronous Lesson - B...
Google Slides

Figure 13.4: A Parent Corner and "What Does 'Done' Look Like?" Checklist in Google Classroom

Communications regarding a Specific Student

You are going to be communicating with caregivers regarding their students.

You may have to personalize this type of communication. As Nikki explained, ask in your parent survey what their preferred mode of communication is and try to match that communication mode as much as you can. For example, you may have a parent whose first language is not English. That parent may not feel comfortable talking on the phone but may reply to written messages because written communication offers more time to translate than verbal communication does.

In summary, there may not be a one-size-fits-all communication solution for the one-on-one communications with caregivers. Keep a spreadsheet of preferred one-on-one communication methods. However, you can still streamline communications regarding course information, as illustrated in *Figure 13.5*.

Figure 13.5: Course versus Student Communications

Summary

This section outlines the most important parts from the chapter:

- In online learning, the grown-ups in your learners' lives take a very active role in their children's formal learning.

- The more prepared and knowledgeable caregivers feel about online learning, the more successful their children will be in an online learning environment.

- As an online teacher, you have to be strategic about supporting caregivers.

- Caregiver support should be addressed as part of all online learning initiatives.

- Strong parent-teacher relationships build the foundation for communication between home and school.

- Provide ongoing support to families as they develop routines to support home learning.

Reflection

After reading "Chapter 13: Supporting Grown-Ups," reflect on how the content can be applied to your unique learning environment.

Share your reflections online using the hashtag **#TeachersGuideToOnline**.

Does your family communication plan need to be tweaked?

Could you survey families about their communication preferences?

What tools are you currently using for family communication? Will you change or streamline the tools you are using?

Are you able to collaborate with other teachers at your educational institution to ensure caregivers are not being asked to manage too many tools across grade levels?

What is your final plan for supporting and communicating with your students' caregivers?

Chapter 14:
Maslow before You Bloom

You have done it. You have made it past two online learning hurdles. Your students are in the homebase and consistency has led to more student success with completing learning tasks. You have tackled caregiver support and have a solid plan for streamlined communication for all. The online learning race is finally off in full force! Now what? Well, Maslow before you Bloom, of course! This leads to our next key takeaway, which was mentioned briefly in a previous chapter:

> Maslow before you Bloom! You must focus on the social-emotional side of learning.

The saying "Maslow before you Bloom" refers to Maslow's hierarchy of needs and Bloom's taxonomy of educational objectives. In short, the saying gets to the idea that humans will be more apt to learn (Bloom) if their human needs such as security and belonging are met (Maslow).

Creating personal connections with students is a critical part of the teaching and learning process across the learning continuum.[26] Teacher interaction with students is clearly linked to student learning.[27] Studies have shown that the student-teacher relationship is an important component of student success in online learning.[28] In addition, online students are more apt to remain active in class if they feel a sense of community with their instructor and/or classmates.[29]

---

26   Michelle Drouin and Lesa Rae Vartanian, "Students' Feelings of and Desire for Sense of Community in Face-to-Face and Online Courses," *The Quarterly Review of Distance Education* 11, no. 2 (2010): 147–59.

27   Swan, "Learning Effectiveness."

28   Karen Swan, "Building Learning Communities in Online Courses: The Importance of Interaction," *Education, Communication, and Information* 2, no. 1 (2002): 23–49, https://doi.org/10.1080/1463631022000005016.

29   Underdown and Martin, "Engaging the Online Student."

The term social-emotional learning (SEL) encompasses many facets of well-being. For the sake of this book, when it comes to the social-emotional side of your online courses, consider these major elements as illustrated in **Figure 14.1**:

- Developing relationships

- Creating personal connections

- Developing a sense of community

Figure 14.1: Major SEL Elements

Online learning is different than face-to-face learning in terms of how you go about developing relationships and a sense of community. This leads to the next key takeaway:

> Relationship building does not come naturally in online learning as it does in face-to-face. Therefore, you have to be intentional about consistently embedding relationship building activities into online learning.

I'll say it again: you have to be intentional about consistently embedding relationship building activities into online learning. It must be continuous; it cannot be a one-off. In other words, you can't complete one relationship building activity the first week of class, check it off your list, and expect that relationships have been built. I "Maslow'ed" before I "Bloom'ed"—my job here is done! It does not work that way. The building of relationships, community, and culture has to be constant. In addition, relationship building goes two ways. As much as you need to get to know your students, your students need to get to know you. A 2010 study on teacher personality in online courses concluded that "teachers should have the opportunity to express their personality in online learning contexts."[30]

> **Your personality is one of your strengths as a teacher - find ways to let it shine in a digital environment!**

The question of every new online teacher is, "How do I develop a learning relationship with students that I never see in person?" It is true that cultivating relationships looks a little different in an online setting than it does in a face-to-face one. When you are physically in the same room with other human beings, making connections with people comes fairly naturally. You can see their facial expressions and have an idea of their overall well-being. You can have unplanned private conversations. You can share fluidly. These are things that don't happen naturally in an online space, whether synchronous or asynchronous. Online teachers must find new ways to express emotion and make connections.[31]

> **Face-to-face learning is more forgiving than online learning. Therefore, you have to be more strategic with online learning.**

You must be more strategic and intentional with relationship building in online settings. This chapter will share a few specific strategies, but it is in no way meant to be a comprehensive list of strategies for cultivating connections with students in online learning. You will notice that many of these strategies overlap with the strategies shared in "Chapter 11: The First Hurdle—Get to Homebase!" for engaging learners with the homebase. Several of the strategies in this book accomplish more than one goal.

> ***Efficiency is key to being an effective (and sane) teacher.***

---

30   Maria T. Northcote, "Lighting Up and Transforming Online Courses: Letting the Teacher's Personality Shine," in *Curriculum, Technology & Transformation for an Unknown Future. Proceedings ASCILITE Sydney 2010* (Sydney, Australia: ASCILITE, 2010), 694–98.

31   Swan, "Learning Effectiveness."

Teacher Presence

I am a member of an online community where I shared an article from *Edutopia* titled "Keys to Success in Distance Learning." One of the key takeaways of the article is to "stay on camera as much as you can; it helps with relationship building."[32] After posting the article, I received a few comments from teachers disagreeing with this key takeaway. The reason for disagreement was concern for teacher well-being. The consensus was that synchronous video calls are draining, and they simply couldn't do any more on-camera time. I realized that I had interpreted this key takeaway completely differently than these other teachers had.

I responded immediately and explained that my interpretation of the statement "stay on camera as much as you can" applied to asynchronous online learning as much as synchronous. For example, I can create videos that include myself on camera. Students are seeing my face and hearing my voice. This is a way to "stay on camera," is it not?

As I reflected, I realized the key takeaway from this article was getting to the idea of **teacher presence**. According to Anderson, Rourke, Garrison, and Archer, teacher presence includes design and organization, facilitating discourse, and direct instruction in order to reach meaningful and educationally worthwhile learning outcomes.[33] Garrison and Cleveland-Innes state that "teaching presence is integral for higher level learning to occur."[34]

A 2010 study investigated the components of teacher presence that online students valued and felt contributed to a successful and satisfying learning experience. The study found that teacher presence in online learning was perceived more broadly by students. Students indicated clear course requirements, the teacher's responsiveness to student needs, and timeliness of instructor feedback as the most important indicators of a successful online learning experience. These elements were ranked as more important than synchronous communication.[35] In online learning, teacher presence is as much

---

32   Nikki Healy, "Keys to Success in Distance Learning," *Edutopia* (blog), August 21, 2020, https://www.edutopia.org/article/keys-success-distance-learning.

33   Anderson et al., "Assessing Teaching Presence."

34   Randy D. Garrison and Martha Cleveland-Innes, "Facilitating Cognitive Presence in Online Learning: Interaction Is Not Enough," *American Journal of Distance Education* 19, no. 3 (2005): 133–48, https://doi.org/10.1207/s15389286ajde1903_2.

35   Kathleen Sheridan and Melissa A. Kelly, "The Indicators of Instructor Presence That Are Important to Students in Online Courses," *Journal of Online Learning and Teaching* 6, no. 4 (2010), https://jolt.merlot.org/vol6no4/sheridan_1210.htm.

asynchronous as it is synchronous. Teacher presence is as much the design and organization of your course as it is your time on camera.

> Face-to-face learning is more forgiving than online learning. Therefore, you have to be more strategic with online learning.

> Organization and consistency are critical to online learning.

SEL Frameworks

If you are looking for a systemic approach to SEL at your school, numerous SEL frameworks exist. In Pamela Livingston Gaudet's *Like No Other School Year*, three different SEL frameworks are highlighted:[36]

- The Institute for Social and Emotional Learning framework takes an experiential approach that focuses on growth mindset.

- The RULER system is more analytical because it has set actions for students to take based on the RULER acronym: recognizing, understanding, labeling, expressing, and regulating.

- The Collaborative for Academic, Social, and Emotional Learning (CASEL) model focuses on five domains: self-awareness, self-management, social awareness, relationship skills, and responsible decision-making.

 Thrively (thrively.com) is a digital tool that includes a CASEL-aligned curriculum and other SEL-focused tools.

---

36   Pamela Livingston Gaudet, *Like No Other School Year: 2020, COVID-19, and the Growth of Online Learning* (n.p.: Product Value Solutions, 2020), 46–47.

All about You

I used to start every class with an "all about you" type of assignment. The idea came from teaching personal finance; students created an item that expressed their values, needs, and wants, because these ideas are the foundation of all financial choices. One of my favorite student creations was a giant superhero figure to express this student's love of everything related to the Comic-Con world. I found this to be a great way to learn about my students and implemented this idea in all of my classes as a first-week-of-class activity.

You can implement an "all about you" project in many ways. Start off with a list of questions for students to answer. Get creative and add questions relating to your content area. Choose a format or, even better, let your students choose. I find that when I let students choose is when I learn the most about their personalities.

 For equity purposes, provide both a digital option (using a tool such as Book Creator, Canva, or Google Drawing) and a physical option. Allow students to craft a physical creation using items they have available to them at home. Students then take pictures and/or video of their creation to share with you. You could also put a modern spin on this and have students create a mock-up of a social media profile, letting them choose the social media tool that is their favorite. Alternatively, what if students created a TikTok-type video to introduce themselves?

 In online learning, I always give a no-tech, low-tech, and high-tech option for equity purposes.

In addition to students creating an "all about you" project, create your own digital "all about you" piece that you can share with your students. You can use the same one for every class year after year! Book Creator is a great tool for this because you can add video and audio.

Embed Sharing Activities

Just as you used fun sharing activities to entice students to open the homebase, choose activities that focus on relationship building. Get to know your students and let them get to know you:

- Host a virtual talent show using a tool such as Flipgrid, where you participate too! This is a great way to learn the strengths and passions of your students.

- Host a virtual show-and-tell during synchronous online time or using a tool such as Flipgrid or Book Creator. Again, you must participate as well! Remember, relationship building goes two ways.

- Initiate a TikTok dance challenge during synchronous online time or use a tool such as Flipgrid. You guessed it. You have to complete the challenge too! Right foot, left foot, anyone? (The "right foot now left foot" dance is a current TikTok sensation.)

- Make sure your students know you are a person too. Share about your life, including kids, pets, and hobbies. What do you do when you are not teaching them?

- Use a tool such as Flipgrid or Padlet to prompt sharing questions. I like to embed questions that give me an idea of incentives to offer, for example, "What motivates you to work hard at something?" Refer to "Chapter 11: The First Hurdle— Get to Homebase!" for more question ideas.

- What do you geek out about? I always share what I geek out about first. What do your students geek out about? I once had a student that was very into everything horses and rodeo and another that was into everything history.

Design Challenge

Have students complete a design challenge. This can easily be linked to your content area. For example, students could design a solution to any of the scenarios below:

- Get clean water to more people in the world.

- Remove plastic from the ocean.

- Improve someone's life.

- Make everyday life more accessible to all.

By seeing what your students create in a design challenge, you will learn more about their personalities, strengths, and weaknesses.

Fun Games

Play fun games with your students that are focused on building community. For example, use the whiteboard feature built within your video conferencing tool to play Pictionary. The words could be vocabulary words or sight words, for instance.

Another game is "Who's the imposter?"—a play on the video game *Among Us* and the game "Two Truths and a Lie." You identify one student as the "imposter." Then, ask students a question about themselves. What is your favorite ice cream flavor? Who is your favorite musician? All students answer truthfully except for the imposter. Students then try to guess who the imposter is. Once the imposter is revealed, that student gives the correct answer. You can play "Who's the imposter?" synchronously or asynchronously.

Bitmojis (Yes, Again)

Yes, Bitmojis again! Bitmojis are a great way to add a personal touch to online learning. Refer to the Bitmojis section in "Chapter 11: The First Hurdle—Get to Homebase!" for more details.

Learning Journals

Have students complete a form of **learning journal**, which is a log of a learner's thoughts, reflections, notes, and more. Learning journals are a great way to have one-on-one conversations and get to know your learners.

Learning journals can take many forms: written, video, audio via a blog, vlog, or podcast. Below are some tools that you can use for each format.

➡ *Written*

- Blog tools such as Blogger (blogger.com), which also has the ability to easily embed video

- Word processing tools such as Google Docs or Word Online

- Slide tools such as Google Slides or PowerPoint Online, both of which also make it easy to embed video

- OneNote (bit.ly/aboutonenote—also has built-in audio record feature)

➡️ *Video*

- Flipgrid
- Screencasting tools
- Book Creator, which can also incorporate written and audio entries

Blogger

➡️ *Audio*

- Web-based audio recording tools such as Soundtrap

OneNote

Learning journals can combine media formats. One entry might be a video, while the next could be written. For example, if using a blog tool, students may record a video reflection using Screencastify and embed that video in their blog.

No matter what format or tool you use, learning journals can be a great way to learn more about your students and use that information to develop relationships. Learning journals can also be used as a strategy to develop metacognition, which we will discuss in depth later in a section on reflection.

Video

Video is a great way to connect with your students in a full online course. A 2016 study on the use of instructor-created video for engaging postsecondary online learners found that instructors who created videos were often able to engage their students even more than they could in face-to-face courses.[37]

I know, I know . . . you don't like to see yourself on video, and you don't like to hear yourself. No one does. As a teacher in modern times, you just have to get over this! There is no other way around it. Work into it slowly. Maybe start with a ten-second video . . . then a thirty-second one . . . and so on. The more you are on video, the more normal it will seem. Video is a strong strategy to let your personality shine.

---

37   Underdown and Martin, "Engaging the Online Student."

> **Your personality is one of your strengths as a teacher - find ways to let it shine in a digital environment!**

In addition to using video to connect with learners and add personal elements, video is an important element for this key takeaway:

> **Use technology to duplicate yourself to all learners regardless of when and where they are learning.**

Recording via video allows you to clone yourself! For example, you can use video to provide instructions or deliver content.

➡ Research on Using Video for Learning

Research regarding using video for learning indicates that you as the teacher trump quality.[38] Your students need to hear and see *you*. The more learners see and hear their teacher, the more likely they are to engage with the content.[39] In addition to engagement, teacher-created videos increase student satisfaction and participation, and they can also help develop a quasi-relationship between teacher and student.[40]

Don't stress about videos being fancy or super high quality. High-quality videos take hours to make. You don't have time for that, and studies show that quality doesn't have a direct impact on engagement.[41] What matters more than having a video that Steven Spielberg would be proud of is that you seem enthusiastic and upbeat.[42] This doesn't mean that you can't use a video that you find on YouTube or Khan Academy (khanacademy.org). However, try to start a lesson with a short video of yourself enthusiastically introducing

38   Phillip J. Guo, Juho Kim, and Rob Rubin, "How Video Production Affects Student Engagement: An Empirical Study of MOOC Videos," in *Proceedings of the First ACM Conference on Learning @ Scale* (Association for Computing Machinery, 2014), 41–50, https://doi.org/10.1145/2556325.2566239.

39   Scott T. Miller and Stephen L. Redman, "Improving Instructor Presence in an Online Introductory Astronomy Course through Video Demonstrations," *Astronomy Education Review* 9, no. 1 (2010), https://doi.org/10.3847/AER2009072.

40   Underdown and Martin, "Engaging the Online Student."

41   Guo, Kim, and Rubin, "How Video Production Affects Student Engagement."

42   Diwanji et al., "Success Factors of Online Learning Videos."

that lesson. Then, you could add another video for the content within that lesson.

Shorter videos increase engagement. Specifically, videos under three minutes in length have the highest engagement rate.[43] In addition to keeping videos short, segmenting those videos has a positive effect on learning.[44] Segmenting means that videos are broken into smaller chunks. This gives learners more control over the pace of learning and provides the opportunity to process information before moving to the next learning task. There is a line of too much segmenting though. Segmenting videos in increments of less than approximately thirty-six seconds was perceived as annoying rather than helpful.

Strategies for Using Video to Connect with Learners

There are many strategies for connecting and engaging with your online learners via video. Take a moment to think of all the things you share with learners in a face-to-face class or during synchronous online time. Now, think about how you can transfer those shares to video. **Figure 14.2** includes some ideas organized by category.

Introductions	Introduce yourself
	Share tidbits about yourself
Instructions	Create a course "unboxing" video that introduces students to the course design and organization
	Overviews of tasks to be completed – this could be daily or weekly
Communication	Updates and announcements for students and/or parents
SEL	Pep talks
Engagement	Create a "trailer" for your course to engage learners
	Make videos around a class theme
Feedback	Feedback on the whole-class or individual student tasks

Figure 14.2: Ideas for Utilizing Video

43   Diwanji et al., "Success Factors of Online Learning Videos."

44   Peter E. Doolittle, Lauren H. Bryant, and Jessica R. Chittum, "Effects of Degree of Segmentation and Learner Disposition on Multimedia Learning," *British Journal of Educational Technology* 46, no. 6 (2014): 1333–43, https://doi.org/10.1111/bjet.12203.

In the study "Engaging the Online Student: Instructor-Created Video Content for the Online Classroom," the authors identify four specific types of video as a starting point for integrating personalized videos into online courses: welcome to class, syllabus overview, embedded feedback, and student feedback.[45] Consider these video types a starting point for integrating video into your online course.

 In addition to you as the instructor creating videos, have your learners create videos to show their learning, reflect on their journey, and more. This is a great way for you to get to know your students.

➡ *How to Create Video*

There are many (many, many, many) tools available for creating videos. In this section, I don't want to overwhelm you with a list of video editors (refer instead to "Chapter 10: Essential Instructional Tools" for a list of video creation tools). Instead, I want to share a few strategies for creating quick and easy videos for your online courses.

A device with a webcam is perhaps the most valuable tool for creating videos in order to make personal connections with your students. If you have a smartphone or tablet, use the front-facing cameras to record quick, informal videos of yourself sharing information (think Snapchat and TikTok style videos). This could be information related directly to the course or videos of you in your daily life.

Screencasting tools are another quick and easy way to make videos to connect with your students. Most screencast tools have a feature to add your webcam to the video. This means it will record you while you are talking and add that to the corner of the screencast video. Many screencast tools will do the opposite as well and allow you to only show your webcam. Refer to "Chapter 10: Essential Instructional Tools" for more details on screencast videos.

Flipgrid is another great tool for recording and sharing videos. A great use for Flipgrid is to use one grid to post daily or weekly course updates.

Remember, when creating videos to connect with your students, do not focus on perfection; instead, focus on being personable. Use your smartphone to take a quick video—nothing fancy! You may even find that a selfie stick does indeed have a useful purpose!

---

45   Underdown and Martin, "Engaging the Online Student."

Sharing Your Videos

If you record a video on a mobile device, you can upload these videos directly to YouTube or a cloud storage tool such as Google Drive or OneDrive (bit.ly/aboutonedrive). Then, share links to the videos, which are hosted on these platforms.

YouTube is the easiest video sharing platform. There are three sharing settings for videos on YouTube, as illustrated in *Figure 14.3*:

- Public—Videos can be viewed and shared by anyone on YouTube. Public YouTube videos will appear in a YouTube search.

- Private—Videos can only be viewed by people you choose. You must share a private YouTube video directly with anyone you want to view it.

- Unlisted—Videos can be seen and shared by anyone with the link to that video. This means unlisted videos do not appear in a YouTube search. You must share the link to the video for someone to view an unlisted video.

 When in doubt, choose unlisted.

Can be viewed by anyone
Searchable

Public

Can be viewed by only those you choose
Must be shared

Private

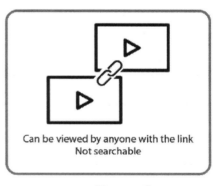

Can be viewed by anyone with the link
Not searchable

Unlisted

Figure 14.3: YouTube Sharing Settings

 To ensure videos are accessible, make sure to add captions to your videos or choose videos that have captions. YouTube is the easiest way to create videos with captions.

Please don't waste your time trying to type a transcript of a video in order to add captions. If you have no other options to get the text for captions, use a little trick of mine. Find a tool that has a dictation feature:

- Google Docs has "Voice typing."

- Microsoft Word and OneNote have "Dictate."

Turn on dictation in the tool of choice, then play the video. The dictation tool will dictate the captions for you! When done, make any needed edits to the transcript. Then, copy and paste the final transcript into the caption tool.

 If you have a video that you want to ensure students watch, you can embed that video into Edpuzzle. Edpuzzle allows you to embed stopping points within a video with reflection questions. It also gives you a dashboard that shows how much of the video each student has watched. Again, I wouldn't do this with every video in your online course—only those that it is super vital that students watch or those that you want to embed with assessments.

Maintain Regular Contact

> You must maintain regular contact with learners.

Regular contact with learners is important for developing a student-teacher relationship that cultivates learning. A study on the success of asynchronous online learning identified three positively contributing factors, one of which is an instructor who interacts with students frequently and constructively.[46]

In face-to-face learning environments, you have the benefit of making contact with your learners each time they enter your physical classroom. Although not always foolproof, physically seeing and interacting with students gives you a fairly good idea of each learner's emotional state. You don't have that benefit with online learning, so guess what? You must be more strategic and intentional about embedding check-ins of various types. Below are three strategies to help you maintain regular contact with your learners. A blend of all three of these strategies is effective.

---

46 Karen Swan et al., "Building Knowledge Building Communities: Consistency, Contact and Communication in the Virtual Classroom," *Journal of Educational Computing Research* 23, no. 4 (2000): 359–83, https://doi.org/10.2190 /W4G6-HY52-57P1-PPNE.

> **Face-to-face learning is more forgiving than online learning. Therefore, you have to be more strategic with online learning.**

Virtual Check-Ins

Virtual check-ins are a solid strategy for maintaining this contact, and after the initial setup, they shouldn't take a large part of your time. Another great thing about virtual check-ins is that they have many more benefits in addition to building relationships. What can you accomplish with a virtual check-in?

- Continue to build relationships with your learners.

- Check on learner well-being.

- Identify learner challenges or points in need of assistance.

- Reach out to learners specifically to assist with their individual needs (learning and/or well-being).

- Receive feedback on coursework and make adjustments where necessary.

So many teacher goals all in one strategy! Notice that these check-ins can cover the entire continuum from academic goals to SEL goals. The frequency with which you have learners complete a check-in will depend on many factors, including the length of your course, your course organization, the age of your learners, and so on. I would recommend at minimum a weekly check-in or a check-in at the beginning, middle, and end of each unit within the course.

 Depending on the age of your learners, you may want to come up with a more age-appropriate phrase other than "virtual check-ins": "How's it going?" for middle and high school students, or "Say hi!" for elementary students.

Forms

I am a fan of using a form tool, such as Google Forms or Microsoft Forms, for virtual check-ins. **Figures 14.4, 14.5,** and **14.6** show an example check-in form that uses Google Forms. Get a copy of this check-in form at intechgratedpd.org/vip.

The breakdown of the form is as follows:

- Message—Consider starting the check-in form with a short message to remind students that you are there for them and you care. In this example, I use a Bitmoji, but you could simply write a message.

- Question 1—This includes the date of the check-in. This is critical if you are going to reuse the same form for each check-in (which I highly recommend).

- Questions 2 and 3—This includes the student's first and last name. I purposefully separate first and last name so I have more sorting and filtering ability when using the data from the check-in form.

- Question 4—This includes the period or class the student is in. This is for teachers who teach multiple classes per day and may not apply to you. If you are online you may not have period numbers, so instead put the class title, section number, or grade level.

- Question 5—This includes the well-being check-in. I like to add pictures here. In this example, I use emojis so this form can easily be copied and used, but you could add your own Bitmojis here as well.

Figure 14.4:
Check-In Form 1

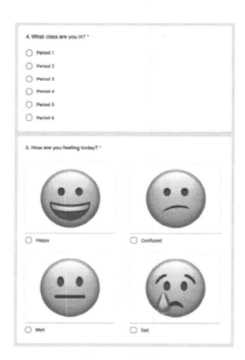

Figure 14.5:
Check-In Form 2

- Question 6—This allows students to indicate if they need help at this time or not.

- Questions 7 and 8—This prompts feedback regarding how the learning tasks are going. In a 2019 study, researchers analyzed the elements of online courses from award-winning faculty. One element of successful online courses was that online teachers used surveys to "gather student feedback on various aspects of their online courses."[47] Use this information to determine what is working and not working. It is okay to make changes in the middle of a course if something is really not working. Fail equals first attempt in learning.

- Question 9—Consider leaving the last question open-ended. I find with this question that students will often leave a fun message.

Figure 14.6:
Check-In Form 3

- Final message—Consider ending the form with an encouraging message that changes every so often. You are creative. Remember you're special. Seize the day! Add your personality here. In this example, I use a Bitmoji, but again, you could type a message or upload another type of image or even a short video.

It is important for you to customize the questions in your check-in form to fit your learners and your course organization; however, at minimum, I would recommend a question that identifies learner progress with the coursework and a question that asks about emotional well-being.

 If your educational institution utilizes a SEL framework, this is a great time to integrate the tenets of that framework.

It is a fine balance to get the information you need without having so many questions that the learner skips over them. Add personal touches, such as Bitmojis, school mascots, school colors, class sayings, or pictures of yourself.

---

47   Kumar et al., "Award-Winning Faculty Online Teaching Practices."

> **Your personality is one of your strengths as a teacher - find ways to let it shine in a digital environment!**

Make a copy of the sample check-in form at intechgratedpd.org/vip. It is a Google Form, so you must be logged into a Google account in order to copy it. Once the copy is made, you can customize the form in any way.

Think about how you can incentivize students to complete the virtual check-in form. Maybe students are entered into a drawing to win a prize every time they complete the form. You could embed a fun easter egg, joke, or riddle. You could even slightly change the check-in form every now and then with something different so learners will want to check the form to see what surprise awaits them this time. Have fun with it!

Virtual check-in forms are only useful if you know how to analyze and implement the data you receive. Most form tools will make charts and graphs automatically from the data, such as in **Figure 14.7**. However, these charts and graphs usually encompass all submissions from the form, which means if you plan to use the same form over and over again these auto-generated charts won't be particularly useful. Most form tools, including Google Forms and Microsoft Forms, allow you to export the results into a spreadsheet. The spreadsheet is where you can really take control of the data and make it useful.

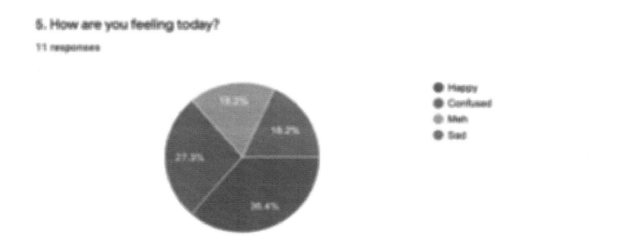

Figure 14.7: Example Pie Chart from Google Forms Responses

Spreadsheets

Once you export the data from the check-in form into a spreadsheet, I recommend sprinkling a little spreadsheet magic that will make you superefficient at analyzing your virtual check-in data. This may seem like a bit much at first, but I promise it will make your data much easier to read. Data is only helpful if you can use it. I will show examples here using Google Sheets, but Microsoft Excel has the same functionality.

When you first open the spreadsheet, it will most likely look similar to **Figure 14.8**. It may be overwhelming depending on how many submissions you have. Note that the column titles are the same as the questions from the form. Each row is a form response.

The first thing you want to do is highlight all the text. If you select the square that is above row one and to the left of column A, it will select or highlight the entire spreadsheet. Once the spreadsheet is highlighted, find the "wrap text" feature. This will make the spreadsheet data easier to read, as shown in **Figure 14.9**.

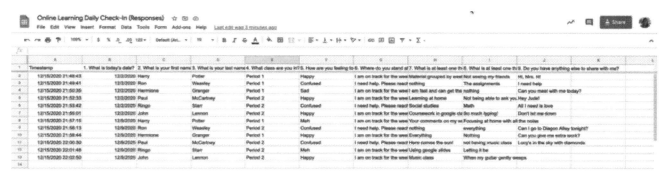

Figure 14.8: Sample Spreadsheet Data from Check-In Form

Figure 14.9: Sample Spreadsheet Data with Wrapped Text

The next step is to create a filter. A filter will add the ability to choose a drop-down menu next to the column titles. Click on the drop-down menu and you can filter out certain responses, such as all dates except for the current date, as shown in **Figure 14.10**. Filters are the key to reusing your check-in form (or other forms for that matter). If I want to see the check-in results from my period 2 class (let's say it is 12/9/2020), I would filter column B to only show "12/9/2020" and column E to only show "Period 2." In addition to filtering by date and student, you can filter by course status or feelings to see only students who have indicated they need help or only students who have indicated they are confused.

At this point, you have what you need to analyze your virtual check-in data. If you are feeling overwhelmed, stop here.

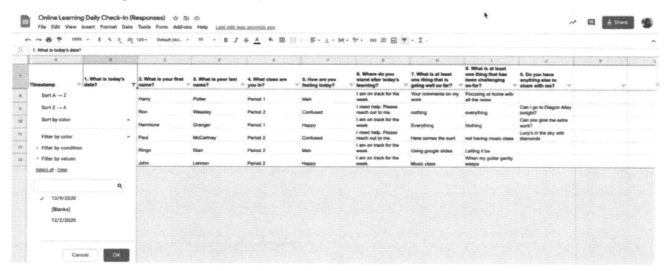

Figure 14.10: Spreadsheet Filters

Figure 14.11: Conditional Formatting Example

If you are like me and geek out when it comes to spreadsheets, stay with me. Now we are going to really add to the spreadsheet magic and use a feature called **conditional formatting**. This is a spreadsheet feature that allows the user to format cells that meet specific criteria or conditions. For example, if a cell contains the word "confused," the cell will be highlighted in red. It may sound complicated, but it really is easy. In *Figure 14.11*, conditional formatting is set for the word "confused" and the phrase "I need help. Please reach out to me." to turn red. This means that I can glance at the spreadsheet and immediately see who I need to contact.

Spreadsheets for Virtual Check-Ins

Another option for virtual check-ins is to utilize a spreadsheet without the form. For example, *Figure 14.12* shows a spreadsheet organized by learning task. Get a copy of this spreadsheet at intechgratedpd.org/vip. You can make a copy of this spreadsheet by selecting File > Make a Copy or download it as a Microsoft Excel file by selecting File > Download > Microsoft Excel. The spreadsheet uses conditional formatting to color code by status. I like that this organizes for the learner while at the same time keeps the teacher updated. However, keep in mind that you would most likely need one spreadsheet per learner, and you would have to open every spreadsheet. If you teach multiple classes, this would not be efficient. However, if you teach only one class and have a smaller number of students, this might be a great option. This option also doesn't have a well-being check-in piece, but that is something you could add. The spreadsheet has three sheets, each with a slight variation of organization—learning task, date, and week.

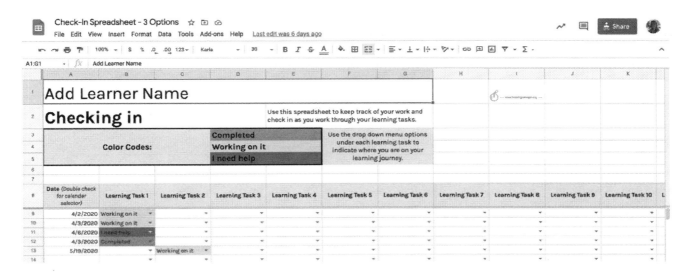

Figure 14.12: Check-In by Learning Task

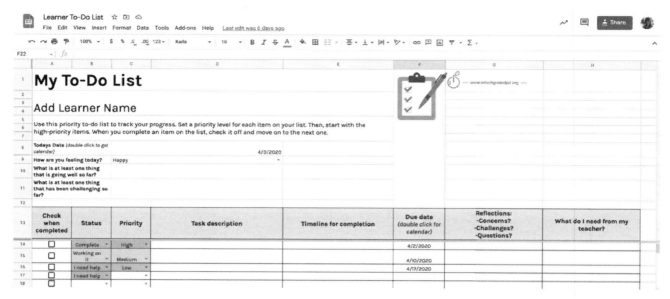

Figure 14.13: My To-Do List

Figure 14.13 shows another spreadsheet check-in option that combines a learner to-do list and check-in. View the "My To-Do List" spreadsheet at intechgratedpd.org/vip and make a copy or download.

➡ *One-on-One Appointments*

Open up your calendar periodically for optional one-on-one appointments with learners where you can join a video or phone call together. Usually, fifteen minutes is an appropriate office hour time slot. Not all students will take advantage of this, but some will; it is a great way to get to know your online learners. I recommend keeping your appointment slots consistent. Always open up one-on-one appointments at specific times and dates, so your students will know when they can get a hold of you.

 Make sure to offer a variety of days and times to accommodate different schedules.

You can request a one-on-one appointment with a student too. You could make one-on-one meetings a requirement of your course, but that could result in a lot of unnecessary tracking. Perhaps a better idea, if you feel that one-on-one meetings with learners should be required, is to work individual meetings with students into an assessment (more on this in "Chapter 18: Assessment in an Online Environment").

Most calendar tools have an appointment feature that will allow you to set up a block of appointments on your calendar that other people can reserve. Calendly (calendly.com) is also a great option.

 Educator Kristin Wolfgang uses SignUpGenius (signupgenius.com) for caregiver meetings, and this could also be used for student meetings.

For one-on-one appointments, you may want to create a new video call link and share the link with only that student. Most calendar tools make creating and sharing a link to a video call easy. Refer to the discussion of video conferencing tools in "Chapter 10: Essential Instructional Tools" for more specifics.

 If phone calls are needed and you are not working from a brick-and-mortar school site, don't use your personal phone number to contact students under the age of eighteen. Use call-in numbers that are built into video conferencing tools or ask your educational institution to provide you with an alternative phone number. Google Voice (voice.google.com) and Grasshopper (grasshopper.com) are two tools that allow another number to be connected to a phone. Note that Google Voice is free for a personal Google account but must be purchased by the educational institution for use with Google Workspace for Education accounts.

As I mentioned earlier, it isn't a great idea to communicate with learners from a personal account or number. Advocate to your school to provide Google Voice for your school Google Workspace for Education account. This is absolutely necessary in the modern education world.

→ *Office Hours*

"Office hours" are a specific, scheduled block of time in which you are available to answer "live" questions (most likely via a video conferencing tool). Offering office hours is beneficial for many reasons:

- Develop personal connections (In fact, you may find some students show up to office hours just to chat!)

- Reduce email

- Set expectations for answering questions

The last bullet is an important point. Something we haven't yet discussed is creating a healthy work-life balance as an online instructor. If you have never worked remotely or outside a physical classroom, you will have to find your own routine. I find that strategies such as office hours help you as an online learning instructor develop that healthy balance, so you don't feel that you are always at the beck and call of your students. This is especially important if your course is mostly asynchronous and learners may be working at varying times of day and night.

 "Office hours" is a term that was borrowed from higher education. If you are teaching online in the K–12 setting, you may want to call office hours something more friendly and fun that is appropriate to the age of your learners, perhaps that relates to the particular content area you are teaching. For example, an art teacher might have "studio hours," and a science teacher might have "lab time."

How often you offer office hours will vary depending on the length of your course, course organization, and the age of your learners. However, for the sake of your sanity, don't offer more than one hour at a time. Offer at least two options of days and times, especially for an asynchronous course where learners may have widely varying schedules. Offer office hours the same days of the week and keep the same hours throughout the course. This will save you time communicating available times with your students and make it easier for your students to plan for these time slots. Again, consistency is key!

 And remember: parents, guardians, or other adults supporting learners at home should not be allowed on a video call with other students in the class.

Summary

This section outlines the most important parts from the chapter:

- Studies have shown that the student-teacher relationship is an important component of student success in online learning.

- Online students are more apt to remain active in class if they feel a sense of community with their instructor and/or classmates.

- You must be intentional about consistently embedding relationship building activities into online learning.

- As much as you need to get to know your students, your students also need to get to know you.

- The more learners see and hear their teacher, the more likely they are to engage with online course content.

- Teacher-created videos increase student satisfaction and participation as well as help develop a quasi-relationship between teacher and student.

- Shorter videos increase student engagement.

- Regular contact with learners is important for developing a student-teacher relationship.

Reflection

After reading "Chapter 14: Maslow before You Bloom," reflect on how the content can be applied to your unique learning environment.

Share your reflections online using the hashtag **#TeachersGuideToOnline**.

? **How will you cultivate relationships with the learners in your online course(s)?**

? **What makes your classes or teaching special?**
How could you incorporate that into your online course(s)?

? **How can you provide opportunities for students to showcase their personalities throughout your online course(s)?**

? **What digital tools will you use to create videos?**

? **How will you maintain regular contact with your learners?**

Chapter 15: Creating Self-Directed Learners

There is one more foundational element that must be considered in online learning: engagement. Keeping learners engaged is vital to learner success but is also one of the most challenging parts of online learning.

Schlechty presents five ways that a student may respond to a learning task:[48]

- Engagement—A student that is engaged is attentive, committed, persistent, and finds meaning and value in the learning task. An engaged learner is intrinsically motivated.

- Strategic compliance—The student is attentive but not committed. The student is extrinsically motivated to complete the learning task. The student may seem engaged at first glance.

- Ritual compliance—The student has low attention and commitment but wants to avoid any negative consequences. This is typically the student that completes the bare minimum of a learning task.

- Retreatism—The student has neither attention nor commitment. The student is completely disengaged and does not comply with the task but is not disruptive to others.

- Rebellion—The student has no commitment and is disruptive to others.

In face-to-face learning, a teacher has proximity in their favor and can set negative consequences for retreatism or rebellion. A teacher can also see if a student is retreating and redirect. Online learning is the opposite. A student can easily retreat; all they have to do is walk away from their device! A teacher can't redirect this retreatism in online learning.

Typically, in K–12 face-to-face learning environments, the teacher has control over most, if not all, aspects of the learning environment, particularly time and space. The teacher

> In order for online learning to be successful, you must shift control from teacher to student.

---

48   Phillip C. Schlechty, *Engaging Students: The Next Level of Working on the Work* (San Francisco: Jossey-Bass, 2011), 15.

controls when class starts, when it ends, where students sit, what they see on the wall, and so on. These types of learning environments make it fairly easy to enforce ritual compliance.

In online learning, control over time and space shifts to the learner, as illustrated in **Figure 15.1**, and thus makes it easy to retreat. Therefore, in order for learners to be engaged in online learning, it is critical that control over other aspects of the learning environment shifts to the student.

Figure 15.1: Time and Space in Face-to-Face versus Online Learning

In order for control to shift from teacher to student, students must become **self-directed learners**.[49] A self-directed learner is a self-starter who takes initiative and responsibility for their learning. In online learning, students must take initiative because the teacher is not physically present. In a 2011 study, it was found that self-directed and self-regulated learning experiences affect the need for learner support in online environments.[50] Students who are the most successful at online learning are not those who have the highest digital literacy skills but those who are the most self-directed.

> In online learning environments, proximity is not in your favor. You cannot stand over a learner's shoulder and ensure a task is accomplished.

49   Şahin and Yurdugül, "Learners' Needs in Online Learning Environments."

50   Sang Joon Lee et al., "Examining the Relationship Among Student Perception of Support, Course Satisfaction, and Learning Outcomes in Online Learning," *The Internet and Higher Education* 14, no. 3 (2011): 158–63, https://doi .org/10.1016/j.iheduc.2011.04.001.

How to Create Self-Directed Learners

Part of teacher presence is guiding students through self-directed learning.[51] The first and most important thing to know about helping your students become more self-directed is that it doesn't happen overnight. You must build **instructional scaffolding**, meaning you must add certain supports for students when concepts or skills are first introduced in order to aid in the mastery of tasks. You must then slowly take away these supports and give students a little more ownership over their learning. Also, in order to create learners who are more self-directed, you must embrace this key takeaway:

> In order for online learning to be successful, you must shift control from teacher to student.

➡️ *Ownership of Technology*

Can your students troubleshoot their own technology challenges?
This one is easy to tackle.

 Create resources such as video playlists that are accessible to your students (and their grown-ups) in their moments of need. This is something your educational institution should offer for any mandated technology tools.

> Use technology to duplicate yourself to all learners regardless of when and where they are learning.

Also, despite being "digital natives" in their leisure time, students typically don't know how to use technology for learning. You have to teach this. Students need to know how to use technology to be productive and organized.

 Google's Applied Digital Skills (bit.ly/exploreapplieddigitalskills) is a great resource that teaches digital skills. You could also provide planner templates or to-do lists for your learners to help them develop organizational and time

---

51   Carol A. O'Neil, "Introduction to Teaching and Learning in Online Environments," in *Developing Online Courses in Nursing Education*, 4th ed., ed. Carol A. O'Neil, Cheryl A. Fisher, and Matthew J. Rietschel (New York: Springer, 2020), 1–10.

management skills. In "Chapter 14: Maslow before You Bloom," the "My To-Do List" spreadsheet (found at intechgratedpd.org/vip) was shared as a resource to complete virtual check-ins but can also be used as a to-do list.

Google's Applied Digital Skills

➡ *Ownership of Resources*

Teach students how to use their resources to answer their own questions. When faced with a challenge, a self-directed learner knows how to solve that challenge without the teacher (or at least attempts to solve the problem). Since one of these resources is the internet, students need to know how to do an effective internet search. Once an internet search is conducted, how do you know if the source is credible?

 Google's Applied Digital Skills curriculum has a lesson for each of these topics.

➡ *Ownership of the Course*

You may see a theme by now that ownership is an important part of building self-directed learners. When students feel a sense of ownership, they are more likely to commit.

In "Chapter 14: Maslow before You Bloom," you learned how to use virtual check-ins. You were encouraged to solicit student feedback on the course as part of the check-in process. Share this feedback with students (anonymously, of course), and explain what changes you are making based on their feedback. Emphasize that this is their course, and you want to make it successful and enjoyable! You could also have periodic course check-ins during synchronous group sessions where you ask for feedback on what is going well and what has been challenging.

Another strategy for increasing student ownership of the course is to give students a job or role. Just as you have the line leader and date changer in the physical classroom, create jobs for students in the virtual classroom. Maybe you have students that are into technology. They may want to become the resident technology guru to help others troubleshoot technological challenges. Maybe you have a student who is in charge of leading the Pledge of Allegiance at the beginning of every Monday synchronous session. Guess what? That kid will probably be present every Monday! Maybe you have a student that loves jokes and is in charge of sharing a weekly or daily class joke. I love the role of "encourager" whose job is to go the extra mile to give others a pat on the back or shoutout. Analyze the tasks that you complete and see if you can transfer the ownership of any tasks to a student. The trick here is to embrace the strengths and interests of students to assign them a role that they will enjoy and take charge of.

> **Organization and consistency are critical to online learning.**

 Organization and consistency are both important elements to increase student ownership of the course.

➜ *Pacing Guides*

Adding pacing guides to asynchronous learning tasks is crucial to building self-directed learners. Students are most likely accustomed to a traditional face-to-face learning environment that directs every second of their school day, from when they eat lunch to when they practice math. Taking a student that is used to this learning environment and dropping them into an online learning setting that requires self-direction may not be successful without scaffolding. Pacing guides are one simple support you can add to build self-direction in your students. Pacing guides will be discussed in detail later in the book and examples will be included.

➜ *Reflection*

Research has indicated that reflection is essential to the learning process.[52] This is especially important in online learning because of the need to shift control over learning from teacher to student. A type of reflection that is essential to online learning is **metacognition**, awareness or analysis of one's own learning and/or thinking processes.[53] Simply put, metacognition is thinking about thinking and understanding the way you learn. Developing metacognition is a key part of becoming a self-directed learner. You may also hear this referred to as self-assessment.

---

52   Muhsin Menekse, "The Reflection-Informed Learning and Instruction to Improve Students' Academic Success in Undergraduate Classrooms," *The Journal of Experimental Education* 88, no. 2 (2020): 183–99, https://doi.org/10.1080/00220973.2019.1620159.

53   *Merriam-Webster*, s.v. "metacognition (*n.*)," accessed November 29, 2020, https://www.merriam-webster.com/dictionary/metacognition.

Self-assessments that prompt metacognition are critical in an online learning environment where teachers are not physically present and students are in charge of their own learning. Learning journals, discussed earlier as a method of cultivating connections with learners, are also a great strategy for embedding reflection into online learning.

Below are some examples of questions that spark metacognition. Once you get to "Chapter 17: Asynchronous Online Learning," think about how you could embed these types of metacognitive questions into asynchronous learning tasks.

- How long did the task take you compared to the recommended pacing guide? If longer or shorter, why?

- How did you do with time management on this task?

- How could you improve your time management for class work?

- Did you spend enough time on the task to produce quality work?

- How well did you do regulating distractions in order to complete the task?

- Did you work as hard as you could have on this learning task?

- Did you seek help when needed?

- What was easy for you with this task?

- What was hard for you with this task?

- What was the most important thing you learned?

- How will you use what you learned in the future?

- If you were to complete this task over again, what would you do the same? What would you do differently?

- What is one goal you would set for yourself for improvement?

- How did you develop the reasoning to back your claims?

- How did your mindset affect your work?

- What have you learned about your strengths?

- What have you learned about your personality and how you learn?

The questions embedded throughout this book exemplify reflection strategies to help you apply the information to your professional life.

→ *Learner Choice*

In online learning, learners must have choice; it is especially important in an asynchronous course to give students a sense of autonomy. One aspect of the learning environment that is fairly easy to shift toward the learner is choice. Luckily, offering choice is especially easy in asynchronous courses since time is not a concern. It doesn't matter if one student chooses a method of learning that takes longer than another because they are working on their own time!

> **Every student does not have to do the exact same thing at the exact same time.**

> **Understanding when to use synchronous learning and when to use asynchronous learning is key to designing successful online learning.**

The strategies below for offering learner choice are all great asynchronous strategies.

Choice Boards

Choice boards (also referred to as learning boards or learning menus) are a great strategy for offering choice to learners. **Figure 15.2** shows an example of a choice board. This example is designed to be similar to a tic-tac-toe board, where the middle square is what is required of the learning task and the student gets to choose one of the other squares. This example was created from the Take Charge Today lesson plan titled "The Basics of Taxes."[54] This lesson had one assessment option of creating a foldable to answer the questions. I took the exact same concept but added several other choices for answering the same set of questions.

John Spencer divides choice boards into four levels:

- Level 1: Embedded choice—Same assignment with one element of choice

- Level 2: Simple choice menu—Same learning target, choice in learning tasks

---

54   "The Basics of Taxes," Take Charge Today, accessed December 29, 2020, https://takechargetoday.arizona.edu/.

- Level 3: Advanced choice menu—Self-selected learning target, choice in learning tasks

- Level 4: Independent project—Completely learner-directed

"Show What I Know About Taxes" Choice Board

Directions: The middle orange block is required and then choose one additional block to complete your learning task! Color the block you choose.

Choose 1	**Choose 1**	**Choose 1**
Foldable Each section of the foldable should include one of the required questions. Submit pictures of your foldable.	**Choose a Tech Tool** Choose a tech tool to answer the required questions. Some examples could include: Slides, Sway, WeVideo, or Powtoon. Submit a link to your creation.	**PSA** Create a public service announcement (PSA) to educate the public about taxes! Your PSA could be in video or flyer form. Submit a link to your creation.
Choose 1 **Political Candidate Social Media Profile** Create a (fake) social media profile using the templates provided for a political candidate who is educating their voter base on how taxes work. Submit a link to your profile. Social media profile templates: Facebook Template Twitter Template Create Fake Tweets	**Required** Answer the following questions: • What are taxes? • What are the benefits of taxes? • What is income tax? • What is payroll tax? • What is property tax? • What is sales tax? • What is excise tax? • What are the two most important things to know about taxes?	**Choose 1** **Political Candidate Campaign Video** Create a campaign video for a political candidate who is educating their voter base on how taxes work. Submit a link to your video. Video tools: WeVideo Powtoon VideoScribe iMovie Windows Video Editor
Choose 1 **Song or Poem** Create a song or poem. Submit a link to the recording, video, or Google Doc.	**Choose 1** **Your Choice! My choice is:** Choose a way to answer the required questions. The only requirement is you must be able to submit a link, file, or pictures to your creation.	**Choose 1** **Interview a Tax Expert** Create an interview video or transcript of yourself interviewing a tax expert such as an accountant or college professor.

 — www.intechgratedpd.org —

Figure 15.2: Choice Board Example
"Show What I Know About Taxes" Choice Board (found at intechgratedpd.org/vip)

The four levels are on a continuum moving from teacher-centered to student-centered.[55] This is a good model for strategically designing choice boards that have the level of choice that works for your situation.

The taxes choice board is an example of a level 2 simple choice menu, as it offers choice in product. If your learners need to be mastering the same learning outcome, this is a great option for providing learner choice. Level 2 simple choice menus are a great place to start with scaffolding choice into learning.

Figure 15.3, created by educator Rebecca Recco for her online art class, shows another example of a choice board. Students start in the Google Doc and choose a topic. Each choice links to a Hāpara Workspace (hapara.com/workspace) that houses the learning tasks. This would be an example of a level 3 advanced choice menu because learners are picking their own learning outcomes based on their choice.

Level 2 and level 3 choice boards can be created with a variety of tools. The examples in **Figures 15.2** and **15.3** use a word processing program. However, choice boards could also be created using slides, design tools, OneNote, Microsoft Teams (via channels), or Google Sites. Refer to "Chapter 10: Essential Instructional Tools" for specific slide and design tools.

Level 4 independent projects move from elements of learner choice to being completely learner directed. A project that piques a student's interest tends to lead to the student taking greater initiative in their learning. Independent projects can take on many forms but are typically a type of **inquiry-based learning**, which utilizes learner curiosity to springboard learning.

Inquiry-based learning can seem overwhelming at first, but Genius Hour and Wonder Day/ Week are both examples of inquiry-based projects that provide a structure that you can follow. It is key with these projects to structure them in a way that has a low entry but a high ceiling. In other words, all learners should find it easy to start these types of projects, but the project also has room for growth for students who want more.

---

55   John Spencer, "4 Ways to Craft Choice Menus in Distance Learning Classes," *John Spencer* (blog), accessed November 20, 2020, https://spencerauthor.com/choice-menus/.

Online Learning Tic Tac Toe – Student Choice Learning
Due May 28, 2020

Instructions: MAKE A COPY OF THIS DOCUMENT. Please pick 3 projects to do to make a Tic Tac Toe. Each square will take you to a workspace. When you complete that workspace, return to this page to choose another workspace. Continue until you have 3 in a row.

When you are finished with all 3 projects, fill out page 2 of this document and share this document with me.

Art From Trash --	The Block --	Political Art --
Learn about artist Aurora Robson and create 2-D or 3-D art from things you would ordinarily throw away. https://j.mp/2QvAvaY *low tech*	Learn about artist Romare Bearden, the Harlem Renaissance, and how artists collaborated to create a movement in American art. https://j.mp/3dqIkZk *low tech*	Artists have always used their work to promote ideas and encourage others to act. What message do you have for the world? Create a work of political art to share your message with others: https://j.mp/2x4QN3X *low tech*
Art and Community -- Learn how artists everywhere create public art to share the stories of their community, improve the value of properties, and encourage people to get out and enjoy a place. Then, create your own mural design and digital maquette! http://j.mp/2OfOoYs	**Creating a Comic Zine --** Learn about artist Thien Pham and how he creates characters and worlds in graphic novels, then create your own graphic zine to share. https://j.mp/3dUgrce *low tech*	**Documenting Life through Photography --** Learn about Dorothea Lange, whose photography captured life in America during the Dust Bowl leading up to WWII https://j.mp/3buw1cy
Lettering Art -- Learn how artist Jessica Hische creates beautiful art with words and create your own word art. https://j.mp/39MBZEI *low tech*	**Digital Citizenship --** Learn how to stay healthy, happy, and productive while working online, and also how to create and share your work responsibly. https://j.mp/2RdJSfT	**Mosaics --** Learn about artist Laurel True and the process of creating mosaics. Then, create your own mosaic using materials from your own home. https://j.mp/2Xbm0NE *low tech*

Figure 15.3: Example Level 3 Advanced Choice Menu for Art
Source: Rebecca Recco. Used with permission.
Online Learning Tic-Tac-Toe (found at intechgratedpd.org/vip)

Genius Hour

Genius Hour is a movement in education based on the idea of passion projects or 20-percent time. Students get to choose what they learn during certain times. Students drive the entire learning experience. Asynchronous online courses and blended learning environments are a great opportunity to conduct passion projects since time is not a constraint. Visit the Genius Hour website (geniushour.com) to learn more.

Genius Hour

Wonder Day or Week

If Genius Hour seems overwhelming, Wonder Day or Wonder Week projects are a great place to start. For online learning, I would suggest a Wonder Week project. Whether you are committing to a day or week, the idea is that students research a topic that they are curious about over the designated period of time. John Spencer has Wonder Day resources on his website.

Wonderopolis

 If your students need a little help coming up with wonders, Wonderopolis (wonderopolis.org) is an excellent resource (and even includes Immersive Reader).

Of course, Genius Hour and Wonder Day/Week are only two examples of inquiry-based learning as a way to develop self-directed learners. In the end, find inquiry-based methods that work for you and your students.

No matter which strategy you choose for offering learner choice, make sure that your choices do not try to replicate face-to-face instruction in an online environment.

> **Do not replicate face-to-face instruction in an online environment.**

Summary

This section outlines the most important parts from the chapter:

- In online learning, control over time and space shifts to the learner. Therefore, in order for learners to be engaged, it is critical that control over other aspects of the learning environment shifts to the student.

- In order for control to shift from teacher to student, students must become self-directed learners.

- Students who are the most successful at online learning are not those who have the highest digital literacy skills but those who are the most self-directed.

- Helping students become more self-directed does not happen overnight.

- Developing a sense of ownership, adding pacing guides, and developing metacognition are strategies that build self-directed learners.

- Online learning must have elements of learner choice.

Reflection

After reading "Chapter 15: Creating Self-Directed Learners," reflect on how the content can be applied to your unique learning environment.

Share your reflections online using the hashtag **#TeachersGuideToOnline**.

What will you do to foster self-direction in your learners?

How can you add elements of choice to your online course(s)?

Face-to-face learning is more forgiving than online learning. Therefore, you have to be more strategic with online learning.

You have to lay the tracks before the train can run.

Part 3:
STRATEGIES

Chapter 16:
Synchronous Online Learning

Now we are ready to dive into the nitty-gritty strategies of making online learning work. In this chapter, we will tackle the synchronous part of this key takeaway:

> **Understanding when to use synchronous learning and when to use asynchronous learning is key to designing successful online learning.**

Remember, synchronous learning is learning that happens in real time. It is the first thought of every new online teacher. This makes perfect sense, because synchronous online learning looks the most like traditional face-to-face learning. To set up this chapter on synchronous online learning, let's bring back this key takeaway introduced earlier:

> **Do not replicate face-to-face instruction in an online environment.**

What Is the Relation of Learning and Seat Time?

As part of the exploration of synchronous online learning, it is important to examine the relationship between learning and seat time. By seat time, I am referring to the amount of time a student spends attending a class in real time, whether virtually or physically. Synchronous online learning assumes some type of seat time, because students are in a virtual space in real time.

What is the result of seat time? Does seat time equal learning? Seat time is not equal to learning and essentially amounts to attendance and not much else. Being in a synchronous space (virtual or physical) does not equate to or guarantee learning. Because of this, learning should not be measured by attendance or seat time. Can you focus on competency-based learning instead? Assess whether your online learners are meeting proficiency of the learning goals rather than staring at a screen for a specific amount of time. When it comes down to it, what else should matter other than learning-goal proficiency?

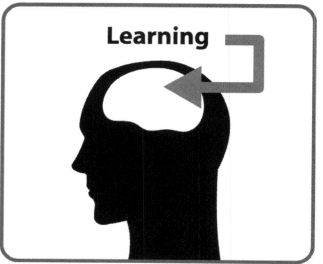

Figure 16.1: Seat Time versus Learning

Synchronous Online Learning in Each Pillar

Understanding when to use synchronous learning and when to use asynchronous learning is key to designing successful online learning.

I teased at this key takeaway earlier but didn't really tell you when each is appropriate. This is partly because some of this you will just have to figure out on your own. Every class has different learning objectives, and what is better for synchronous learning in one class may not be best for another. However, I can give you some general guidelines of when synchronous online learning is appropriate based on the pillars of teaching.

Content Delivery

If your face-to-face classes have typically consisted of mostly direct instruction for content delivery, your first instinct with online learning may be to simply transfer this direct instruction to a video conferencing platform. Done! You have an online course.

By now, though, you should know that it's not that easy! There are several challenges with delivering content via synchronous online learning. The first challenge is rooted in the truth that video calls are more fatiguing than face-to-face interactions are. Many people around the world can relate to this after experiencing the phenomenon firsthand in 2020. In fact, a new term entered the pop culture arena to explain this feeling—"Zoom fatigue." An article in the *Harvard Business Review*, "How to Combat Zoom Fatigue," explains why video calls are more tiring: it has to do with how our brains process information over video and through screens. In a nutshell, video calls require two things that make us tired: more focus in order to comprehend information and staring at a screen without visual breaks.[56] In an early 2021 review of the literature, Bailenson presents four additional explanations for Zoom fatigue: "Excessive amounts of close-up eye gaze, cognitive load, increased self-evaluation from staring at video of oneself, and constraints on physical mobility.[57]

What does this mean for you as an online teacher? This means that a student who struggled to focus and absorb information in an hour-long lecture in a face-to-face learning environment will likely absorb even less (if any) of the same lecture via video.

Face-to-face learning is more forgiving than online learning. Therefore, you have to be more strategic with online learning.

The second problem is a lack of physical proximity to learners. With direct instruction in a face-to-face environment, teachers have the advantage of proximity to gain attention. Without physical proximity, direct instruction tends to be fairly ineffective online, unless it occurs in very small bursts.

In online learning environments, proximity is not in your favor. You cannot stand over a learner's shoulder and ensure a task is accomplished.

Additionally, nonverbal cues guide direct instruction in face-to-face learning environments.[58] Video tends to lack nonverbal cues. In fact, video not only lacks nonverbal cues but also makes those cues more complex. Bailenson explains that nonverbal communication in face-to-face interactions is natural and effortless, while nonverbal

56   Liz Fosslien and Mollie West Duffy, "How to Combat Zoom Fatigue," *Harvard Business Review*, April 29, 2020, https://hbr.org/2020/04/how-to-combat-zoom-fatigue.

57   Jeremy N. Bailenson, "Nonverbal Overload: A Theoretical Argument for the Causes of Zoom Fatigue," *Technology, Mind, and Behavior* 2, no. 1 (2021), https://doi.org/10.1037/tmb0000030.

58   Gurley, "Educators' Preparation to Teach."

communication via video requires people to work harder to send and receive signals.[59] The complexities of nonverbal cues in synchronous online learning make direct instruction challenging.

> **Within the same time period, you cannot cover as much in online learning as you can in face-to-face. You must whittle your curriculum down to the most essential learning objectives.**

Finally, synchronous online learning is notoriously plagued with technical issues. If your course is reliant on synchronous video calls, you may be causing yourself unnecessary headaches. Personally, I try to avoid unnecessary technical headaches at all costs. The reality is, there comes a point when technology becomes a hindrance instead of a catalyst to learning. Any instructional technologist will tell you that is absolutely not the goal of using technology as part of the learning process.

So, what can you successfully do with content delivery via synchronous online learning?

- Introduce a topic, gain excitement, and "hook" learners. If you remember back to your teacher education training, this is referred to as the anticipatory set. What can you do during synchronous class time to get students excited for learning more about a particular topic? After getting them hooked, they can then dig deeper asynchronously.

- Present "mini" chunks of content. Make sure to embed brain breaks (more about that in a bit) to give both learners and yourself visual and mental time away from the screen. Later in this chapter, I will present some ideas to help with this idea of chunking content in video calls.

- Switch from direct instruction to an active strategy for gaining content knowledge. For example, let's say my students are learning about animal cells. Instead of explaining the organelles of an animal cell, I send students into virtual breakout rooms to work in small groups. Each group is assigned a different organelle of the animal cell to research. Groups research their assigned organelle and use a collaborative digital tool, such as Google Jamboard, to share their findings. Then, everyone comes back to the main virtual room and each group shares what they learned about their assigned organelle.

---

59   Bailenson, "Nonverbal Overload."

These are just a few ideas. If you need to deliver content via a synchronous online format, make it short, make it active, and try to gain excitement for the topic at hand before moving the remainder of the learning to asynchronous strategies.

 As you determine what strategy to use for your content delivery, ask yourself, "Could this be accomplished with a video?" If the answer is yes, could you create a video of the content and then use your synchronous time to accomplish other goals? Note that the last thing you want to do is fatigue your learners with too much video content. If the lesson or unit is already video-heavy, then maybe synchronous is the way to go for this particular case.

Assessment

Formative assessment is assessment for learning. I like to think of formative assessments as checks for understanding. **Summative assessment** is assessment of learning. For me, formative assessments are what guide my instruction, with no grades attached. Summative assessments indicate competency of learning goals. Through summative assessments, I can tell if a student is nearing proficiency, has reached proficiency, or has exceeded proficiency of a learning goal.

Later in the book, "Chapter 18: Assessment in an Online Environment" will discuss assessment in depth, so I am going to make this section brief. You can accomplish some formative assessment synchronously, typically with "in-the-moment" checks

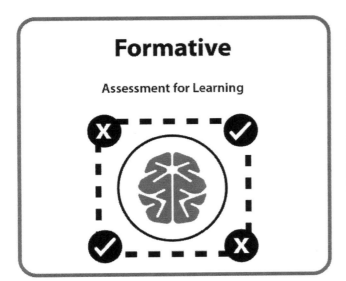

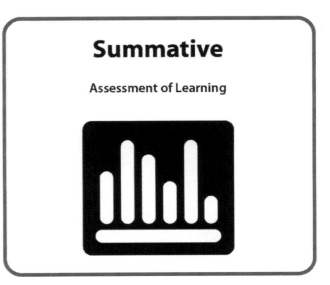

Figure 16.2: Formative versus Summative Assessment

for understanding. Below are some examples of formative assessments during a group video call:

- The teacher uses a digital tool such as Quizizz or Pear Deck to facilitate formative assessment. Students answer questions, and the teacher receives a summary of the responses.

- Students give a "fist to five," where showing a fist or adding a 0 to the chat means they feel they do not understand a concept. Holding up five fingers or adding a 5 to the chat means they could teach the concept to someone else.

- Students use the "raise hand" feature in a video conferencing tool to indicate their understanding. Some video conferencing tools have additional features that can be used for formative assessment, such as a yes/no feature or a survey tool.

These types of group synchronous assessments should never have a grade attached to them and should only be used to guide teacher instruction. Synchronous online instruction has too many variables that can affect individual performance to attach a grade to this data. In addition, use these types of formative assessments to check overall group status in learning, not the status of individual students.

Earlier in the book, I introduced one-on-one appointments as a strategy for getting to know your students and developing relationships. One-on-one synchronous meetings can also be used for assessment, either formative or summative. Sometimes there is no better way to check a student's understanding than to have a personal conversation with that student and ask questions that assess the student's depth of knowledge on a subject. This can be time-consuming, yet it is an incredibly powerful way to assess. Some would argue that teachers should focus on these types of assessments in online learning environments. A bonus is that it works as an extra relationship building strategy and an opportunity to check on learner well-being.

 By the way, assessment via personal conversations is a popular strategy for individualized and personalized learning environments.

My final strategy for assessment in synchronous online learning is to use synchronous time to introduce an assessment that will be completed asynchronously. This can be a good time for students to ask questions as well.

Feedback

Giving effective feedback to learners is vital to the learning process and a large part of a teacher's job description.[60] In a group synchronous virtual session, you can give general feedback directed toward the group. Maybe several students made the same error on an assignment, so you can address this error to the group.

I would never give feedback directed toward an individual in a group virtual session. In a face-to-face learning environment, you can easily have side conversations or pull a learner away from the group to have a private conversation, but this is not possible in a group video call.

 You never want feedback to seem like a reprimand instead of part of the learning process.

In the assessment section, we discussed having one-on-one personal conversations as an assessment strategy; personal conversations can be a great feedback strategy as well. Again, this can be time-consuming but also very powerful. You can even combine assessment and feedback into personal conversations. Let's say that, through a personal conversation with a learner, you find they do not have a grasp on a particular learning goal. Pivot and use the time to provide feedback and redirect the student.

As with content delivery, you should analyze if feedback could be accomplished asynchronously with a video instead of synchronously.

Social-Emotional Learning

 Maslow before you Bloom! You must focus on the social-emotional side of learning.

This one is easy. You should spend as much of your synchronous online learning time as possible on building relationships, developing a sense of community, and making connections with your students. This is where synchronous online learning shines.

---

60   Paul Orsmond, Stephen Merry, and Kevin Reiling, "Biology Students' Utilization of Tutors' Formative Feedback: A Qualitative Interview Study," *Assessment and Evaluation in Higher Education* 30, no. 4 (2005): 369–86, https://doi .org/10.1080/02602930500099177.

You can do this with whole groups, small groups, and individually. You can do this in your chair. You can do this everywhere! Below are some ideas for social-emotional-focused synchronous activities.

- Always start class synchronous sessions with a well-being check. Make it fun!

- Find a tool that has a draw feature (for example, Padlet, Pear Deck, or Nearpod). Have students draw how they are feeling.

- Have students share a **GIF** or meme describing their current mood. A GIF is basically an animated image. A bunch of images are strung together and put on a loop to look a little like a video. If you use social media, you have most likely seen lots of GIFs as they are very popular in the social media world. Some video conferencing tools, such as Microsoft Teams, have GIFs built into the tool. Padlet is also a good tool for this as you can use the "search the web" feature which has a "choose GIF" option.

- Let students pick a favorite "something" to share—movie, game, song, sport, or food. This is also a great way to entice students to show up to synchronous class sessions. Bonus!

- If you have access to a student messaging tool, such as Hāpara Highlights (hapara.com/highlights), send students personalized messages during synchronous time, especially if students are in breakout rooms or working on a task.

> Relationship building does not come naturally in online learning as it does in face-to-face. Therefore, you have to be intentional about consistently embedding relationship building activities into online learning.

Figure 16.3 summarizes the main takeaway from this section. Focus synchronous time in the SEL pillar. If you find yourself struggling to decide what learning objectives are appropriate for synchronous online learning, take a step back and look at the big picture. Determine your ultimate learning goal. I always ask myself, "Can this learning goal be accomplished asynchronously?" If yes, then I do as much as I can asynchronously, and save precious synchronous time for objectives that are better met in real time.

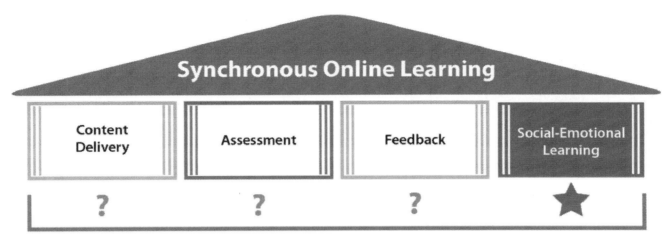

Figure 16.3: Synchronous Online Learning in Each Pillar

Tips for Effective Synchronous Group Sessions

➡ *Split the Class into Smaller Groups*

If at all possible, split your class into smaller groups for synchronous sessions. The smaller the group, the easier and more fluid video calls become. In addition, it is much easier to engage a small group of learners in a synchronous session.

➡ *Make It Optional*

There are at least two reasons why synchronous group sessions should be optional: equity and assessment.

 Synchronous online learning is not equitable: even if your educational institution has thoughtfully tackled the large equity issue of access, there are still home environments and personal lives to consider. They will never be equitable.

- What if you have a student that can only complete their learning tasks at night because they have to watch their younger siblings while their caregiver(s) works during the day?

- What if you have a student that has to work a job outside the home and needs a flexible learning schedule?

If attendance in synchronous sessions is tied to a course grade, these students have already failed your class.

The second reason why synchronous group sessions should be optional is that, as we discussed earlier in the chapter, group synchronous assessments should never have a grade attached. Synchronous online instruction has too many variables that can affect individual performance to attach this data to a grade. If a student doesn't attend a synchronous group session and their grade is docked as a result, you are measuring attendance, not learning. Instead, have an asynchronous assessment that measures learning and attaches to a grade.

Remember that synchronous group sessions can always be recorded and watched at a later time. Of course, a student is not receiving the full benefit by watching a recording compared to attending live, but if the student is showing proficiency in the course learning goals in other ways, does it even matter?

What if synchronous group sessions are optional and no one comes?

If you build it, they will come.

In other words, if you make your synchronous online sessions engaging, fun, interactive, and focused on social-emotional well-being, your students will show up! Will all of them come? Probably not, but remember that attendance does not equate to learning. Every student may not be able to attend. If a student that doesn't attend the optional group sessions is reaching proficiency with all learning goals, does it matter that the student doesn't show up to synchronous group meetings? Make an intentional effort to connect with that student in other ways.

Maslow before you Bloom! You must focus on the social-emotional side of learning.

There are other strategies you can use to increase attendance at optional synchronous group meetings. Earlier in the book, as a method for building self-direction, I presented the idea of assigning students jobs or roles based on their interests. This can also be a strategy for boosting attendance. If a student knows they are in charge of a certain aspect of the meeting, they are more likely to come.

 Of course, this is optional, and you should never call out a student that isn't there to accomplish their "job."

In "Chapter 14: Maslow before You Bloom," I introduced the idea of seeking course feedback from students as a way to develop course ownership and therefore increase self-direction. This is also a great strategy for getting students to show up to optional group meetings. Give ample warning that you will be seeking feedback on the course at the upcoming virtual meeting. Students may want to show up to air grievances, and you should let them (within reason of course)! Don't take this personally. Set up the session in a way that feedback is shared productively.

You can also reach out to students individually and make them feel wanted in group synchronous sessions. Tell students that you really need their input at the upcoming class meeting. You could mention, "I saw that you needed help with the assignment you submitted today. Come to the group meeting tomorrow, and I will answer those questions for everyone."

 ## *Technical Setup*

In order to successfully lead synchronous group sessions, you need to have a technical setup that helps you teach well in this type of online environment. There are several factors to consider.

Monitors

You need to have two monitors or screens. Having two screens allows you the flexibility to share one screen with the students in the video call and view student webcams, the chat box, and any polling features on the other. Alternately, you can view your students' webcams and the chat on one screen and your notes on the other. If you plan to share your screen in video calls, a second monitor is critical. There is no way you can share resources large enough for students to be able to see, view student video, and monitor the chat all on one screen, especially if you have a smaller device. More screen space makes your life easier and enhances the screen sharing experience for learners.

Having two monitors means that you have your device, such as a desktop or laptop computer, attached to an external monitor or even a smaller television to act as a second screen. You could also have two external monitors that attach to your device. This is the setup I use. To make it even more convenient, I have those two monitors on monitor mounts that are fully adjustable, so I can move the monitors up, down, left, and right and even rotate them.

If you don't have an extra computer monitor or small television, you can use two devices instead. This setup works but is not ideal. Maybe your school provides you with a tablet in addition to a laptop. If you need to use two devices, you will have to sign into the video call on both devices. Use the larger device for any screen sharing and the smaller device for the video call features, such as chat, viewing webcams, and so on. Make sure to mute and turn your camera off on the smaller device or else you will get high-pitched feedback through the video call.

 Two Screens for Teachers (twoscreensforteachers.org) is a project of DonorsChoose that focuses specifically on matching teachers with donors who will gift you a 22-inch monitor.

Webcam and Microphone

Two more pieces of the technical setup are a webcam and microphone. You may be able to use the built-in webcam and microphone on your device, but this will depend on their quality as well as the environment or room you are in. For example, my old office was a bit echoey, so I always had to use an external microphone. My new office has better acoustics, and I can now use the built-in microphone on my device for all my video calls.

Figure 16.4: Sample Two-Monitor Setup

Many people have earbuds with a microphone on the cord. I have found that this microphone can brush up against your clothing or a necklace and make unwanted background noise. Wireless headphones work well, as the microphone is built into the headset. If you share a working space with others, using headphones during video calls may be a requirement.

If you determine that you need to purchase an external microphone, keep in mind you may also need or want to use that microphone for recording videos. I have found that my built-in microphone works great for video calls but does not work so well for creating videos. Therefore, I have a microphone I use for video creation and also keep close to my computer as a backup for video calls.

For video recording, I have found that a good old-fashioned headset with the microphone that wraps around to your mouth works the best for me. And, as an added bonus, it makes me look and feel like an air traffic controller. You can't beat that! Honestly, I have multiple microphone options on hand at all times, because you never know with video calls.

The webcam you use will depend on the setup of your device and monitor(s). I used to use an external webcam that was mounted on top of my main monitor. This worked well until I upgraded to a larger monitor. Then, the webcam was so far up that it was pointing down at the top of my head. I didn't care for the view others were getting, so I moved back to using the built-in webcam on my laptop by placing my laptop under my monitor. Now, when I am on a video call, I move my large, main monitor up a bit (this is where the adjustable mounts come in handy) to reveal the webcam on my laptop. I use this screen for the video call chat, participant list, and webcam views. The larger monitor is used for anything I need to share or notes I need to access.

One word of advice if you do plan to buy an external webcam: I made the mistake of buying a wide-angle webcam. What I didn't consider is that you want to show as little of your background as possible to avoid distractions for your learners. A wide-angle lens does exactly what it says—shows a wide angle! It wasn't my wisest choice as an online teacher.

What is in the background of your video does matter. The last thing you want is your background to be distracting. Try to make your background as simple, clean, and uncluttered as possible. Most video conferencing tools now have virtual background or background blur options, although this may not be an option if your internet connection has low bandwidth.

You will have to do some adjusting to find the perfect technical setup for your monitors, devices, microphones, webcams, headphones, and backgrounds. Oh my!

Document Camera

A **document camera** presents a real-time image to an audience; in essence, it is the digital version of an old-school overhead projector. Having a document camera is optional and depends on both what you teach and your teaching style. Hands-on topics (e.g., art, music, career and technical education, and science) as well as topics such as math may benefit from a document camera.

There are many portable document camera options on the market for under $100.

 You can also mimic a document camera with a smartphone or tablet. I have a stand that holds my iPad. Then, Airplay (apple.com/airplay) allows me to display my iPad screen on my computer. Once I open the camera of my iPad, anything I place underneath appears on the computer screen.

Software

One final element to consider for your synchronous online teaching setup is software or functionality that helps when you are sharing your screen in a video call. Personally, I want two functionalities to assist screen shares: zoom and focus.

The ability to zoom in on something on your screen is important during screen shares. For example, if I am explaining instructions for an asynchronous learning activity, I may need to zoom into those instructions in order for my students to see what I am referring to. Mac OS has an amazing built-in zoom feature that you can control with keyboard shortcuts.

 You may have to go into the accessibility section of the settings to turn this feature on. The default keyboard shortcut is the control key + using the scroll gesture (sliding two fingers up and down) on the trackpad (up for zooming in and down for zooming out). You can do some customization of this feature in the settings.

Windows OS has a setting called Magnifier that has similar functionality. You can find Magnifier in the Ease of Access center of the settings.

Focus means you can draw attention to a specific area of your screen. I am a fan of a mouse spotlight tool, as shown in **Figure 16.5**. Most likely you will have to purchase a tool that has this feature. I use Mouseposé (boinx.com/mousepose) for Mac OS. Windows OS has a few different tools you can purchase. Do a search for "mouse spotlight tool for <enter your operating system>."

Custom cursors are another tool you can use for focusing, as shown in **Figure 16.6**. There are many free custom cursor tools out there. I use a Google Chrome extension called Custom Cursor for Chrome (bit.ly/chromecustomcursor).

 Windows 10 OS's "Ease of Access" center includes cursor color and size changing options.

Custom Cursor for Chrome

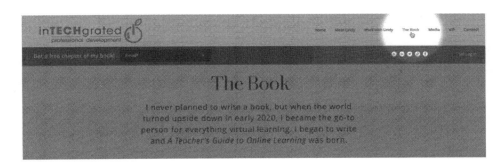

Figure 16.5: Mouse Spotlight Tool Example

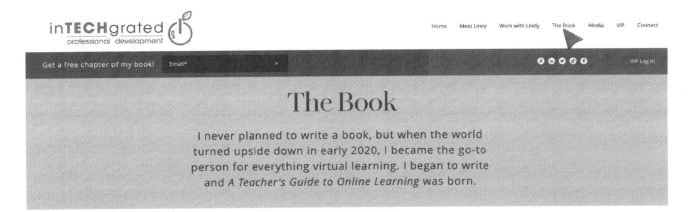

Figure 16.6: Custom Cursor Example

Norms and Expectations

You have to lay the tracks before the train can run.

Just as in face-to-face learning, you must set norms and expectations for synchronous time. In fact, transparency of norms may be even more important in online learning since typical face-to-face norms are not available to either student or teacher.[61]

Norms and expectations look a little different in online learning. Have as few of them as possible, and make them as simple as possible. Better yet, crowdsource them from your students. If students feel ownership, they are more likely to follow those norms and expectations. Start every synchronous video call with a reminder of what they are.

Organization and consistency are critical to online learning.

Below is an example norm list:

- I would love to see your face, but video is always optional.

- Stay muted until you are ready to share.

- Stay on topic in the chat box.

Create a graphic of the norm list to display at the beginning of every video call. View an example in **Figure 16.7**.

---

61   Anderson et al., "Assessing Teaching Presence."

Figure 16.7: Example Norms Graphic

By the way, you should never require that cameras be on during video calls. One, it is an equity issue.

Two, a privacy issue. And three, remember our discussion of seat time and ask yourself what purpose requiring webcams is serving. I know, I know: it is awkward talking to a screen. This is something you will get used to with time if synchronous video calls are an important or required part of your online course. Educator Tracey Nesrallah in Ottawa, Ontario, Canada, shared the following regarding her grade 6 class as part of the Ottawa Catholic School Board Virtual Academy:

> "I have never asked my students to turn on their cameras. It is hard for me to teach to a blank screen, but I do so I can protect my students' privacy. Many of my students don't have a private and quiet space to work; there are many things going on behind them. Their toddler siblings are playing or sitting on their lap. Their parents are washing dishes or cooking lunch. I don't want someone taking a screenshot of their face and then using it against them. I don't want my students with ADHD to be overwhelmed by thirty tiny faces staring at them on the screen. I still know my students. I would walk right past them on the street, but if they spoke, I would know it is them. I know their voices. I know which ones are outgoing and which are shy. I don't need to see their face to know that about them. I have gotten to know them through their writing, their projects, their emails, their conversations. Is it hard for me? Yes! Sometimes I feel lonely, and I wonder if I am reaching them. But I can see that they are engaged through their work, through interactive platforms like Pear Deck, the Google Meet polls, hand gestures, and in small group breakout rooms. When I talk to their parents and they tell me that on Sunday nights their child is so excited for the Google Meet the next day, I don't think a tiny image on a screen will help me know that student better."

Earlier I mentioned a response I received in the learner survey that made me think about webcams in a different way: "I do not enjoy sharing my camera. I understand that the teachers feel weird without the other face online, but has it ever occurred to them that I might feel weird sharing my face?" I have to say that honestly had not occurred to me until now! Even in pre-COVID times, being on a video call with my camera on was second nature to me. I had to think back to my first video calls and remember that it can be a little awkward.

Have a Key for Chat Communications

Set a handful of standard chat communications for specific actions. **Figure 16.8** provides an example. Make sure not to have too many, or else they will be confusing instead of helpful.

Chat Communication	Meaning
BRB	I need to step away (like a virtual hall pass)
Back	After a hall pass, indicate when you are back and engaged in the virtual call
Claps or 👏	Virtual claps when others share or when you like something shared
See you soon!	Indicate when you leave a virtual call

Figure 16.8: Sample Key for Chat Communications

Use Hand Gestures

In addition to standard chat communications, if students have their webcams on, use hand gestures or hand signals to communicate common information as well as to sneakily incorporate some movement into your synchronous virtual sessions.

 Make sure you have a chat box alternative for any hand gestures. For example, in addition to the virtual claps in the chat box, you and students who have their video on could do a golf clap anytime someone shares during a virtual group session. You could also borrow from American Sign Language (ASL) to develop hand signals for when students understand/don't understand or agree/disagree. Have students help come up with these hand gestures to create ownership and buy-in.

Hand gestures are a good idea for several reasons. The mute/unmute process can be incredibly awkward during video calls. Hand gestures allow students to participate in the call without having to unmute.

 This can also help with equity if you have a student that is not comfortable unmuting due to their environment. This is also a way to entice students to turn on their cameras, if you feel that is important.

Some video conferencing tools have features that mimic hand gestures. Participants can raise a hand, give a thumbs up/down, or indicate yes/no.

 ## *Brain Breaks*

Earlier in the chapter, we discussed how video calls require two things that cause fatigue, one of which is staring at a screen without visual breaks. This means it is imperative to build breaks into video calls. A brain break can be as quick as you want to make it and can be anything that gets eyes off the device and bodies moving, as illustrated in **Figure 16.9**.

Move

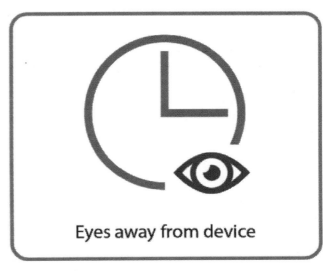

Eyes away from device

Figure 16.9: Brain Breaks

Drawer Dash or Run and Grab

Challenge students to go find an item and bring it back to their computer to show everyone or mention what the item is in the chat.

 Note that for equity purposes, never call out a kid that doesn't bring back an item or require that webcams be turned on to view the item. You can take this in many different directions:

- Relate to your content area or the topic you are currently learning. For example, a world language teacher could say, "Run and grab an everyday household item and tell me what it is in X language." A literature or reading teacher could say, "Drawer dash to find an item that reminds you of the story we just read."

A math or science teacher could say, "Drawer dash to find an item that is smaller than 1000 millimeters" or "Run and grab something that is square in shape."

- Focus on something for relationship building. For example, you could say, "Drawer dash to find something that makes you happy" or "Run and grab something that shows a little of who you are."

- Choose something random and fun. For example, students could run and grab something that is red, something from the kitchen, something that smells good, or something from a junk drawer.

Copycat

GIFs can inspire fun and productive brain breaks. To find GIFs, conduct an internet search or use a website such as GIPHY (giphy.com).

Note that GIPHY is an adult-only website and not one that you want your students visiting.

GIPHY

Search GIPHY for "cats stretching" or conduct an internet search for "cat stretching GIFs." Find the GIF of choice and tell students to "copycat." The concept is really difficult . . . you have to copy the cat! This gets them stretching side to side or stretching their arms up. Of course, it doesn't have to be a cat, but I find students really like the animal stretching GIFs. It's a win-win! To get started, try searching for "stretch," "move," "cat," or "dog." Make sure to add "GIF" to the search if conducting a generic internet search and not using a tool such as GIPHY.

If you are a Microsoft Teams user, GIFs are embedded into the "Posts" feature for quick and easy access. You can also adjust the GIFs setting for the Team to "Strict" mode to ensure only kid-friendly GIFs appear in the search.

Dance Break

Search for a dance GIF for students to copy. Another approach is to play a song and prompt students to dance along to the beat.

If you do play a song, be aware of copyright laws and ensure you are legally able to play that song.

TikTok Dance Challenges

This is similar to "dance break" but focused on viral social media dances. Find a video of a dance (it doesn't have to be a TikTok video), such as the right foot, left foot dance. Challenge students to follow along or learn the dance by the next group session.

 You can find many of these on YouTube. Of course, not all viral dances are school appropriate, so don't pick one on the fly.

Just Breathe

 If you need to focus the group, use a breathing GIF. Search for "breathing" or "breathing exercise" GIFs. This is a great option for students with physical limitations.

Minute to Win It

These are basically goofy challenges like those from the game show *Minute to Win It*. For example, see how many seconds you can balance your pen or pencil on your nose. Stand on one leg for one minute. Try to touch your tongue to your nose.

Move It Extension

Move It (bit.ly/moveitchromeextension) is a Google Chrome extension that you can set to any five-minute interval. Move It will automatically pop up on your screen at the set time with a prompt of something active to do, such as climb the ladder on the spot for a count of ten.

*Move It
Chrome Extension*

 If you need more movement ideas, Sanford Health's website *fit* (fit. sanfordhealth.org) includes a tool that shuffles and generates random activities, such as running in place, mountain climbers, and tricep stretches. There is also a set of cards that you can print and use.

Experiments with Google

Experiments with Google (experiments.withgoogle.com) is a website where coders showcase projects. There are a few experiments that get kids moving and are also learning opportunities:

- Move Mirror (experiments.withgoogle.com/move-mirror)— Move Mirror is an **artificial intelligence (AI)** experiment. AI is the capability of a machine to imitate intelligent human behavior.[62] In this AI experiment, GIFs are created based on your movements. Place yourself in the webcam frame and move around. The system matches images of your poses and puts those images together into a GIF.

Experiments with Google

- Body Synth (experiments.withgoogle.com/body-synth)— This experiment turns your body into an instrument. Move around to make music with your body!

- Semi-Conductor (experiments.withgoogle.com/semi-conductor)— This is another AI experiment where you conduct your own orchestra by moving your arms.

Movement Videos

- GoNoodle (gonoodle.com)—This is a collection of movement- and mindfulness-focused videos and a solid option for younger kids.
- Super Movers (bit.ly/bbcsupermovers)—Super Movers is from the BBC and is a collection of videos, again particularly suited to younger children, to get them moving while they learn.

GoNoodle

 If you can't access the videos from the Super Movers website, many of the videos are available on YouTube.

---

62   *Merriam-Webster*, s.v. "artificial intelligence (*n.*)," accessed January 10, 2021, https://www.merriam-webster .com/dictionary/artificialintelligence.

Sculpt It! Draw It!

If you have provided students with Play-Doh as part of their learning-at-home kits, use it for brain breaks. This is an easy one to integrate into your content area as well. For example, you have two minutes to sculpt . . . a noun, national landmark, vocabulary word, or animal. Another approach is to integrate the brain break into a social-emotional focus; you have two minutes to sculpt your pet or the pet of your dreams. The possibilities are endless! If students don't have Play-Doh, you can have them draw instead. For example, draw a diagram of photosynthesis or a sight word.

This list of brain breaks should get you started. Brain breaks really come down to moving and having fun! Get creative and ask students for ideas.

 ## *Have a Class Schedule*

Bring a little structure to synchronous online learning and create a schedule for group sessions. Divide the schedule into common themes. This helps keep learner engagement in group video calls. Remember our discussion of how video calls are fatiguing. With synchronous video sessions, you must keep your learners busy and on their toes. *Figure 16.10* on the next page illustrates an example for a one-hour class:

 For engaging learners in synchronous group sessions, I have found using the backchannel wall of Padlet to be beneficial as it has more interactive features compared to the chat in most video conferencing tools. For example, Padlet has a draw feature, as shown in *Figure 16.11* on the next page. This image is an example from a synchronous group session where I asked participants to draw how they were currently feeling. The draw feature offers lots of options to engage learners, and the camera feature is useful for sharing even if students don't turn on their video. Plus, the draw feature adds a small hands-on strategy to synchronous online time. Pear Deck has similar features.

 ## *Embrace the Awkward Teacher Pause*

All teachers have experienced the awkward teacher pause in a face-to-face environment. You ask a question and . . . silence. When I was a new teacher, I didn't understand that this silence didn't necessarily mean students did not know the answer or were not engaged. Many learners need this silence to process information, especially students who are English-language learners (ELL). The same is true for synchronous virtual learning.

Approximate Time	Schedule	Description
As students are joining the virtual session	Fun share	Have a fun share up on the screen. I like to do yes or no questions for this purpose. For example, pineapple on pizza? Yes or no? This is a good way to spark conversations and set a positive, collaborative tone for the call from the beginning.
2 minutes	Review norms and expectations	Quickly review the norms list.
15 minutes	Check-in	Focus on SEL. How is everyone? Make it fun!
3 minutes	Brain break	Stand up and touch your toes ten times.
5 minutes	Instructions for learning activity	Introduce the learning activity for today's session.
15 minutes	Breakout rooms or hands-on activity	Send students off to complete the learning activity. Make it collaborative or hands-on. Remember it doesn't have to be in front of the computer! Set a timer.
3 minutes	Brain break	Bring everyone back together and refocused. Use a breathing GIF.
10 minutes	Share, Reflect, Questions	Reflect on the learning activity, share, and answer questions.
5 minutes	Overview of asynchronous learning tasks for the week	Review learning tasks for the week (or day).
2 minutes	Wrap up and bye!	Final call for questions. Give a little pep talk, encouraging message, or inspirational quote.

Figure 16.10: Example Class Schedule

I always joke when I am facilitating synchronous virtual professional development sessions that the awkward teacher pause over a video call is even more awkward, but this really is so true! If participants are all muted, you may literally have complete and utter silence in response to your question. This is ok! Embrace the silence and allow students time to process.

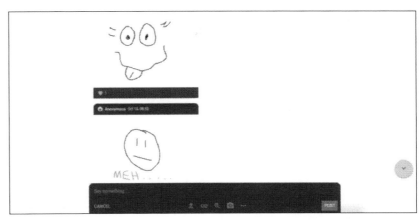

Figure 16.11: Drawing Feature in Padlet

Just Say No

In general, when it comes to synchronous group sessions, just say no to the strategies below:

- Direct instruction

- Student presentations

- Large group discussions

Virtual meetings just don't work for these strategies. In "Why We're Exhausted by Zoom," the author explains why large group discussions don't work via video calls. It is stated that in order to achieve conversation, "all the tools of human interaction are recruited."[63] Video calls lack human interaction cues and are meant for one speaker at a time.

There are more effective strategies for spending your precious virtual synchronous time.

63   Susan D. Blum, "Why We're Exhausted by Zoom," *Inside Higher Ed* (blog), April 22, 2020, https://www.insidehighered.com/advice/2020/04/22/professor-explores-why-zoom-classes-deplete-her-energy-opinion.

More Synchronous Learning Strategies

Sometimes you may want to shake up your synchronous group sessions and add a virtual guest speaker or virtual field trip. Both of these strategies can be used to entice attendance to group video calls.

Virtual Guest Speakers

Virtual guest speakers are bound to generate excitement and will encourage learners to attend a group synchronous session. Just as you would connect with guest speakers to bring them into the physical classroom, do the same for your virtual classroom. Send guest speakers the link to the video call.

However, ensure your video conferencing tool allows outside guests to join. This is a perfect question for your school technology director.

You may want to provide your emergency contact information in case the speaker has technical issues joining the video session.

Virtual Field Trips

Virtual field trips can add a level of engagement to online learning. There are more options out there than you could imagine, and more are being added every day. There are many virtual field trip options in the list below. However, depending on the exact format of the virtual field trip, some of these may be better as asynchronous activities. You could use the synchronous time to introduce the virtual trip and gain excitement, and then send students off to complete the virtual trip on their own.

Google Arts and Culture

If you don't want to spend time tracking down virtual experiences, look no further than Google Arts and Culture (artsandculture. google.com), which includes national parks, museums, art galleries, opera houses, and more. Note that all Google Expeditions are being migrated to Google Arts and Culture in 2021.

Google Arts and Culture

Zoos and Aquariums

Many zoos and aquariums around the world have live camera footage in exhibits. For example, the San Diego Zoo had over twelve live cams available in 2020. Below is a non-exhaustive list of other zoos and aquariums in alphabetical order that have live cams as of 2020:

- Alaska Zoo
- Aquarium of the Pacific
- Calgary Zoo
- Chattanooga Zoo
- Cleveland Metroparks Zoo
- Dublin Zoo
- Edinburgh Zoo
- Georgia Aquarium
- Greater Cleveland Aquarium
- Houston Zoo
- Indianapolis Zoo
- Kansas City Zoo
- Maryland Zoo
- Memphis Zoo
- Milwaukee County Zoo
- Monterey Bay Aquarium
- National Aquarium
- The National Zoo
- Omaha Zoo
- Pittsburgh Zoo
- Seattle Aquarium
- Trevor Zoo (this is a zoo inside a high school in Millbrook, New York, USA)
- Woodland Park Zoo
- Zoo Atlanta

Museums and Art Galleries

In addition to the museums and art galleries that are part of Google Arts and Culture, many museums and art galleries around the world have virtual tours of their exhibits on their own websites:

- The Georgia O'Keeffe Museum
- The Louvre
- The Met
- National Museum of Natural History
- National Women's History Museum
- The Rock and Roll Hall of Fame
- Salvador Dali Museum
- The Vatican Museum
- Vizcaya Museum and Gardens
- Boston Children's Museum

Websites

- AirPano (airpano.com) has virtual journeys from around the world in the form of 360 videos and interactive 360 images. Explore the Taj Mahal, Niagara Falls, Machu Picchu, the Great Wall of China, and more.

- Explore.org (explore.org/livecams) streams live cams from around the world. Visit the bald eagle cam on Catalina Island, the polar bears in Wapusk National Park, or the underwater manatee camera from Homosassa Springs Wildlife State Park.

- Xplorit (xplorit.com) is filled with virtual tours of cities, monuments, and more.

- HistoryView (historyview.org) includes historical virtual tours, such as the Lincoln Memorial, Liberty Bell, Titanic, and more.

Google Maps and Google Earth Street View

Both Google Maps (google.com/maps) and Google Earth (google.com/earth) have a street view feature. In both tools, street view is accessed via the peg man as shown in **Figure 16.12**. Pick up the peg man with your mouse and drag to anywhere you want to view. Drop the peg man on that location, and Google Maps or Earth will instantly send you into street view, if available. Not every place in the world has street view content.

Google Maps

Google Earth

Other

- Cities and monuments—Stonehenge and New Orleans, Louisiana, are two examples of cities and monuments that have created virtual tours.

- National parks—Yellowstone National Park has virtual tours created by the park. Yosemite National Park has Virtual Yosemite (virtualyosemite.org/virtual-tour), an interactive tour of the park.

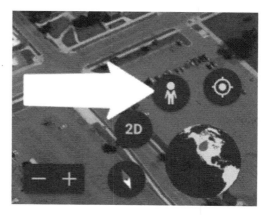

Figure 16.12: Google Earth Peg Man

Many more national parks have tours on Google Arts and Culture, including Bryce Canyon National Park, Carlsbad Caverns National Park, Dry Tortugas National Park, Hawaii Volcanoes National Park, and Kenai Fjords National Park.

- Conservation and/or educational organizations—National Geographic, The Nature Conservancy, and the United States Botanic Garden all have some form of virtual tour.

- Universities—Oxford University (bit.ly/oxforduniversityvirtualtour) has a very detailed virtual tour and other universities are beginning to follow suit.

- Research centers—The NASA Glenn Research Center (nasa.gov/glennvirtualtours) has several virtual tours.

- Access Mars (accessmars.withgoogle.com) is a virtual tour of Mars recorded from NASA's Curiosity rover.

Summary

This section outlines the most important parts from the chapter:

- Being in a synchronous space does not equate to or guarantee learning, so learning should not be measured by attendance or seat time.

- Synchronous online learning is not equitable. Even if your educational institution has thoughtfully tackled the large equity issue of access, there are still home environments and personal lives to consider.

- Synchronous group sessions should be optional.

- If at all possible, split your class into smaller groups for synchronous sessions.

- Focus synchronous time on SEL.

- There are several challenges with delivering content via synchronous online learning.

- Video calls are more fatiguing than face-to-face interactions.

- Direct instruction tends to be fairly ineffective online, unless it occurs in very small bursts.

- You can accomplish some formative assessment synchronously, but synchronous online instruction has too many variables that can affect individual performance to attach a grade to this data.

- In a group synchronous virtual session, you can give general feedback directed toward the group but never give feedback directed toward an individual.

Reflection

After reading "Chapter 16: Synchronous Online Learning," reflect on how the content can be applied to your unique learning environment.

Share your reflections online using the hashtag **#TeachersGuideToOnline**.

What role will synchronous learning play in your online course?

How can you ensure learning is not measured by attendance or seat time?

What can you do during synchronous time in your online course to build relationships, develop a sense of community, and make connections with your students?

What type of brain breaks will resonate with your learners?

Chapter 17: Asynchronous Online Learning

As a reminder, asynchronous learning is when learners complete work related to the course on their own schedule. Asynchronous online learning is much fuzzier than synchronous learning. It is easy to explain that synchronous online learning is typically a video call and occasionally a live chat, but it is hard to describe what asynchronous online learning looks like. This is because you can accomplish so many different learning tasks with asynchronous online learning. There are almost endless ideas and options! That makes this chapter both the most challenging and the most exciting to write. The last thing I want to do is overwhelm you, so I have decided to focus the chapter on the asynchronous instructional strategies that I feel will be the most helpful no matter what age or content you teach. Once you master these strategies, you can easily branch off into other asynchronous strategies.

Teacher Well-Being

It is important to start the chapter on anytime, anywhere learning with a short discussion on teacher well-being. Remember that even though your students may be working at all times of day and night, this does not mean that you have to be available all the time to be an effective asynchronous online instructor. Set boundaries and make it clear to students when you will and will not answer emails, respond to instant messages, video call with them, and so on.

 Remember that creating office hours is a good strategy to help create a healthy balance.

Asynchronous tasks can be time-consuming to create. You may find yourself spending a lot of time creating asynchronous learning tasks the first time you teach a course online. However, there is a good chance that the first time you teach a course online, you will also assign too much asynchronous work. Remember:

> Within the same time period, you cannot cover as much in online learning as you can in face-to-face. You must whittle your curriculum down to the most essential learning objectives.

Every online course has limited synchronous time, and you may find yourself using asynchronous time to try to fulfill all the learning objectives that you didn't get to synchronously. Try to resist this urge for the sanity of both you and your students! Less truly is more in online learning.

In a traditional face-to-face learning environment, you may find yourself with what I refer to as "time burn." We have all been there. There are thirty minutes left of a class period and students have completed everything you have planned. What do you do with that extra thirty minutes?! Every teacher at some point has been guilty of giving "busy work" to burn time. Time burn is nonexistent in online learning, especially with the asynchronous part of online learning. If you give your students "busy work" for asynchronous online learning tasks, they will call you out for it. Most likely this callout will come in the form of not doing any work that looks even slightly like busy work!

If you find yourself frantically putting together a lesson so students will have something to do the next day ... stop.

Asynchronous online learning must be targeted and purposeful. Instead, what if you put the prep work back onto the students and have a "Wonder Day"?

Asynchronous Online Learning in Each Pillar

Understanding when to use synchronous learning and when to use asynchronous learning is key to designing successful online learning.

Let's answer the second part of that takeaway: when should you use asynchronous online learning? The explanation of when asynchronous online learning is appropriate based upon the pillars of teaching (**Figure 17.1**) is much simpler than the explanation for synchronous learning. The short version is:

This is the easy part of asynchronous learning; it can be effective in all four of the pillars. The key word in that sentence is "can." If not executed correctly, asynchronous learning can easily be ineffective. The real challenge with asynchronous learning is engagement. Therefore, it is critical that the foundational elements covered in "Part 2: Foundations" are implemented if any asynchronous learning is part of your online course.

Content Delivery

Should you focus asynchronous learning on content delivery? Yes, yes, and yes. Bring in lots of choice in asynchronous content delivery formats—videos, podcasts or audio recordings, websites, and articles. The wonderful tool called the internet gives teachers many options for content delivery formats. Refer to "Chapter 10: Essential Instructional Tools" for open-source content resources.

Assessment

Should you focus asynchronous learning on assessment? Yes, yes, and yes. Remember, synchronous online learning is limiting in terms of assessment options.

Will you have to think differently about assessment as a piece of asynchronous online learning? Possibly. It depends on the types of assessments you typically assign in

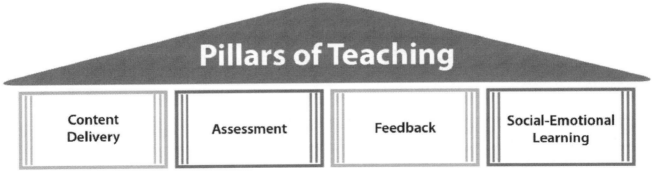

Figure 17.1: Pillars of Teaching

face-to-face learning. If you typically assign assessments that are more project-based, these assessments will work wonderfully in an asynchronous environment. You may need to make some small tweaks, but overall, project assessments work great in this type of environment. If, however, you typically give "closed-notes" or memorization-focused assessments, you will need to rethink assessments for your online course. We will discuss assessment in online learning in detail in "Chapter 18: Assessment in an Online Environment."

Feedback

Should you focus asynchronous learning on feedback? Yes, yes, and yes. Unless you are facilitating synchronous one-on-one meetings with students, you won't be providing individual feedback synchronously. Most feedback will be completed asynchronously.

In order to avoid online teacher burnout, you need to think strategically about which learning tasks do and do not receive detailed feedback. Just as with face-to-face learning, you don't have to give feedback on every single learning task your students complete. In fact, research supports this idea. The study "Teacher and Student Attitudes toward Teacher Feedback" indicated that students considered limited feedback more motivating than an overabundance of feedback.[64]

Educator Tracey Nesrallah uses stickers to provide asynchronous feedback. I will let Tracey explain:

"My sticker books have been pretty successful this year. I started them last year during the spring remote learning. This year, my grade 6 students love them. The sticker book is a few Google Slides with a cute background (usually from SlidesMania). I make custom stickers using a script from Alice Keeler. They are custom, because I put my feedback right on the sticker. I use the stickers to show the kids I have looked at their work (in virtual I do not access everything, but I do try to look at all their work and at the very least, put a sticker on it). I tag the student's email in the sticker, so it forces them to read my feedback that I've left on their work. The student then copy-and-pastes the sticker into their sticker book, which is housed in our homeroom [Hāpara] Workspace. I also use the stickers as incentives when we play math games or virtual bingo. There are coveted stickers, for example if I share their work on my Twitter they get a special sticker for that. It is a fun thing to do that helps my students with engagement and gets them to read my feedback."

---

64   Nugrahenny T. Zacharias, "Teacher and Student Attitudes toward Teacher Feedback," *RELC Journal* 38, no. 1 (2007): 38–52, https://doi.org/10.1177/0033688206076157.

Social-Emotional Learning

> Relationship building does not come naturally in online learning as it does in face-to-face. Therefore, you have to be intentional about consistently embedding relationship building activities into online learning.

We learned that synchronous online learning shines with SEL, but there are still many opportunities for SEL during asynchronous online learning as well. In fact, a study on using asynchronous activities to build a sense of community concluded that "well-designed asynchronous activities can help to promote sense of community among online students."[65]

For asynchronous SEL, it's likely you will intentionally embed these strategies within the other three pillars: content delivery, assessment, and feedback. Many of the strategies shared in "Chapter 14: Maslow before You Bloom" can be completed asynchronously. As a quick reminder, below is a summary of some asynchronous social-emotional strategies:

- "All about you" assignment—This doesn't have to be a one-off. Add little "getting to know you" questions throughout asynchronous tasks.

- Embed sharing activities—There are endless ways of embedding sharing activities asynchronously, whether within the homebase, learning tasks (content and assessment), or feedback.

- Bitmojis, learning journals, video, and virtual check-ins are all completely asynchronous SEL strategies.

 Adding SEL tidbits to feedback is a quick and easy way to embed within asynchronous tasks. Microsoft has an app called Praise (bit.ly/microsoftpraise) which includes SEL badges (e.g., persistence and empathy) that can be provided at various points in the learning process.

Flipgrid is a great tool for creating a synchronous-like environment asynchronously, since it is all about video. Use some of the same SEL strategies you use during synchronous learning, but transfer them to a Flipgrid board instead.

---

65   Jesús Trespalacios and Jennifer Rand, "Using Asynchronous Activities to Promote Sense of Community and Learning in an Online Course," *International Journal of Online Pedagogy and Course Design* 5, no. 4 (2015): Article 1, https://doi.org/10.4018/IJOPCD.2015100101.

> Maslow before you Bloom! You must focus on the social-emotional side of learning.

Brain Breaks

Before we dive into strategies, I want to return to the concept of brain breaks as an important part of asynchronous learning tasks. Remember, we need breaks from staring at screens, so brain breaks are important for digital asynchronous work as well. A brain break can be as quick as you want to make it and can be anything that gets bodies moving. Below are some of my favorite brain break activities for asynchronous learning. You will notice many are similar to synchronous brain breaks.

How Fast Can You . . . ?

Challenge students to do "something" and tell you how many seconds it took.
How fast can you touch something orange at least five feet away from your computer?
How fast can you stand up and do ten jumping jacks?

Drawer Dash or Run and Grab

Yes, this works asynchronously as well. Instead of students sharing what they bring back via the video call, have students take a picture of the item.

Copycat

GIFs are great to use asynchronously, as shown in **Figure 17.2**. This is a GIF of Winnie the Pooh touching his toes over and over. Remember, a GIF is an animated image of sorts. Therefore, you can insert a GIF into many digital platforms as an *image*. The easiest way to add a GIF is via the URL to that GIF. All the Google Docs tools have this feature, and GIPHY has a "Copy link" feature that makes this process simple:

1. Navigate to GIPHY to find the GIF you want to use.

2. Copy the link to that GIF by clicking the button that states "Copy link."

3. In any of the Google Docs tools, navigate to Insert > Image > By URL, as shown in **Figure 17.3**.

4. Paste the GIF's URL and click "Insert." Easy peasy!

Figure 17.2: Asynchronous Brain Break Using GIFs

Minute to Win It

These challenges can also be done asynchronously using pictures or video. For example, try to touch your tongue to your nose and take a picture. Pat your head and rub your stomach at the same time and take a video.

Experiments with Google

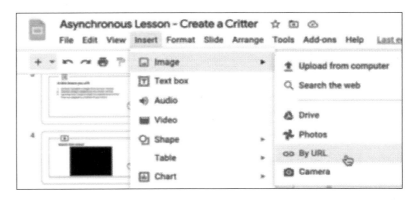

Figure 17.3: Inserting an Image or GIF via URL

Many of the Experiments with Google can be exported and shared. For example, have students make a Move Mirror and share.

Movement Videos

GoNoodle and Super Movers videos are probably even better for asynchronous brain breaks than synchronous ones!

Remember, many of the Super Movers videos are available on YouTube as well.

Sculpt It! Draw It!

You can really integrate this into your learning objectives. The choices are endless: sculpt a character from the story . . . a water molecule . . . a tripartite leaf . . . and take a picture of your sculpture. If Play-Doh isn't available, draw a vocabulary word, and take a picture of your drawing.

Asynchronous Strategies

As we dive into asynchronous strategies, let's bring back two key takeaways to set the tone:

> Every student does not have to do the exact same thing at the exact same time.

> Use technology to duplicate yourself to all learners regardless of when and where they are learning.

 These key takeaways stress the importance of flexibility with asynchronous online learning. At the beginning of this book, we discussed course timelines, and I recommended that you not plan for individual days in online learning. I want to revisit that idea and focus it on building asynchronous learning tasks. As you become familiar with the asynchronous learning strategies in this book, think about how you could use them to build out a week's worth of learning.

With these strategies, you will notice many can be used for content delivery, assessment, and feedback all in one. It is likely that asynchronous learning will encompass a large portion of your online course; therefore, it is important to get as much bang for your buck as possible.

Asynchronous Lessons

Asynchronous lessons, also known as self-paced lessons, are my number one asynchronous online learning strategy. Asynchronous lessons include content delivery, assessment, and feedback all wrapped up into one convenient bundle. An asynchronous lesson includes everything a learner needs to complete the lesson on their own. Imagine them as lesson packages you wrap up and hand to your students. Within that package is everything they need to be successful with learning on their own. That package allows you to duplicate yourself in digital form to all learners regardless of when and where they are learning.

Figure 17.4 on the next page outlines the pieces that need to be included in a self-paced lesson. By including all the elements of an asynchronous lesson, you will accomplish the goals below:

- Create self-directed learners.

- Reduce the number of questions all around: to you from learners, to grown-ups from learners, and from grown-ups to you!

Before we dive into discussing the elements of an asynchronous lesson, you need to view some examples. Note that while the examples provided use Google Slides, there are many tools you can use to create asynchronous lessons. I typically use Google Slides and Google Forms. I will discuss Google Form examples later in the chapter. I have listed the examples below in order of age appropriateness, although there could be some overlap. These examples can be found at intechgratedpd.org/vip:

- Primary ages 6–8—Become a Weather Forecaster

- Intermediate ages 8–11—Create a Critter

- Middle school ages 11–14—Become the Character

- High school ages 14–18—Intro to Design Principles

Now that you have seen an example or two, refer to *Figure 17.4* on the next page. This visual includes all the elements that need to be included in an asynchronous lesson "package" in order for your learners to be successful. Let's break down each element.

Learning Target

In order for your students to buy in to online learning, it is essential that they know the purpose of a learning task. Make sure the learning target (also known as goal, objective, outcome, or intention) is clear and visible.

 Start with only one learning target per lesson.

Elements of an Asynchronous Lesson

LEARNING TARGET

Clear and visible

OVERVIEW OF LESSON

In this lesson you will...

VIDEO INTRODUCTION

Your face and voice!

LEARNING RESOURCES

Give choices!

LEARNING TASK

More choices!

WHAT DOES DONE LOOK LIKE?

Answer this question as simply as possible

REFLECTION

Bring it all together

**TEMPLATES found at
intechgratedpd.org/vip**

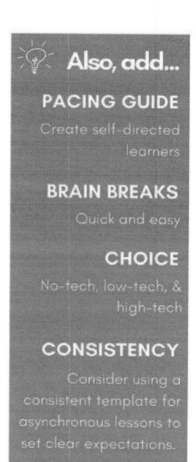

Also, add...

PACING GUIDE

Create self-directed learners

BRAIN BREAKS

Quick and easy

CHOICE

No-tech, low-tech, & high-tech

CONSISTENCY

Consider using a consistent template for asynchronous lessons to set clear expectations.

@lindyhockenbary
www.intechgratedpd.org

Figure 17.4: Elements of an Asynchronous Lesson

Overview of Lesson

Do you write on the board of your physical classroom what students will be doing that day, period, or block? Instead of writing a lesson summary on the board, put it in the asynchronous lesson so students can access it anytime, anywhere. I recommend using consistent language each time, such as "In this lesson you will . . ."

Video Introduction

We learned in "Chapter 14: Maslow before You Bloom" that in terms of video, you as the teacher trump quality. The more that learners see and hear their teacher, the more likely they are to engage with the content. Therefore, I find it crucial to begin asynchronous lessons with a video of the teacher introducing the lesson. Think of this like a lesson introduction in a face-to-face learning environment where you stand in the front of the room and say something like, "today we will be doing this, and I want you to focus on such and such." The introduction video for an asynchronous lesson is the same idea.

I typically create a quick, informal screencast video sharing the asynchronous lesson on my screen with my webcam embedded in the corner of the video. Make sure the video is short, sweet, and to the point.

Introduce the lesson. Explain anything that may be confusing.
Give a little pep talk.

Use technology to duplicate yourself to all learners regardless of when and where they are learning.

Learning Resources

This includes any resources that help meet the learning target.

Make sure to provide choices of various formats if possible.

I try to give at least one visual resource, such as a video, and one written resource, such as an article.

Learning Task

This is the assessment. How will students show proficiency of the learning target outlined at the beginning of the lesson? It is important to provide choices here as well, and it is easy to integrate choice boards into asynchronous lessons, as shown in **Figure 17.5**.

What Does "Done" Look Like?

I find that answering the question "What does 'done' look like?" is extremely helpful to both the student and any caregivers who are potentially assisting the student.

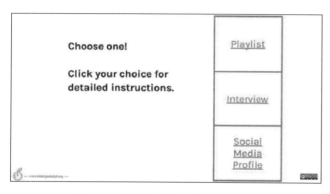

Figure 17.5: Choice Board in an Asynchronous Lesson

This is also known as a checklist of completion.

Answer this as simply as possible. I find a simple checklist is effective, as shown in **Figure 17.6**. To help caregivers, you can also add this checklist to the homebase or whatever tool you are using for home communication. **Figure 17.7** shows an example parent corner with the checklist of completion in Google Classroom.

Reflection

Adding a short reflection at the end is crucial to bringing the lesson together. The reflection serves as valuable feedback for you because what the learner shares in the reflection is usually a tell-tale sign of whether they met the learning target or not.

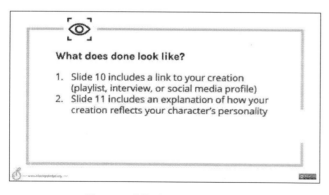

Figure 17.6: What Does "Done" Look Like? Example

The reflection is also an important self-assessment strategy to build metacognitive skills. If you have students that tend to rush through asynchronous tasks or need assistance with time management, you can use the reflection to embed self-assessments that require students to reflect on their time management skills. Refer to "Chapter 15: Creating Self-Directed Learners" for specific metacognitive prompts.

Pacing Guide

Remember that pacing guides are a strategy for building self-directed learners. Therefore, including pacing guides throughout an asynchronous lesson is a crucial element to ensure student success.

Pacing guides for asynchronous lessons can be approached in two ways—approximate time of completion or minimum time of completion, as illustrated in *Figure 17.8*.

 I find it easier to gauge a minimum time of completion as opposed to trying to guess an average time across all learners and all choices provided.

When using Slides for asynchronous lessons, I add a timer icon to the slide as shown in *Figure 17.9*. The time provided is a *minimum* time to complete the entire lesson, as it is on the lesson overview slide.

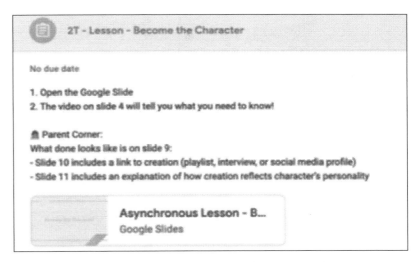

Figure 17.7: Checklist of Completion for Parent Corner

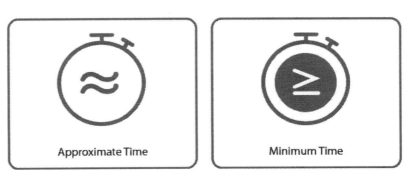

Figure 17.8: Pacing Guide Options

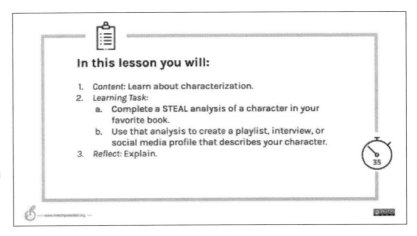

Figure 17.9: Pacing Guide Example

Learning Task Overview

1. Complete a STEAL analysis for a character in your favorite book/story
2. Use your STEAL analysis to create one of the following:
   - *Playlist* describing the character
   - *Interview* with your character
   - *Social media profile* of your character
3. Add a link or picture of your completed product to slide 10
4. Reflect on slide 11

Figure 17.10: Pacing Guide Example per Task

In addition to providing the minimum time for completion of the entire lesson, I add a minimum time for completion of each task or part of the lesson, as shown in **Figure 17.10**. Notice the timer is also a link, as indicated by the underline. The link opens a timer already set to the minimum time indicated, as shown in **Figure 17.11**.

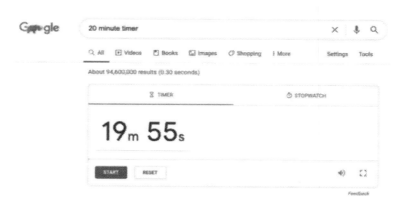

Figure 17.11: Timer within a Google Search

It is incredibly easy to add a timer. Navigate to Google.com and complete a search for "20-minute timer," as in this example. Once you click "enter" on the search, the timer will automatically appear and start counting down. This works for any time period in minutes or hours. To add that timer as a link to the lesson, simply copy the URL of the Google search. Then, add that URL as a link to the timer in the lesson.

> Use technology to duplicate yourself to all learners regardless of when and where they are learning.

Brain Breaks

I feel that I have talked about brain breaks enough by now that you shouldn't be surprised to hear that they are an essential element of an asynchronous lesson! Refer back to the brain breaks section of this chapter for specific ideas.

The tool you are using for your asynchronous lessons will determine what type of brain break you use. One of the reasons I like Google Slides is that it is easy to embed multimedia such as videos and GIFs. Add a GoNoodle video, insert a GIF, or type a simple message. Have students add a picture, as shown in **Figure 17.12**.

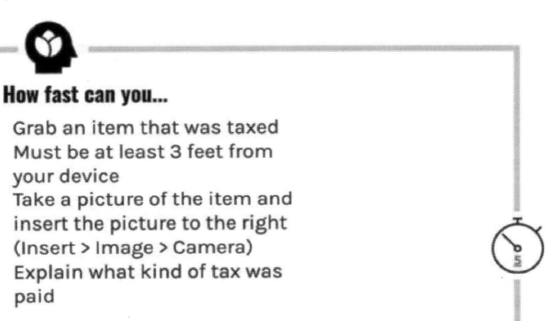

How fast can you...

- Grab an item that was taxed
- Must be at least 3 feet from your device
- Take a picture of the item and insert the picture to the right (Insert > Image > Camera)
- Explain what kind of tax was paid

  *Figure 17.12: Asynchronous Brain Break Example*

Choice

In order for online learning to be successful, you must shift control from teacher to student.

It is important with asynchronous tasks to give students autonomy over their learning. Offering choice is especially easy in asynchronous lessons since time is not a constraint. For equity purposes, always offer a no-tech, low-tech, and high-tech option for the assessment piece. Since assessments are typically more project-based, this provides a chance for every student to successfully complete the assessment regardless of the resources available to them at home. In the "Become the Character" lesson, the three choices for the learning task were to create a playlist, interview, or social media profile mock-up. **Figure 17.13** illustrates how these choices could fall within the no-tech to high-tech spectrum. Notice there is even choice within the choice!

No-Tech	Low-Tech	High-Tech
Playlist	Playlist	Interview
	Interview	Social media profile

Figure 17.13: Equitable Choices

Consistency

Organization and consistency are critical to online learning.

You may have noticed that all the asynchronous lesson examples I provided use the same Google Slides template with the same structure, layout, design, and icons. This is intentional both for the sake of consistency as well as saving time when creating the lessons.

 Create a template for your asynchronous lessons and copy it over and over to save you time. I have created asynchronous lesson templates that you are welcome to copy and use. I will discuss these templates in detail in the next sections.

The more you are consistent in the format of your asynchronous lessons, the more successful your students will be.

Asynchronous Lesson Template—Slides

I have created an asynchronous lesson template using Google Slides, which has everything you need to complete this strategy. The template can be found at intechgratedpd.org/vip. If you are a Google Slides user, File > Make a Copy > Entire Presentation will copy the Google Slide template into your Google Drive. I recommend saving this as your template that you can copy again and again. If you are a Microsoft PowerPoint user, File > Download > Microsoft PowerPoint will download these slides into Microsoft PowerPoint form.

The template includes a key for the icons used. Customize these icons so that they work for your learners, but no matter what you use, keep the icons consistent. Refer to the list of icon resources provided in "Chapter 12: The Second Hurdle—I Can't Find . . . " Delete the teacher tips and examples from the template. Then, insert your own content to create engaging asynchronous lessons.

 I recommend starting with one learning target and a short lesson, say twenty minutes maximum. If appropriate, you can slowly make the lessons longer.

Distributing Asynchronous Lessons

How you distribute asynchronous lessons to each student will depend on what homebase tool you use, but the goal is always the same: that each student gets their own copy of the lesson. If you use Google Slides, Google Classroom is the easiest way to distribute the lesson. You add the lesson as an assignment and set the permissions to make a copy for each student. Hāpara Workspace accomplishes the same goal by adding the slide to a card and setting the card as an individual task.

 If you ever need to force students to make a copy of a Google Doc file type, here's a little Google trick. First, copy the URL. At the end of that URL, you should find either "view" or "edit." Change "view" or "edit" to "copy." Now, when the link is followed, the user will receive the message shown in **Figure 17.14**. The user must be logged into a Google account in order to copy.

If you are a Microsoft PowerPoint user, the Microsoft Teams Assignment feature is the easiest way to distribute a copy to each student.

Figure 17.14: Google Force Copy

Providing Feedback on Asynchronous Lessons

How you provide feedback will depend on the tool used as well. In Google Slides, it is easy to provide feedback via comments, as shown in **Figure 17.15**. To make adding feedback with comments efficient, make sure students are only adding information to one or two slides. Then, when you are ready to provide feedback, open the document, click on the designated slide, review, add comments, close, and repeat. You could also add feedback via the comments section of the homebase tool used.

Asynchronous Lessons Using Forms

I also like to create asynchronous lessons using a forms tool, such as Google Forms or Microsoft Forms. Let's start by looking at some examples of asynchronous lessons using Google Forms. These examples use the same content as the slide examples to make comparing the two platforms easier. All examples are found at intechgratedpd.org/vip:

- Intermediate ages 8–11—Create a Critter two-part lesson: Create a Critter: Part 1 and Create a Critter: Part 2

- Middle school ages 11–14—Become the Character

There are pros and cons to using forms over slides. A pro is that using forms makes the lesson very linear. A con is that forms by their very nature are more limited in terms of what you can and cannot do. I find that the choice of format depends on both personal preference and content area taught. For example, art teachers tend to like the free-flowing nature of slides more than the linear, structured nature of forms.

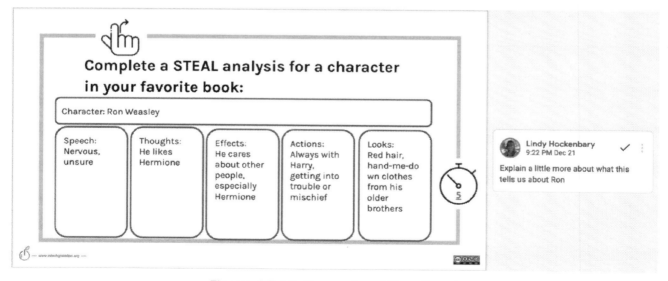

Figure 17.15: Example of Feedback

I do have a template for creating asynchronous lessons using Google Forms. However, I don't feel the forms template for asynchronous lessons is as comprehensive as the slides template due to the nature of forms as a tool. There are two things to consider before you decide to use the forms template. If you have never used Google Forms, I would not suggest starting with this template. The template makes more sense if you have previously used Google Forms. The second consideration is that it is not as easy for me to give you a copy of a Google Form as it is for me to give you a copy of a Google Slide. The link to copy the Google Form can sometimes be a bit fussy.

Sometimes the link won't work for Google Workspace for Education accounts due to domain settings; if that is the case, try a personal Google account.

- Asynchronous Lesson Template Using Google Forms—Found at intechgratedpd. org/vip. You must be logged into a Google account in order for this to work.

Asynchronous Lessons Using Other Tools

Of course, there are unlimited other tools to create asynchronous lessons. You may want to check out Pear Deck and Nearpod. These tools are similar and allow you to create interactive lessons. Use the elements of an asynchronous lesson to provide the pedagogical structure within either tool.

Choice Boards

In "Chapter 15: Creating Self-Directed Learners," we learned all about choice boards. Choice boards can be used as a standalone asynchronous strategy or a part of an asynchronous lesson.

Hyperdocs

A **Hyperdoc** is an interactive digital lesson. *Figure 17.16* shows an example Hyperdoc used for Earth Day. Typically, a Hyperdoc is created using a Google Doc but could also be created using a variety of other tools, such as Google Slides, Google Drawing, OneNote, Word Online, Microsoft Teams (via channels), or Google Sites.

Hyperdocs

Hyperdocs can be easily organized to add elements of choice as well. Learn more about Hyperdocs on the official Hyperdocs website (hyperdocs.co),

Earth Day - How Can You Make Earth a Better Place?

Explore	Your Task
1. **Watch** "Save the Planet!" 2. **Read** "5 Reasons Why You Should Love Earth."	Find one resource about Earth Day. **Add** the link here: **Explain** why you chose this resource:
Explain	**Your Task**
1. **Read** "How Can You Make Earth a Better Place?" 2. **Watch** "What's So Great about Going Green?"	What are five ways you can make Earth a better place? 1. 2. 3. 4. 5.
Apply	**Your Task**
Create a public service announcement (PSA) that answers the question, "How can you make Earth a better place?" Your PSA can be in the form of a video, poster, podcast, book, or article. Pull from your resources to choose the tool that works best for the job!	**Add** a link to your creation here:

Figure 17.16: Hyperdoc Example

Earth Day Hyperdoc (found at intechgratedpd.org/vip)

which has a plethora of examples and templates. **Figure 17.16** uses one of the templates provided on the Hyperdocs website.

→ *One Slide*

One of my most commonly used strategies is also the simplest. Students are given a single slide that contains a prompt or a question. Students have one slide to answer the question or complete the prompt. The slide could be blank, could have the question/prompt at the top, or could have a simple template, as shown in **Figure 17.17**. This strategy could be used for any of the teaching pillars: content delivery, assessment, feedback, and SEL. Below is a list of example prompts:

- Tell me on one slide what you learned this week.

- Tell me on one slide what you know about credit cards.

- Research photosynthesis and explain what you learned on one slide.

- Answer this question on one slide: How is the periodic table organized?

- What are a few of your favorite things? (Example in **Figure 17.17**)

When first introducing your students to the one slide activity, you may want to scaffold by providing a template as a guide. The "What Are a Few of Your Favorite Things?" template shown in **Figure 17.17** is a low-stakes introduction to the one slide activity.

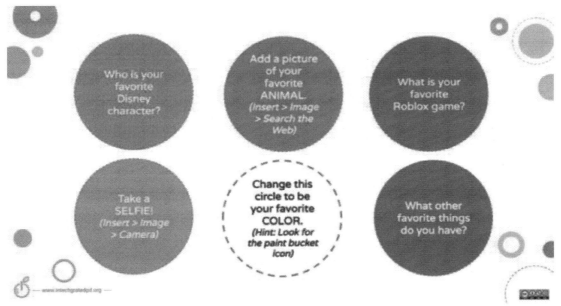

Figure 17.17: What Are a Few of Your Favorite Things?

Figure 17.18: Getting to Know You

 This activity also doubles as a way for students to learn different features of the slides tool of your choice. As previously discussed, this can easily be tweaked to a "getting-to-know-you" activity, as shown in **Figure 17.18**.

Once students are comfortable with the one slide activity, transition to a template focused on a specific learning goal. For example, **Figure 17.19** could be used for students to analyze the characters, setting, and plot of a reading. **Figure 17.20** is a generic template that could be used for many different learning goals.

Notice the addition of a pacing guide in both examples as another optional support.

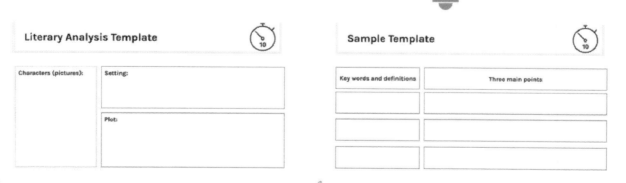

Figure 17.19: One Slide Literary Analysis Template

Figure 17.20: Sample Template

The templates above, plus the templates and examples listed below, may be found at intechgratedpd.org/vip. These are Google Slides, so File > Make a Copy will keep the examples in Google Slide form. File > Download > Microsoft PowerPoint will download the templates into Microsoft PowerPoint form.

- One slide templates and examples

- "What Are a Few of Your Favorite Things?" template

- "Getting to Know You" template for grades 4–12—Note that this template is set up to be a collaborative activity (which will be explained below). Erase slide one if you want it to be an individual activity.

- "Getting to Know You" template for adults—If you lead professional development sessions, this template is a great way to introduce teachers to the one slide activity.

Collaborative One Slide

The one slide strategy can easily transition from an individual to a collaborative activity. Each student is assigned a number and that number becomes the number of their slide. For example, if Kinley is assigned number 7, slide number 7 becomes Kinley's slide. Students are instructed that they can only edit their slide. The great part about this collaborative activity is that each student has their own "space" (a.k.a. slide). However, they can look at other slides to get ideas, knowledge, or guidance. Another benefit of a collaborative one slide activity is that it is quick and easy for you to review because you only have to open one document. For that reason, this strategy is a great way to conduct a formative assessment.

To scaffold, when first starting the one slide collaborative activity, students are only allowed to touch their own slide. Then, as students get more comfortable with the collaboration, students can add a constructive comment to another student's slide.

 I recommend providing a framework for comments, such as the RISE model (risemodel.com). **TAG** is another feedback model that is simple and therefore great for younger kids. TAG stands for **T**ell something you like, **A**sk a question, and **G**ive a suggestion, as illustrated in **Figure 17.21** on the next page.

To set up a collaborative one slide activity, create a collaborative slideshow using the tool of your choice, Google Slides or PowerPoint Online. On slide 1, I typically add the instructions for the activity for reference. An example is shown in **Figure 17.22**. Add a

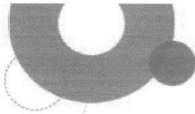

TAG
You're It!

Tell something you like

Ask a question

Give a suggestion

Figure 17.21: TAG You're It!

second slide. This slide will become the template for whatever you want your students to do. For collaborative one slide activities, I typically create a spot for students to add their name to the slide. Take the number of students and add a few more slides. For example, if I had twenty students, I would create twenty-five slides. The reason I add a few extra slides is in case someone forgets their number during synchronous time; I can tell them to jump to the bottom and take the last slide. In Google Slides, it is easy to duplicate a slide by pressing control (on Windows OS) or command (on Mac OS) plus D. This will duplicate slide 2 over and over again until you get the number of slides needed.

To assign each student a number, I use a form to collect names, then open the spreadsheet attached to the form. The student's number becomes the row of the spreadsheet for their name. For example, in **Figure 17.23**, Ginny Weasley would be slide number 5.

Do this once and have students memorize their number to use over and over.

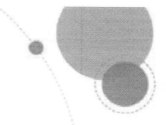

Getting to Know You!

1. Find the slide of your assigned number: this is now your slide.
2. Answer the questions on the slide and make the slide your own!

Figure 17.22: Collaborative One Slide

	A	B	C
1	Timestamp	What is your first name?	What is your last name?
2	12/27/2020 15:01:30	Harry	Potter
3	12/27/2020 15:01:38	Hermione	Granger
4	12/27/2020 15:01:44	Ron	Weasley
5	12/27/2020 15:01:50	Ginny	Weasley
6	12/27/2020 15:01:56	Luna	Lovegood
7	12/27/2020 15:02:03	Neville	Longbottom
8	12/27/2020 15:02:09	Draco	Malfoy

Figure 17.23: Quick Numbering Using a Spreadsheet

Asynchronous Collaboration

Encouraging peer interaction in online learning helps students to feel a sense of community.[66] It seems when many people think of asynchronous collaboration, visions of discussion boards dance in their heads. These discussion boards are typically a feature of an LMS, but there are many other tools that foster collaboration asynchronously. Asynchronous collaboration can be used for assessment, content delivery, and SEL. I want to highlight three important points about asynchronous collaboration:

1. There are tools that offer more engaging asynchronous collaboration experiences than a standard LMS discussion board.

2. Asynchronous collaboration does not have to be a "discussion."

3. Students who feel a strong sense of community in an online course are more likely to participate in asynchronous collaboration.[67]

4. To be successful, you must slowly scaffold asynchronous collaboration into your online course.

---

66   Lee et al., "Examining the Relationship."

67   Wing Sum Cheung, Khe Foon Hew, and Connie Siew Ling Ng, "Toward an Understanding of Why Students Contribute in Asynchronous Online Discussions," *Journal of Educational Computing Research* 38, no. 1 (2008): 29–50, https://doi.org/10.2190/EC.38.1.b.

Let's discuss that last point a little more. As teachers, we always want to set our students up for success. You can't expect students to go from never having experienced asynchronous collaboration to having to do an entire group project asynchronously. You have to instructionally scaffold. There are three factors you should consider when planning successful asynchronous collaboration:

- Group size—Begin with small groups and slowly work up to full-class collaborative activities.

- Structure—When first beginning with asynchronous collaboration, it is important to provide structure to the task. If the first asynchronous collaboration your students experience involves a blank Google Doc, it's likely the collaboration won't be successful. I say this from experience! Where will each student write? How will they ensure they aren't typing over each other? How will their sharing be organized? These are elements of structure to consider when designing your collaborative tasks. There are tools that will provide structure automatically, such as Padlet and Flipgrid. These types of tools are a great starting point.

- Purpose of collaboration—What is the purpose of the asynchronous collaboration? Relationship building? Reflection? Developing collaboration skills? Review? Research? Content development? I recommend starting with a low-stakes purpose such as relationship building. This gets back to the idea of having a practice before the big game. Let students explore the collaboration tool with a low-stakes task first. Then, for the next collaborative task, provide a simple reflection prompt that students respond to but without necessarily responding to each other's posts. If students succeed at that, then introduce a collaborative task where students respond to each other using the RISE or TAG frameworks. Then, if students are successful at responding to each other, give them a collaborative activity where group members have to work together to produce a common goal.

Below is a step-by-step example of a scaffolded approach to asynchronous collaboration:

1. Students are placed in small groups and answer the question, "What song best describes you?" on a Padlet board. Padlet provides the structure required for an introductory collaborative task because it is similar to a digital sticky board wall. Each student adds a "sticky note" to the digital Padlet wall.

Define the purpose of the collaboration and choose a tool that meets that goal.

2. In small groups, students post to Padlet an answer to the question, "What was your top takeaway from the women's suffrage unit?" If you want to try a different tool, Flipgrid also provides structure, as each student adds a recording to the Flipgrid board.

3. In small groups, complete the one slide collaborative activity. Each student gets their own slide in a collaborative Google Slide or PowerPoint Online. Each student is assigned part of an animal cell to explain on their slide. Other group members add one comment to each group member's slide to explain how that part of the cell relates to their part of the cell. By using slides, structure is provided, as each student has their own space.

4. Using Padlet or a slides tool (Google Jamboard or Microsoft Whiteboard would work as well), students complete the following: What questions will you ask our guest speaker about being a children's book author? Work together in your group to come up with the top five questions to ask the guest speaker.

5. If students are successful at all of the above, then, and only then, we could complete a more comprehensive asynchronous group project. For example, students could work together using a slides tool to create a structured presentation about a particular topic.

To start, I suggest mastering a couple of tools you can use for asynchronous collaboration. Padlet and Flipgrid are both great options. Refer to "Chapter 10: Essential Instructional Tools" for more details.

I highly recommend the Google Docs tools (Docs, Slides, Sheets, Drawing) if your school uses Google Workspace for Education and the Office Online tools (Word, PowerPoint, Excel, OneNote) if your school uses Microsoft 365 Education. These tools give you a lot of bang for your buck because you can use all of these tools for asynchronous collaboration as well as many other learning tasks.

 Furthermore, for collaborative activities, I highly suggest starting with slides over a word processing tool such as Docs or Word. This is a quick way to add structure to the collaboration. Slides also make it easy to add different types of media, such as text and pictures. The more you use these tools for collaboration, the more natural this type of digital collaboration will become for you and your students.

If you want students to partake specifically in an online discussion, check out Parlay. Parlay facilitates online discussions in an engaging way. Remember that if you use an LMS, a discussion board feature is most likely included.

→ Virtual Tours

Google Earth Tour of Montana

Even though your students may not be leaving their homes, you can still add engagement by bringing the world to them. Virtual tours may be used for content delivery, assessment, and SEL.

Google Earth has a feature called "Projects" where you and your students can create virtual tours. I created this simple Google Earth Tour of Montana (bit.ly/tourofmt) to introduce you to where I live as well as to guide you through some of the features within Google Earth projects. Google Maps also has a feature called "My Maps" (mymaps.google.com) that can be used to map out specific routes.

Virtual tours can be created for many different content areas. You could create virtual tours for content delivery, or students could create virtual tours as an assessment option. Below are a few ideas for integrating virtual tours into asynchronous online learning:

- Create a "lit trip" for historical fiction and nonfiction reads.

- Create a tour of your community noting things that are paid for by taxes.

- Use the measure feature to calculate distance and area.

- Create a map of the Axis versus the Allied troop movements through World War II.

- Create a map to show the spread of an infectious disease.

→ Non-Digital Asynchronous Learning Activities

Just as in a physical classroom, there are many learning opportunities that can happen away from a device. Depending on the mix of synchronous and asynchronous time for your online class, you may want to be strategic about embedding non-digital learning activities for asynchronous time. You could also have a learning task that blends non-digital and digital. For example, students make observations about their environment and then come back to their device to create a video that summarizes these observations. Asynchronous, non-digital learning activities can be used for content delivery, assessment, and SEL.

Asynchronous online learning does not have to be digital.

These non-digital learning activities may require the use of items. Remember from "Chapter 7: Considerations for Learning Design" that there are two ways to handle this:

1. Can you create learning opportunities that use regular household items but don't require anything specific?

2. Can you send home "learning kits" that include items your students could use over and over again?

 Below is an extensive list of non-digital learning activities based upon typical household supplies, environments, and tasks. For all of these, make sure to be flexible for the sake of equity.

Pictures from Your Environment

"Your environment" can mean a house, apartment complex, neighborhood, and so on.

- Take pictures from around your environment and find a word in Spanish, French, German, or another language.

- Create a field guide identifying the plants and animals in your environment.

- Record the shapes around you.

- Create an inventory of household items—toys, cleaning supplies, and so on.

Art

- Draw, paint, cut, glue, and construct using items from around the house.

Reading

- Write a book review.

- Record yourself reading aloud.

Interview

- Conduct an in-person or phone interview.

Maker Projects

Hacking STEM

- Create an invention from household items to help people, the environment, or something else.

- Create a freestanding tower from household items.

- Create a habitat for an animal.

- Create a plan to reduce your household's impact on the environment: water, food, garbage, electricity, gas, and more.

- Hacking STEM (bit.ly/hackingstem) includes tons of **STEM** project ideas using low-cost items (STEM stands for science, technology, engineering, and math).

Cooking

- Cook a meal.

- Film a cooking show.

- Double or half a recipe.

- Conduct cooking experiments (e.g., change the cooking process and record temperature or ingredients).

- Rewrite a recipe to make it easier to follow.

- Create a daily/weekly/monthly menu and make a corresponding shopping list within a set budget.

Exercise

- Plan a PE class for your household.

- Take a "wonder walk" through your environment and record wonders via writing, pictures, and/or video.

Weather

- Create a local weather guide.

- Predict the weather for the next week.

Acting/Recording Video

- Act out a story you have read.

- Write a story and act it out.

- Create a public service announcement (PSA) or commercial to explain why it is important to eat healthily or exercise every day.

Video Creation

- Create a stop-motion video using anything from around your house—toys, Play-Doh, kitchen utensils, and more.

Unplugged Coding

- Code.org includes ideas for non-digital coding activities.

Summary

This section outlines the most important parts from the chapter:

- Asynchronous tasks must be targeted and purposeful.

- You can accomplish many different learning tasks asynchronously. There are almost endless ideas and options.

- Asynchronous learning is great for content delivery, assessment, and feedback.

- You can intentionally dip into social-emotional learning via asynchronous tasks.

- The real challenge with asynchronous learning is engagement. If not executed correctly, it can easily be ineffective.

- Even though your students may be working at all times of day and night, this does not mean that you have to be available all the time to be an effective asynchronous online instructor.

- Brain breaks and flexibility are important parts of asynchronous learning tasks.

- Asynchronous lessons include everything a learner needs to complete the lesson on their own.

- To be successful with asynchronous collaboration, you must scaffold. You can't expect students to go from never having experienced asynchronous collaboration to having to do an entire group project asynchronously.

- Asynchronous online learning does not have to be digital. Just as in a physical classroom, there are many learning opportunities that can happen away from a device.

Reflection

After reading "Chapter 17: Asynchronous Online Learning," reflect on how the content can be applied to your unique learning environment.

Share your reflections online using the hashtag **#TeachersGuideToOnline**.

What role will asynchronous learning play in your online course?

How will you ensure learner engagement with asynchronous tasks?

What type of asynchronous learning tasks will be successful for your online course(s)?

How will you embed SEL into asynchronous tasks?

Can you embed non-digital tasks into your online course(s)?

Chapter 18: Assessment in an Online Environment

Assessment has already been touched on a few different times throughout the book. This chapter will bring it all together and focus solely on assessing student learning in online environments.

When I asked teachers what they needed to know about online learning, one of the top requests was how to assess in remote environments. This question makes perfect sense, because traditionally, assessments in face-to-face learning environments have a memorization or "closed-notes" focus in the form of a test or quiz. Therefore, the first question from many teachers when it comes to assessment outside of traditional face-to-face learning environments is:

> **How do you assess students when there is no way to know if they are looking up all the answers?**

> In online learning environments, proximity is not in your favor. You cannot stand over a learner's shoulder and ensure a task is accomplished.

Now, you may not like the answer to the above question at first, but stick with me through this chapter. The answer is: you can't. You have to think differently about the goal of assessments in online learning. In turn, this means you may also have to reevaluate your learning goals. After all, the goal of assessment is to determine if learning goals have been met or not.

> Face-to-face learning is more forgiving than online learning. Therefore, you have to be more strategic with online learning.

Redefine "Cheating"

Somewhere along the educational journey of humans, the idea that you can "cheat" at learning came along. I get it. Before modern technological advances, we did need to memorize information; therefore, memorization became the focus of learning goals. And if the goal of learning is to memorize, then researching an answer or using notes would be cheating.

Technology has completely changed modern society. Almost every one of us carries a computer in our pocket everywhere we go in the form of our smartphone. We can instantly search for information anytime, anywhere. We can also ask computerized assistants for answers. For example, I have an Amazon Echo in my kitchen. Now, when I am baking, instead of having to memorize how many tablespoons are in a cup or pints in a gallon, I simply ask Alexa and get an instant answer faster than my brain could recall the information anyway! This is only one example of content that previously needed to be memorized but is now at our fingertips.

Because of this, we, as educators, need to redefine cheating.

Knowing how to use resources to find information quickly and efficiently is a skill in itself. This skill has changed over time from understanding library card catalogs to understanding how to conduct an effective internet search using a search engine. Therefore, if an assessment includes an answer that a student can find in seconds by conducting an effective internet search, we must ask ourselves as educators: is this *really* cheating?

Instead, could the ability to conduct an effective internet search be the learning goal that is assessed?

The International Society for Technology in Education (ISTE) has standards for students. Standard 1: Empowered Learner states, "Students leverage technology to take an active role in choosing, achieving, and demonstrating competency in their learning goals, informed by the learning sciences."[68] What if the ISTE Standards for Students helped drive your learning goals and therefore your assessments?

---

68   "ISTE Standards for Students," ISTE, accessed December 20, 2021, https://www.iste.org/standards/for-students.

What does this mean for assessment in online learning? Assessments in online environments cannot solely assess rote memorization. You can't (sanely) enforce "no-Google" assessments. In other words, if students can complete (and pass) an assessment by Googling all the answers, it is your assessment that probably needs to be reworked.

> **Do not replicate face-to-face instruction in an online environment.**

When thinking about assessment in your online course, analyze your learning goals with a critical eye and determine if the goal must absolutely be met with a closed-notes or memorization-based assessment.

> ### Could you increase the rigor of the assessment?

Both Bloom's taxonomy and Webb's depth of knowledge model are frameworks that help determine the complexity or rigor of learning tasks.[69] The revised version of Bloom's taxonomy, as shown in **Figure 18.1** on the next page, is illustrated by a pyramid where complexity generally increases with each level of the pyramid. At the top of the revised version of Bloom's taxonomy is create, followed by evaluate, analyze, and apply.[70]

Dr. Norman Webb's depths of knowledge framework consists of four levels of complexity, with level 1 being the simplest and level 4 the most complex:[71]

1. Level 1—Recall and reproduction

2. Level 2—Skills and concepts

3. Level 3—Strategic thinking

4. Level 4—Extended thinking

---

69   Karin K. Hess et al., "Cognitive Rigor: Blending the Strengths of Bloom's Taxonomy and Webb's Depth of Knowledge to Enhance Classroom-Level Processes," ED517804 (2009), https://eric.ed.gov/?id=ED517804.

70   David R. Krathwohl, "A Revision of Bloom's Taxonomy: An Overview," *Theory into Practice* 41, no. 4 (2002): 212–18, https://doi.org/10.1207/s15430421tip4104_2.

71   Katherine Miller, "Bloom's Taxonomy and Webb's Depth of Knowledge," *Synergis Education* (blog), January 5, 2018, https://www.synergiseducation.com/blooms-taxonomy-and-webbs-depth-of-knowledge/.

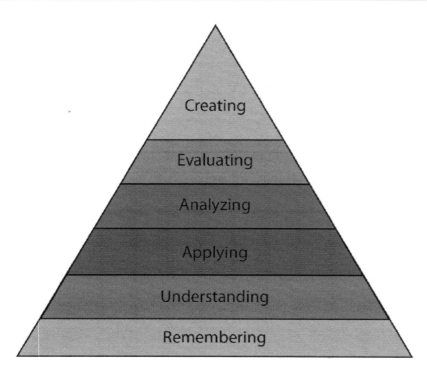

Figure 18.1: Revised Version of Bloom's Taxonomy

Using the revised version of Bloom's taxonomy and/or Webb's depth of knowledge framework as a guide, can you tweak learning objectives to focus on applying, analyzing, evaluating, or synthesizing information instead of simply remembering it? More on this later in the chapter.

Ask yourself what you are assessing—memorization, compliance, or learning? Make sure the focus of assessments is on learning. Consider moving from a point-based grading system to a competency-based or standards-based system.

 If you are searching for an online teaching position, make sure to ask about the educational institution's approach to assessment and grading.

Before moving on, I think it is important to address the idea of "locking" students into specific websites. There are tools that your educational institution may purchase that will allow this to happen. This always comes up as a potential solution to proctoring "exams" in virtual learning environments. But here is the deal: these tools were created for face-to-face learning environments. When the student moves from face-to-face to a remote environment, these types of tools open up a host of potential challenges and concerns.

 Privacy is one of those concerns. For example, even if a student is on a school-issued device, are they using their home internet? Are students signing into their school-issued accounts from a personal device? Do students share a device with other members of their family?

When it comes to using these types of tools for online learning, I always ask, "Will this cause more headache than help?" In other words, using these types of tools remotely opens up a host of potential technological challenges.

> *Is learning being positively affected*
> *enough to make up for those potential challenges?*

➡ Start with Why

This one is simple. Students should always know why they are learning something. In fact, explanation of purpose was identified as an element of award-winning online courses.[72]

Simon Sinek has a great TED Talk called "How Great Leaders Inspire Action."[73] Spoiler alert: the point of the TED Talk is to "start with why." No matter what you are doing, always first ask, "Why?" I use this to guide everything I do and every decision I make. Intrinsic motivation is essential to success in online learning; therefore, understanding the "why" behind a learning goal is critical.

What does all of this mean for assessment in online learning? It boils down to developing assessments that meet the below characteristics:

- Encourage the finding of information

- Require original thoughts and creations

- Are competency-based

Assessment Strategies

Before we dive into new assessment strategies, remember that many of the asynchronous learning strategies covered in "Chapter 17: Asynchronous Online Learning," such as asynchronous lessons, choice boards, and Hyperdocs, have an assessment component. One slide activities and virtual tours can both be used as assessment strategies. Many of the non-digital asynchronous learning activities shared could become assessments as well.

---

72   Kumar et al., "Award-Winning Faculty Online Teaching Practices."

73   Simon Sinek, "How Great Leaders Inspire Action," filmed September 2009 in Puget Sound, WA, TED video, 17:49, https://www.ted.com/talks/simon_sinek_how_great_leaders_inspire_action?language=en.

Encourages the finding of information

Requires original thoughts and creations

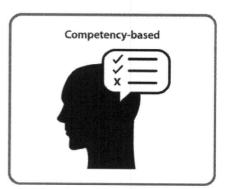
Competency-based

Figure 18.2: Assessment Development

Project Assessments

Figure 18.2 above outlines three characteristics of assessments for online learning. **Project assessments** can encompass all three of these characteristics.

Project assessments are not to be confused with **project-based learning**. Project assessments (also known as project-based assessments) are hands-on projects that require students to apply knowledge. Project-based learning is a form of inquiry-based learning. According to the Buck Institute for Education, project-based learning is a teaching method in which students learn by actively engaging in real-world projects.[74] An astute presenter I once had the pleasure of hearing explained the difference between the two by using the analogy of a meal: project assessments are the dessert, project-based learning is the main course.

Project assessments are easily integrated into asynchronous lessons, choice boards, and Hyperdocs. In fact, the examples provided throughout this book are examples of project assessments. The "Show What I Know About Taxes" choice board in **Figure 18.3** is full of project assessments:

- Create a foldable.

- Create a PSA.

- Create a political candidate's social media profile or campaign video.

- Create a song or poem.

- Interview a tax expert.

---

74   "What Is PBL?," PBLWorks, accessed December 28, 2020, https://www.pblworks.org/what-is-pbl.

"Show What I Know About Taxes"
Choice Board

Directions: The middle orange block is required and then choose one additional block to complete your learning task! Color the block you choose.

Choose 1
Foldable
Each section of the foldable should include one of the required questions. Submit pictures of your foldable.

Choose 1
Choose a Tech Tool
Choose a tech tool to answer the required questions. Some examples could include: Slides, Sway, WeVideo, or Powtoon. Submit a link to your creation.

Choose 1
PSA
Create a public service announcement (PSA) to educate the public about taxes! Your PSA could be in video or flyer form. Submit a link to your creation.

Choose 1
Political Candidate Social Media Profile
Create a (fake) social media profile using the templates provided for a political candidate who is educating their voter base on how taxes work. Submit a link to your profile.

Social media profile templates:
Facebook Template
Twitter Template
Create Fake Tweets

Required
Answer the following questions:
- What are taxes?
- What are the benefits of taxes?
- What is income tax?
- What is payroll tax?
- What is property tax?
- What is sales tax?
- What is excise tax?
- What are the two most important things to know about taxes?

Choose 1
Political Candidate Campaign Video
Create a campaign video for a political candidate who is educating their voter base on how taxes work. Submit a link to your video.

Video tools:
WeVideo
Powtoon
VideoScribe
iMovie
Windows Video Editor

Choose 1
Song or Poem
Create a song or poem. Submit a link to the recording, video, or Google Doc.

Choose 1
Your Choice! My choice is:
Choose a way to answer the required questions. The only requirement is you must be able to submit a link, file, or pictures to your creation.

Choose 1
Interview a Tax Expert
Create an interview video or transcript of yourself interviewing a tax expert such as an accountant or college professor.

— www.teachgateofpd.org —

Figure 18.3: "Show What I Know About Taxes" Choice Board

Choose one!

Click your choice for detailed instructions.

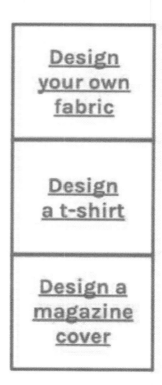

Figure 18.4: "Introduction to Design Principles" Asynchronous Lesson Assessments

In the "Introduction to Design Principles" asynchronous lesson, the choices for assessments are all project assessments, as shown in **Figure 18.4**.

In "Chapter 17: Asynchronous Online Learning," I provided a hefty list of non-digital asynchronous learning activities. Many of these were examples of project assessments. A few examples are highlighted below:

- Create a field guide identifying the plants and animals in your environment.

- Write a book review.

- Create an invention from household items to help people, the environment, or something else.

- Create a habitat for an animal.

- Create a plan to reduce your household's impact on the environment: water, food, garbage, electricity, gas, and more.

- Cook a meal.

- Film a cooking show.

- Double or half a recipe.

- Rewrite a recipe to make it easier to follow.

- Create a daily/weekly/monthly menu and corresponding shopping list for a set budget.

- Create a local weather guide.

- Act out a story you have read.

- Write a story and act it out.

- Create a PSA or commercial to explain why it is important to eat healthily or exercise every day.

- Create a stop-motion video using anything from around your house —toys, Play-Doh, kitchen utensils, and more.

If you need more project assessment ideas, reference the list of products below:

- Presentations
- Animated videos
- Stop-motion animated videos
- Choose-your-own-adventure stories
- Digital storytelling or story books
- Book covers
- Poems
- Comic strips
- Songs
- Soundtracks
- Interviews
- Commercials
- TV shows
- Movies
- Movie trailers

- Guides
- PSAs
- News broadcasts
- News articles
- Radio broadcasts
- Educational materials
- Maps
- Concept maps
- Sketchnotes
- Timelines
- Trading cards
- Mock social media profiles
- Games
- Journal or diary entries

Moving from memorization-based assessments to project assessments may require learning goals to shift to applying, analyzing, evaluating, and creating. Examples of revised learning goals are illustrated in **Figure 18.5** on the next page.

Original Learning Goal	Original Assessment	Revised Learning Goal	Revised Assessment
Define the principles of design.	A test where students define each principle of design.	Apply the principles of design.	Design a fabric, t-shirt, or magazine cover.
Define behavioral and physical adaptations.	A multiple-choice test where students identify whether each example is a behavioral or physical adaptation.	Analyze behavioral and physical adaptations.	Create a hypothetical animal that has adapted to a habitat of choice.

Figure 18.5: Revising Learning Goals for Project Assessments

With project assessments, a solid strategy for determining if a student has met the learning goal is by using a rubric. Make sure to provide the rubric to students *prior* to completion of the learning task.[75]

I am a fan of **single point rubrics** in particular. A single point rubric includes a single column that indicates expectations for proficiency. **Figure 18.6** is an example of a single point rubric for the "Introduction to Design Principles" asynchronous lesson found at intechgratedpd.org/vip. There are many benefits of a single point rubric over other rubric types:

- Less text
- Easier for students to read
- Easier for students to find expectations
- Easier and faster for teachers to make
- Easier and faster for teachers to provide feedback

---

75   Fisher, Frey, and Hattie, *The Distance Learning Playbook.*

Areas for Improvement:	Proficiency of Learning Goals Is Indicated By:	Areas That Exceed Expectations:
	Design reflects balance	
	Design reflects proportion/scale	
	Design reflects emphasis	
	Design reflects rhythm	

Figure 18.6: Single Point Rubric Example

 ## *Checks for Understanding*

A check for understanding is like a nongraded quiz and is an excellent formative assessment strategy. Checks for understanding quickly gauge learners' comprehension of a concept and give immediate feedback to learners regarding what they understand versus what they need to spend more time on.

Earlier in the book, it was shared that in order to whittle your curriculum to the most essential learning objectives, you must become a master at ensuring you are not teaching what students already know. Checks for understanding are a great strategy for this. Fisher, Frey, and Hattie state, "use technology for great diagnosis of what students need to learn."[76]

Checks for understanding are not intended to be the only assessment of a learning goal. Nor are they graded, because they are truly a formative assessment strategy that immediately corrects any errors in knowledge. Once content knowledge is solidified, a student can complete a summative assessment (say a project assessment) to illustrate proficiency of the learning goal.

Since learners receive immediate feedback, this is also a great metacognition strategy. However, don't expect your students to automatically know how to use checks for understanding for metacognitive purposes. You will most likely need to teach students how to interpret the data. Since immediate feedback is given to learners, this is also a low-touch strategy for teachers.

---

76   Fisher, Frey, and Hattie, *The Distance Learning Playbook.*

Forms are a great tool for creating checks for understanding. **Figure 18.7** shows an example of checking for understanding questions in a Google Form.

Both Google Forms and Microsoft Forms have a "quiz" feature. Once a form is set up as a quiz form, it allows for the marking of correct answers, as shown in **Figure 18.8**. Note that this feature does not work for short-answer questions.

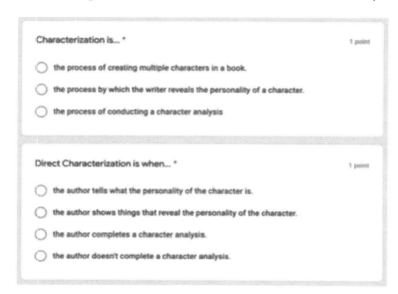

Figure 18.7: Example Check
for Understanding Questions

*Example: Check Your Understanding—Become the
Character (found at intechgratedpd.org/vip)*

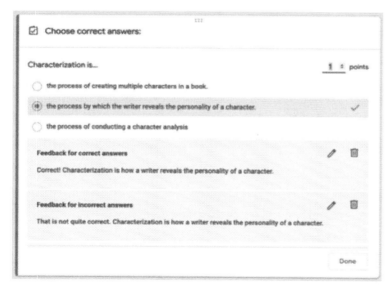

Figure 18.8: Marking Correct Answers
in Google Forms

Once the form is submitted, students receive an option to view their score. **Figure 18.9** shows what this looks like in Google Forms. Once "View score" is selected, the student will see an overall point score (**Figure 18.10**), as well as which of their answers were correct (**Figure 18.11**) and incorrect (**Figure 18.12**).

The form creator has several options to choose from, such as the option to choose if the correct answer will be shown (as in **Figure 18.11**). The form creator can also set feedback for correct and incorrect answers and set point values for a question, as shown in **Figure 18.12**. Even though checks for understanding are "ungraded," I still use points because it provides both me and students a quick metric of their comprehension. For example, **Figure 18.10** shows that the overall point value is 2 out of 4 and only half of the concepts are fully understood.

As the teacher, I can view a summary of scores in the form responses and the response spreadsheet.

Most form tools also allow for the addition of images as questions and answers. This is a great feature for younger students.

Online quiz games, such as Quizizz and Kahoot!, are other tools that can be used for creating check for understanding formative assessments. These tools usually have a gamification element that adds an extra level of engagement. Quizizz takes engagement up a notch by adding custom themes, memes, and music. These tools can be used in either a self-guided individual mode or a teacher-guided group mode; therefore, these tools can be used for formative assessment during group synchronous sessions as well. I like that Quizizz brings back any incorrect questions as "redemption questions" at the end. This forces students to revisit the questions they did not get correct.

Kahoot! adds color and shapes to the answer options, which is a useful feature for younger students. Responses are tallied in a dashboard view for easy viewing and analysis.

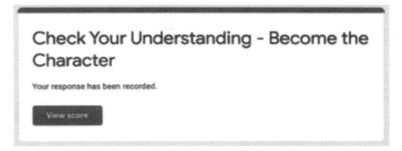

Figure 18.9: View Score Example in Google Forms

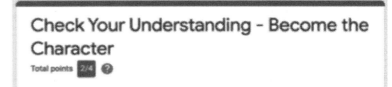

Figure 18.10: Total Point Score in Google Forms

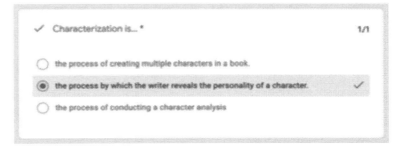

Figure 18.11: Correct Answer in Google Forms

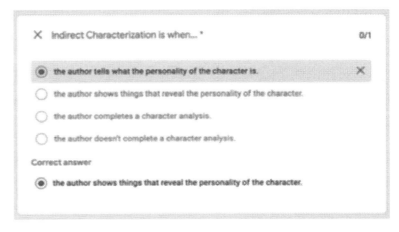

Figure 18.12: Incorrect Answer in Google Forms

Observation Assessment via One-on-One Meetings

Sometimes the best way to assess learning is to observe a student explaining a concept.

In fact, the word "assess" has Latin roots from the word "assidere," which means "sit by."[77] Observation assessment gets back to the root of assessing learning.

Using a form of observation assessment via one-on-one meetings with students can be a powerful assessment strategy in online environments. This is a good assessment strategy if you have content that you must ensure a student has mastered on their own, such as math or reading skills. It is also easy to embed self-assessment questions that boost metacognition within these types of observation assessments.

 For equity purposes, make sure to be very flexible when scheduling one-on-one assessments.

This is a common assessment strategy for personalized and individualized learning environments. I once observed a teacher in a blended environment conduct this type of assessment in her face-to-face classroom. As students worked through the course material at their own pace, one student at a time came to a round table to have a conversation with the teacher about the content at hand. The teacher was able to quickly gauge understanding and redirect if needed. She would instruct students to move on to the next level or go back and review a resource or task.

In "Chapter 14: Maslow before You Bloom," one-on-one appointments were introduced as a strategy to maintain regular contact with learners. If you feel one-on-one appointments should be mandatory for your course, integrating these appointments into an assessment is an excellent approach. Make sure to set clear criteria for proficiency of the learning goal at hand and use the criteria to develop questions to ask students. This is a very personalized strategy as you can reteach and redirect in the moment. Examples are shown in *Figure 18.13*.

---

77   *Latin Dictionary*, s.v. "assidere," accessed March 6, 2021, https://latin-dictionary.net/search/latin/assidere.

Learning Goal	Assessment Question(s)	Proficiency Criteria
Construct a scientific explanation based on evidence from rock strata for how the geologic time scale is used to organize Earth's 4.6-billion-year-old history. (This is Next Generation Science Standard MS-ESS1-4.)	Explain how rocks provide a record of Earth's history.	Explanation includes: • Reference to rock formations and the fossils they contain used to establish relative ages of major events in Earth's history. • At least one piece of evidence in Earth's history (note recalling the specific names is not within the bounds of the assessment).
Given a two-digit number, mentally find 10 more or 10 less than the number, without having to count; explain the reasoning used. (This is Common Core Math Standard 1.NBT.C.5.)	What is 10 less than 26? How did you find that number?	Correct answer was provided. Explanation includes place value understanding.

Figure 18.13: Example Observation Assessments

⇨ Videos

While one-on-one observational assessments are the gold standard, they are also time-consuming and not always feasible. However, in the same way that you can use video to duplicate yourself to your learners, you can also use video to capture learner thought processes.

This is simple. Ensure learners have access to a video tool. This could be a screencast tool, so learners are able to record their webcam and/or their screen. Have learners start the video, share their screen (if applicable), and explain a concept:

- Explain how a math problem was solved.

- Explain the organization of a piece of writing.

- Explain the inspiration behind a piece of artwork or music.

- Explain a creation in another language.

- Explain the diagram of photosynthesis or the water cycle.

You can also use this strategy in conjunction with other asynchronous and assessment strategies:

- Using the one slide strategy, students create a slide showing what they know about a specific topic, then screen record to explain the thinking behind the slide.

- Students explain the map they created to show the Axis versus the Allied troop movements through World War II.

- Explain how a project assessment was created.

Flipgrid is a great tool to accomplish this strategy. What if each student had an assessment board in Flipgrid? Students could record themselves and/or share their screen using the built-in screen recorder feature. At the end of the class, not only would you as the teacher have a clear understanding of where your students were, but students would also have a record of their learning to share with the grown-ups in their lives. To take it one step further, have students record a pre-assessment in addition to a post-assessment. This would provide solid evidence of learning. In the post-assessment video, students could address any misconceptions from the pre-assessment. If you don't want to have to check a different board for each student, use one Flipgrid board for an assessment and turn the "topic moderation" setting on for that board. When this setting is on, the teacher has to approve any videos to be visible to others; therefore, keep the videos "hidden." You now have one Flipgrid board with an assessment video for each student!

This strategy is an excellent way to boost metacognition. What better way to think about your thinking than to explain it to someone else? To ensure self-assessment happens, you could easily embed a metacognitive prompt into the assessment.

The only downside to video is you don't have the ability to immediately redirect and extend questioning, compared to a one-on-one. However, you could follow up the video with questions.

Become the Teacher

There is no better way to learn a concept than to teach it to others. Give students a concept, topic, or learning goal. Instruct them to teach it to others. Students could create a Google Form, Quizizz, Pear Deck, or Edpuzzle on the subject. Students love to use the same tools that you use! Pair students up to take each other's "assessments."

Summary

This section outlines the most important parts from the chapter:

- Assessments in online environments cannot solely assess rote memorization.

- Develop assessments that encourage the finding of information and require original thoughts and creations.

- Develop assessments that are competency-based.

- Make sure the focus of assessment is on learning and not memorization or compliance.

- Knowing how to use resources to find information quickly and efficiently is a skill in itself.

- Consider moving from a point-based grading system to a competency-based or standards-based system.

- Project assessments are an effective assessment strategy for online environments.

- Observation assessment can be a powerful assessment strategy in online environments.

Reflection

After reading "Chapter 18: Assessment in an Online Environment," reflect on how the content can be applied to your unique learning environment.

Share your reflections online using the hashtag **#TeachersGuideToOnline**.

How could you develop assessments that encourage the finding of information and require original thoughts and creations?

Could you use observation assessments in your online course(s)?

Think of a learning goal from your online course(s). How could you edit that learning goal to focus on applying, analyzing, evaluating, or creating?

Chapter 19:
Classroom Management in an Online Environment

Along with assessment, classroom management was on the list of top questions received from teachers when it came to online learning. I have really good news regarding this topic!

> *The foundational elements and strategies shared in this book set the stage for positive classroom management in an online environment.*

This chapter won't be introducing new information; rather, it will reframe much of what has already been covered throughout the book in the context of classroom management.

Classroom management is hard. It is one of the hardest parts of being a teacher. Classroom management in online environments is even harder than it is in face-to-face learning environments. Why is that? Proximity.

> In online learning environments, proximity is not in your favor. You cannot stand over a learner's shoulder and ensure a task is accomplished.

> *How does the online teacher handle classroom management?*
> *By being proactive, not reactive.*

It is difficult to enforce reactive classroom management in remote learning environments. If a student says something inappropriate in a group video call, you can't send that student to the office! Therefore, like assessment, your classroom management strategies may have to be reworked for an online environment. Your teaching methods may have to change in order to create a learning environment that does not need reactive classroom management.

> Face-to-face learning is more forgiving than online learning. Therefore, you have to be more strategic with online learning.

Earlier in the book, I used the analogy of "laying the tracks before the train can run" to refer to being proactive by setting norms and expectations. There are lots of pieces to the classroom management train track. In other words, there are several proactive measures you should take when designing your online course.

Create Engaged, Self-Directed Learners

> In order for online learning to be successful, you must shift control from teacher to student.

What is the ultimate goal of classroom management? Every educator might answer this question a bit differently, but it would be fair to say that most would mention something along the lines of avoiding disruptive behavior of students. Referring back to Schlechty's framework of engagement (engagement, strategic compliance, ritual compliance, retreatism, and rebellion), classroom management aims to avoid rebellion.

Engaged, self-directed learners rarely cause disruptions that require reactive measures. Schlechty explains that the highly engaged classroom "has little or no rebellion, limited retreatism, and limited ritual compliance."[78] Create engaged, self-directed learners by implementing the strategies in "Chapter 15: Creating Self-Directed Learners," such as offering choice and giving students a sense of ownership over the class.

---

78   Schlechty, *Engaging Students.*

Focus on SEL

> Maslow before you Bloom! You must focus on the social-emotional side of learning.

Building strong relationships is one of the best proactive classroom management strategies across the learning continuum. Think about it:

> **If your students feel connected to you, they won't want to disappoint you.**

Follow the strategies in "Chapter 14: Maslow before You Bloom" to create a strong SEL course backbone.

> Your personality is one of your strengths as a teacher - find ways to let it shine in a digital environment!

Design an Organized and Consistent Course

> Organization and consistency are critical to online learning.

Organization and consistency are preventative classroom management strategies. If students are set up for success, less frustration will arise. Less frustration leads to fewer negative reactions. Use the tips for consistency provided in "Chapter 12: The Second Hurdle—I Can't Find . . ." as the backbone for your entire course organization.

Focus on Learning

> Every student does not have to do the exact same thing at the exact same time.

Remember to focus on learning, not seat time, attendance, compliance, or perceived engagement. By placing focus on the latter, unnecessary classroom management issues are created.

> ## Don't set norms or expectations that you can't enforce.

For example, requiring webcams to be on. For one, how would you ever enforce this expectation? Secondly, what is the purpose of requiring webcams? This expectation shifts the focus from learning to compliance and perceived engagement. Webcams don't correlate with learning. Move toward competency-based grading that measures proficiency of learning.

Set Up Synchronous Group Sessions for Success

Synchronous group sessions are likely to be where the majority of classroom management issues will arise. Students can be easily fatigued, distracted by each other, or distracted by their physical environment. Refer to the tips for effective synchronous group sessions in "Chapter 16: Synchronous Online Learning." Below are a few tips that I find particularly useful for proactive classroom management:

- Setting norms and expectations and repeating them at the beginning of every session

- Incorporating brain breaks

- Having a key for chat communications

- Having a schedule that keeps learners busy

Gamify

Gamification is an excellent proactive classroom management strategy. Refer to the section about gamifying the learning experience in "Chapter 11: The First Hurdle— Get to Homebase!"

Incentivize

Personally, I am a fan of positive reinforcement. Why not reward students for positive behaviors? You may have to think differently about incentives for online learning. PBIS Rewards has an extensive list of PBIS Incentives for Distance Learning (bit.ly/pbisincentivesonlinelearning). The list can be filtered by grade level, price (there are many free options), category, and value.

Greater Restrictions Are Not the Answer

When it comes to using digital tools in the learning process, the knee jerk reaction of most school personnel is to restrict. However, research in the area does not support this. Drexler explored research in the area of personalized learning and summarized that "greater restrictions are not the answer."[79] Instead, communication of expectations and community support were cited as critical aspects of digital learning environments.

---

79   Wendy Drexler, "Personal Learning Environments in K–12," in *Handbook of Research on K–12 Online and Blended Learning*, ed. Richard E. Ferdig and Kathryn Kennedy (n.p.: ETC Press, 2014), 447–66.

Summary

This section outlines the most important parts from the chapter:

- It is difficult to enforce reactive classroom management in remote learning environments. Therefore, online teachers must be proactive, not reactive.

- Your classroom management strategies may have to be reworked for an online environment.

- Your teaching methods may have to change in order to create a learning environment that does not need reactive classroom management.

- The foundational elements and strategies shared in this book set the stage for positive classroom management in an online environment.

Reflection

After reading "Chapter 19: Classroom Management in an Online Environment," reflect on how the content can be applied to your unique learning environment.

Share your reflections online using the hashtag **#TeachersGuideToOnline**.

? **Will your typical classroom management approach need to shift for your online courses?**

? **What foundational elements and strategies will you implement to set the stage for positive classroom management in your online course(s)?**

? **What classroom management strategies will you implement?**

Join an online community. There are dozens of Facebook groups out there where teachers share ideas, ask questions, and suggest great resources.

You will find **endless INSPIRATION.**

Make sure to communicate with and care for your students and families.

Part 4:
BEST PRACTICES

Chapter 20: Teachers Share Best Practices

20

"The smartest person in the room is the room." —David Weinberger

This quote summarizes why I planned this chapter as part of this book. This book is designed as a guide to online learning, not a rulebook, for a reason. Online learning has no step-by-step instructions. Every online teacher has to find what works best for their unique mix of teaching style, content area, age of learners, and learner personalities.

This chapter shares the perspectives of online teachers from around the world. Their thoughts are organized by age of learner, starting with third grade, moving to high school and postsecondary, and ending with the views of those in teacher support roles, such as instructional technologists. I emailed teachers the list of questions below but stressed that I wanted them to share what they felt would be helpful to other teachers who are teaching online:

- What do you teach? How long have you taught?

- In early 2020, what situation was your school in?
  What situation is your school in now?

- What have you found to work well with online learning?

- What did you find to not work well?

- What lessons did you learn (if any)?

- Do you have any success stories from online learning?

- Did you find any strategies that worked well for online learning?

- Were/are there resources that are invaluable to teaching online?

- Do you have any resources to share that are specific to
  your content area and/or grade level?

- If you are in a situation where you have some kids face-to-face, some online, some only certain days of the week, and so on, do you have any tips for how to manage this?

- If you have had to suddenly switch from face-to-face to online learning this school year, do you have any tips for how to navigate these sudden changes?

Many shared their experiences with emergency virtual learning during the COVID-19 pandemic. No matter what the state of the world is at the time you are reading this, the tips offered here by these educators are applicable whether you are online learning or crisis learning.

Keyleigh Hennessy,
Grade 3, Billings Public Schools, Montana, USA

"I currently teach third grade distance learners. I have been teaching third grade for seven years. In spring of 2020, we suddenly found ourselves trying to navigate distance learning. I was lucky in that I had been involved in TILT (Teachers Integrating and Learning Technology) for the past two years (which is a professional development group in my school district) and had set up several routines while we were in person. My students were very familiar with navigating Google Classroom, Google apps, and Seesaw. We spent one hour a week on computer skills, coding, and troubleshooting prior to the shutdown, which made a great difference in their ability to navigate online learning from home. This fall, families were given the option to request remote learning, and I was asked to teach a group of those that opted for full remote learning.

"One of the things that works so well for distance learning is the ability for students who have more independence to spend extra time on subjects they are passionate about. I also have a lot more contact with families, and those that are very involved have a better idea of what their child is learning and areas in which they are struggling or excelling. One of the biggest challenges is working with students who have poor attendance and participation. This can happen for a variety of reasons (e.g., poor internet, no parent or adult oversight, student or families struggling to adhere to a schedule, etc.). Without the oversight of the physical classroom, I fear many students are 'falling through the cracks' and will be so far behind when we return to in-person learning. Communicating often and early about expectations and reaching out to families to offer assistance is critical. It is also difficult to build relationships through a computer. Distance learning has challenged me to be very thoughtful and intentional with ways to build community and relationships, as it does not happen as naturally as it would in a physical classroom.

"I think one of the most beneficial things we can do for families is to give them a 'one-stop shop' for all of the information they need. I make sure to push out a schedule to my students each week that has every assignment linked, Zoom times linked, and accompany it with a screencast video in which I discuss anything that might be new, different, or that I have been receiving questions about. This schedule is embedded in a Google Site that has links to other resources and contact information. Many schools are utilizing multiple different websites and learning platforms (they all have their strengths), and it is overwhelming to both students and parents if they have to check multiple different places for assignments. Another important thing to do for students and families is to regularly ask for their input. I use Google Forms to survey students and parents about distance learning. I think this shows the families that I care about making this work for them, and I get helpful feedback about what is and is not working.

"One of the most amazing things to come about during this pandemic is the teacher groups on Facebook that I have joined. Teachers are creating and freely sharing their work with one another as well as offering advice and teaching each other. I have some incredible resources now that are the culmination of work by lots of different teachers from all over the world. It has expanded my professional community and allowed me access to resources that I never would have had time to create entirely from scratch. Another benefit is how much contact I have with families. I feel that I know the families of my students so much better than when I am in the physical classroom.

"The best strategies for online teaching I have found are having video meetings at regular times, having video meetings with smaller groups of students (not the whole class, as too many of them disengage), giving students a link to an interactive or live activity they can work on and complete during video lessons to keep them engaged, getting regular feedback from students and parents, and creating a one-stop shop for parents and families (in my case it is a Google Site).

"Google apps, Seesaw, Zoom, and GoGuardian have been my most invaluable tools during distance learning. The record feature that is built into Seesaw allows me to be sure that students are doing independent work themselves and have them explain their thinking. It is also a place I can easily use to communicate with family members. I use Google Sheets to track the attendance of my students. I use Google Slides for collaborative activities during small groups and creating my weekly linked schedule. I use Google Forms for quizzes, exit tickets, and surveying my students and parents. I have a Google Site that houses all of the important information and links for students and families. Zoom is what allows me to see them face-to-face and truly build relationships! GoGuardian allows me to see their screen while they are working. This allows me to help them troubleshoot.

I can open tabs for them if they close out of an activity, I can block and allow certain sites to help keep them on track, and I can even use it to call them on their device! A new feature in GoGuardian allows me to group students, so I can easily open differentiated assignments on their computers!

"I am a Seesaw Ambassador and publish activities to the community library. You can view my Author Page (bit.ly/keyleighseesaw). I also have a YouTube channel (bit.ly/keyleighyoutube) in which I have made tutorials for other teachers. I made a mental health check-in for my students to complete each morning called 'Good Morning' (bit.ly/formgoodmorning—it was the culmination of work by other teachers in professional groups as well). This is my class site using Google Sites (bit.ly/mrshennessysclass)."

> **Relationship building does not come naturally in online learning as it does in face-to-face. Therefore, you have to be intentional about consistently embedding relationship building activities into online learning.**

Tracey Nesrallah,
Grade 6, Ottawa Catholic School Board, Ontario, Canada

"I teach grade 6 for the Ottawa Catholic School Board. I have taught elementary for eight years. Prior to that, I was a high school drama teacher. In March 2020, the province of Ontario was told we would close for two weeks after our March break. That closure notice was extended many times until the entire school year was spent away from the school buildings. Elementary schools were directed to give 5 hours of asynchronous online work each week during the initial school closure. I was able to deliver this through Hāpara Workspace.

"Currently, my school board has offered two choices to parents—face-to-face or virtual academy. I am presently teaching grade 6 entirely through a virtual platform as a part of the virtual academy.

"I have found that interactive and engaging activities work the best with online learning. Using any kind of activity that students can interact with elicits the most engagement from my students. Using platforms like Pear Deck, where students can interact with my presentations synchronously or asynchronously instead of passively looking or watching a presentation, works really well. I can see the students who are engaging in the learning, and I can check in with those students who are not participating. I also found with my elementary students that they struggle with using Google Docs, but they can better navigate and use Google Slides to show their thinking, especially in math. In Google Slides, students can make a text box anywhere, without fear of changing the entire format of the document. They can also easily add pictures or videos of their thinking. My students also seem to respond to any group task. During this time, my students crave interaction with each other. Even during the time of asynchronous learning during the initial pandemic shutdown, I found using a group shared Google Slide, Padlet, or Flipgrid would get the most buy-in and engagement from my students.

"I have found that reading or listening to lecture-style learning of new materials does not work for my students. If I share math lessons, in particular, where the students have to read through a slide deck, I have found that they will not actually read any of the material. Although, they listen if I add my own voice reading the material. My students also respond less to premade presentations. My students have trouble learning from 'premade courseware.' If I personalize the material using my own voice or a screencast of the lesson, they seem to be more engaged and understand the content more. I also find that any printed activities are difficult to offer feedback on and track. Activities that are digital and usable by the students are much more efficient instead of trying to decipher emailed photos of worksheets."

Your personality is one of your strengths as a teacher - find ways to let it shine in a digital environment!

Billie Johnson,
Grade 6, Pasadena Unified School District, Pasadena, California, USA

"This is my third year teaching middle school history and English in Pasadena, California. COVID has had a significant impact on my teaching practice and has tested the mettle of educators and students alike across the country.

"The 2019–2020 school year started like any other except I was teaching 6th grade instead of 8th grade like I silently hoped for. In December 2019, I began discussing coronavirus with my students, and we stayed up to date with the unfolding events after we returned in 2020. In 2020, it was clear that there was a shift in the complexity of the virus and how it was impacting different regions. Soon we were faced with the reality that we would be hit head-on and our lives were going to change forever. It was a slow progression, like dominoes falling in slow motion. First, we did not allow certain visitors on campus. Then, all visitors were not allowed to visit campus. Finally, we were sent home early for spring break and subsequently told that we were not returning. It all happened so fast, which revealed many of our technological capabilities.

"Currently, for the 2020–2021 school year, my district is strictly teaching online with a TBA return date. With this swift transition from in-class to online learning, I have had to adjust and reflect on how I can best meet the needs of my students.

"As a teacher with my own elementary-school-aged children at home, I have a firsthand perspective of what many other parents are going through. What I found that works well in terms of engaging students is transparency, consistency, honesty, and professionalism.

"Being transparent with how we are feeling, acknowledging where we are, and then discussing how to adapt until life is right side up again is important. My students and I discuss solutions and remain solutions oriented.

"I have routines in place for my classes, so students know how class opens and how it closes each day. Students also have a feel for how our lessons will be carried out and where I will share information with them and on which platforms they can access said information. I post information at different access points so students will be confronted with information wherever they should log in to join class.

"Honesty is key in any relationship and that does not change with teacher-student relationships. The most frequent questions I get are about returning to school and the virus itself. I respond with truth to ease their minds.

"In regard to professionalism, I show up to work dressed and prepared as if we were in the classroom together. It is important to me that I present as a professional, because even though we are home, I am a role model for my students just the same. I have garnered the respect of my students and families by staying true to my teaching practices online as if we were in the classroom. More importantly, my expectations have not changed. However, my level of creativity for engagement has had to level up.

"Engagement is a challenge particularly in middle school. My middle schoolers do not turn their cameras on during lessons but will participate in assignments that require them to post recordings of themselves. Students chat with me during lessons and show up to study sessions or schedule one-on-ones with me for additional support or feedback. I make myself as available as possible, but I am also explicit in my instruction and as clear as possible so students are not confused by what they are expected to produce. I have also modified lessons to make sure students are not overwhelmed by the number of assignments. Virtual field trips have been amazing for engaging students and breaking the monotony of the daily grind.

"Here are a few online apps that have worked amazingly well: Hāpara (progress monitoring/planning/resource sharing), Anchor, Padlet, Google, Flipgrid, Kahoot!, Thrively, Seesaw, and Nearpod. It is critical that the techscape changes to provide students with a different aesthetic similar to the outside world. Other huge wins have been blending videos with content delivery, inviting guests to drop in and open class, and injecting some comedy into the class period when possible. We must remain flexible and understanding with ourselves and our students during this unique time.

"Excellent digital resources that I have used in class and online are Global Oneness, YouTube, Teaching Tolerance, National Geographic, and Cal Global Ed. These resources include lesson plans, videos, and podcasts to offer different perspectives about the lives and realities of the people who exist within the real world they live in. For the record, these are all resources that I have used and will resume using when we return to face-to-face instruction.

"Making the transition from online teaching to in-class or hybrid instruction will be met with open arms. I will certainly cross that bridge when the time comes. However, I will continue to improve upon my teaching practice to meet the needs of all students without location being a factor. What I miss, that has not worked well virtually, is my students prewriting and brainstorming on paper with pen or pencil in hand. I will return to this practice when we return. Another one that we really tried but didn't work was group reading. With so many different internet glitches and misfires it was difficult to keep the rhythm and flow of the reading intact for comprehension and effectiveness. We scrapped the idea and watched the film of the play we attempted to read.

"Overall, I am proud of my students. There are many who were the subjects of bullying who, now that they feel safe, are excelling. Others have stepped up big time and have surpassed my expectations and their own for sure. To encapsulate my frame of mind in all of this and how I want to impress upon my students in the most resounding way possible is that we will focus on what we can do and keeping the line of communication open. Leading with both of these positive methods has forged relationships that even the digital realm cannot deny us."

> **Face-to-face learning is more forgiving than online learning. Therefore, you have to be more strategic with online learning.**

Lana Hekkel,
Music, Grades 6–8,
Sidney Public Schools, Montana, USA

"I am in my 11th year as a K–12 music teacher, currently teaching at the middle school level. In March of last year, our school switched to online learning via Microsoft Teams and the Microsoft 365 suite. As a middle school staff, we were instructed to lessen the workload for our students and do our best to keep things simple. Grades became pass/fail and electives like music rightly took a back seat to core classes. We finished the year that way.

"Over the summer, our school switched to using Google tools in order to be consistent with the other three schools in our district. We began with in-person instruction in the fall of 2020. Our schedule was heavily modified; students stayed in cohorts and made no rotations between rooms except for PE and technology classes. All our core classes were taught over Google Meet so that each teacher could stay in his or her room while teaching to the whole grade level simultaneously. Late fall, electives teachers were allowed to pull small groups of students from study hall for band, choir, art, etc. As of December 2020, it looks like we will remain in this schedule through the end of the year. Because of this setup, our school has had very few COVID-19 cases and little or no spread within. One of the other helpful decisions by our administration was that all students who opted for a full year of distance learning were assigned to Acellus (acellus.com) and separated from the in-class curriculum. This limited the need for teachers to manage in-person and online classes simultaneously. In-person students who were eventually quarantined did log into Google Classroom and Google Meet from home.

"I have little in the way of online classroom management tips, but I do have advice to offer teachers who are new to these online teaching tools. As school began in the fall of 2020, I presented a few training sessions to teachers about the Google Workspace for Education tools and online music teaching. My Google presentations were for beginner-level teachers, who told me they needed someone to 'take the fire hose down to a trickle.' Navigating new online tools can be a challenge; add the pressure of a sudden switch to distance learning and factor in that these teachers do not consider themselves 'techies,' and it's easy to see why they were overwhelmed. We joked that most of these teachers had already transitioned to use computers and then the internet, so this was the final step to ensure the last years of their careers were completely different than the first. My mission was to help them define and understand cloud-based storage and Google tools but also give them permission to 'keep' and 'throw' the tools they would and would not need for successful teaching. Teachers often think they don't have permission to decline a new tool; I advised them to deliberately decide not to stress over what they should be using. Start small and do what works for you. Your students will likely appreciate simplicity.

"Since most of the teachers were familiar with Facebook, I told them, 'Google Classroom is just Facebook for education.' Before Google Classroom existed, you could have created a Facebook group, added your whole class, and shared interesting videos or documents that way. There are obvious problems with that, so we're grateful to have secure LMS tools now, such as Google Classroom, Microsoft Teams, and Schoology, to help us distribute content. The reason I drew this parallel is that the teachers felt comfortable with posting and sharing via Facebook or even texting photos and videos to family. The concept of Google Classroom became less confusing when they thought of it as 'social media for school.'

"I also shared the following analogy to define the most useful Google Workspace tools. Imagine I'm hosting a Thanksgiving dinner party. You and your students are coming to my house, and we're eating buffet style. My house is Google Chrome; you have to enter my house to get to the party. You could go to someone else's house (i.e., Firefox, Safari) but things would be slightly different and probably less fun. The buffet table is Google Drive; everything we need is stored here. (We also called Drive an 'online file cabinet'). The bowls you see on the table are Google tools such as Docs, Sheets, Slides, etc. The foods within those bowls—the nutrition you'll share with your students—are the content you've created as lessons and homework (Docs, Slides, Sheets, Word documents, PowerPoint files, PDFs, videos, etc.). Now comes the interaction. Google Classroom is the plate; you walk to the table and choose what to put on the plate for each student. Within Classroom, each time you attach files to an assignment, you're loading a new plate for your students to consume. Now, you could have shared all these files in an email, but using email to send lessons to students would be like spooning the mashed potatoes and gravy onto a napkin. It's possible, but it won't function nearly as well as using Google Classroom. After the party, you can even ask Classroom to wash the dishes for you (i.e., quizzes made in Google Forms can be graded automatically). Even if you choose not to use that feature, Google will prompt your student to 'bring the dishes to the kitchen' for you by clicking the 'Turn In' button to submit their work.

"These are my recommendations to teachers hoping to become more comfortable with online tools:

- Join an online community. There are dozens of Facebook groups out there where teachers share ideas, ask questions, and suggest great resources. You will find endless inspiration.

- Clean up your workspace to be more efficient. You might have several open Google Chrome tabs and unwanted emails making things look untidy. Pin your tabs, filter your emails, and change your Drive settings to make your list of files look more familiar.

- Spend time playing around with the tools you need. Do you ever tell your kids to practice a new concept so they can wrap their head around it themselves? That's what you need, too. Trainings and tutorials can be information overload, so take the time to process things on your own.

- Spend time looking at the settings in your Google Drive, Gmail, Google Classroom, and Google Chrome. You'll become more informed, plus you can turn on/off whichever settings you choose.

- If you run into a snag that you can't solve, Google it! Add the current year at the end of your Google search to ensure that you'll find a current tutorial.

- Finally, I've dealt with a few teachers who are frustrated with themselves for their own lack of knowledge. If that is you, stop! Not even the techies (or the kids!) were ready for this kind of challenge, and you're actually doing great. Your lack of familiarity with these new tools does not diminish your worth as a great teacher. Please don't be reluctant to ask for help."

Rebecca Recco,
Art, Grades 6–8, Oakland, California, USA

> Within the same time period, you cannot cover as much in online learning as you can in face-to-face. You must whittle your curriculum down to the most essential learning objectives.

"I am an art teacher in a bustling inner-city middle school in East Oakland, California. This is my twentieth year teaching art. I have taught art for my entire career from grades kindergarten through twelfth grade, in public, private, and charter schools. I also have a Masters' Degree in Digital Learning and Leading from Lamar University. I have seen a lot of things in my career and have faced a lot of challenges but nothing like the immediate and long-term shift to online learning in March of 2020.

"It started not long after the announcement about COVID-19 reaching the West Coast. My husband and I were sitting on the sofa watching the news when he said, 'You know, I think you might want to start planning some lessons for students to do from home.' At first, I thought he meant for the potential of students getting sick and needing to be absent for a day or two, but I realized that he actually meant he thought we might shut all the schools down. 'What?' I said, 'No . . . they'll never shut schools down.' 'You might want to think about it, at least,' he said. And so, I decided to build an online lesson using Hāpara Workspaces, a tool that I use for in-person learning to organize resources for my students. I created a two-week learning unit for my students to start in class, but students could complete [it] at home, if needed. Sure enough, it was announced that Friday that we would, in fact, be shutting down. First for two weeks. Then, another two weeks. No online instruction happened for a while, because we had no overall plan to deliver lessons online.

"When it became obvious that we would not be returning to the classroom anytime soon, many teachers struggled with how to teach from home. Schools were allowed to create and submit their own distance learning plans to the district. This allowed schools to respond to the unique needs of their student populations, but it also left many schools struggling with how to address this mammoth problem. On one hand, our school system is surrounded by Silicon Valley giants—SalesForce, Apple, Google, Microsoft, Pixar, LucasFilm. On the other hand, many of our teachers lacked the home technology and expertise to suddenly switch their practice from in-person to online learning.

"For the next two months, teachers struggled to move their lessons online. Teachers who had the technological expertise assisted those who needed help. Over Zoom, teachers collaborated to share best practices, tutor other teachers, provide tech support, and assist students and parents as well. Schools distributed loaner technology to students, while community groups worked to secure Wi-Fi and basic technology needs for families. Textbooks, food, school supplies, and toiletry kits were sent home with students. Wellness check-in calls were made. It was a pretty piecemeal effort to respond to such a major shift in the way we addressed all the needs fulfilled by our schools, but over time, a pretty successful system emerged.

"Over the summer, some efforts were made to tighten up our online learning systems, but unfortunately, those efforts seemed to be more localized. Most of the time and energy was spent planning in-person school reopening and not looking at our spring efforts with a critical eye. There were no efforts to train teachers in digital learning best practices or to share successes or tips for other teachers to learn from. So, when schools opened virtually in August, there was still a lot of confusion and inconsistency.

"I feel that my students were prepared for learning online because we had a strong digital culture in my classroom. Though my classes have always been in person, I utilize a digital learning environment in my practice. This is helpful for many reasons, but I do it mainly to organize carefully curated resources in one place for students, specialists, and parents to have access at any time. Having a well-designed digital learning environment also creates a sense of ownership for my students. They can access it at any time, even if I'm not there to tell them what to do (although there are so many ways I can facilitate their learning, even from afar). And, in doing so, they are learning digital literacy skills that are so needed in adulthood, especially if they would like to work for one of these Silicon Valley giants. In this case, having this practice helped my students to transition from in-person to online learning without too much trouble. They were already familiar with using these tools to learn, so I didn't need to try to teach them how to log in, navigate the online learning environment, and submit work. This gave me more time to do wellness checks with families, support parents in learning how to access the Workspaces, and create rich content for new lessons.

"Another reason that my virtual Workspace worked well for students is that I constantly ask for feedback from my students:

- What worked?
- What didn't work?

- Do you like this layout?

- Can you find what you're looking for in this learning environment?

"By asking these questions, I have been able to identify and fix problems that students might not have mentioned. This also helps with student engagement, because when students feel confused and are learning from home, sometimes they just check out. It's frustrating to not be able to look around the room for confused faces or off-task behaviors, so the next best thing is to simply ask students. Google Forms are great for this as well as Google Jamboard, Padlet, Flipgrid, and Pear Deck. There are so many ways to solicit student feedback and make it really fun. Students love having some say in how class operates, and their solutions help me immensely!

"Speaking of collaboration, perhaps the biggest takeaway from this time is that collaboration wins every time. Schools that seemed to fare the best during distance learning tended to be the schools that held space for authentic collaboration, feedback, reflection, and redesign between teachers, students, and the community to create systems that work for all. Allowing teachers to share their knowledge instead of filling up professional development time with training allowed teachers to meet the needs of students and their families. What works for one community may not work for another.

"Another big takeaway from the shift to online learning is that you really can't take a regular school day and make it digital. In schools where teachers were expected to simply broadcast an in-person lesson to students for the same amount of time they would be in the classroom, teachers quickly found that student engagement dropped and more students struggled with content. That's because online learning isn't simply broadcasting a lesson. Learning is active, but watching a broadcast of a classroom is passive (and boring). Instead, students should be learning through carefully crafted online activities that promote student ownership of their learning. This is important with in-person learning but especially crucial during online learning because students are learning at home and must direct their own activity. Students must be empowered to take control of their own learning, and that's never going to happen when they are watching a blurry video feed from a classroom webcam. Having a successful online learning program means rethinking everything from class schedules to assessments to learning activities, and this requires specialized knowledge and major changes in what we think learning looks like.

"My last takeaway from the shift to distance learning is perhaps the most important one. It is so simple that it sounds flippant, but it has been the ruin of so many expensive and time-consuming plans. Here it is: even the best system will fail if students can't access it. Many school systems across the country have found that online learning was a failure because students did not have access from home. I am fortunate to be teaching in a district where both public and private programs have worked to get every student online, but I also know that this is not true everywhere. But access doesn't only mean having a device and Wi-Fi. Access can be thwarted by a difficult log-in protocol, as well as lack of visual cues for non-readers or English language learners. Access can be stopped cold by incompatibilities between platforms and devices or by lack of student (and parent) technical literacy skills to work around problems. Even if a school put in place the best, most well-funded online learning system that could exist, if students can't access it, it's a failure. A district should never require students and teachers to learn on any system that has major obstacles for users to be able to access it, no matter how many great features it has to offer.

"If I could give one piece of advice to decision makers right now, it would be to collect as much feedback as possible from teachers, students, and parents and use the lessons learned to inform future decisions about learning design. Whether we go back to in-person learning tomorrow or continue to use digital learning or a hybrid of both, it would still benefit all stakeholders to have a solid digital learning system in place, whether it's a shiny new LMS or other learning platforms. After all, we do live in a digital world, where so much of the work and collaboration we do is aided by technology. By building the best system for your school, you are giving students and teachers the tools needed to manage learning, build important digital skills, empower students to become lifelong learners, and build a solid digital culture to prepare students for learning and working after graduation. Taking this rare opportunity to get so much feedback from so much experimentation will certainly steer you toward a better system that suits all learners (and teachers)!"

> Do not replicate face-to-face instruction in an online environment.

Lindsee Tauck,
English, Grades 9–12, Chula Vista, California, USA

"My name is Lindsee Tauck, and I currently teach high school English in Chula Vista, California. I have been involved in education for over 12 years and have taught in a variety of locations, including south central Los Angeles, the Barrio Logan neighborhood of San Diego, Wyoming, Montana, and Mexico.

"In the first few months of 2020, my school was still conducting classes face-to-face as usual. My students and I would discuss the news we had heard about coronavirus spreading and how certain schools throughout Asia were transitioning to remote learning. My students would jokingly say that they wanted that to happen here so they could go to school in their pajamas, all the while believing that it would never actually happen. Then, in mid-March, when our school was on spring break, we were informed that we would not be returning to school after the vacation, and we would begin distance learning indefinitely. My colleagues and I found out that we essentially had one week to set up our classes in a totally new online environment and began scrambling to re-create our courses.
Up until then, I had never participated in a video chat in my life, but luckily I have been using Google Classroom and the Google Workspace for Education tools for the past several years with my classes, so I was already set up for distance learning. That occurred ten months ago, and as we currently wrap up the fall semester of 2020, our district is still one hundred percent online.

"This certainly has been a school year like none other; distance learning has posed several challenges, but I believe my students have also experienced many successes as well. Due to the demographics of the area that I teach in, there have been significant issues with student accessibility to functioning technology, Wi-Fi access, and some students even have reported that they are currently residing either in different states or are south of the border. Many of my students' parents are essential workers and are unable to stay at home when distance learning is taking place. A number of my students are completing distance learning with no adult supervision and are responsible for helping their younger siblings with their online learning. Even with these challenges, we have adapted the best that we can.

"For me, regardless of being face-to-face or in a remote classroom, building strong student relationships is the key to successful learning. This has proven to be particularly more difficult during distance learning because students are very reluctant to share their video screens or speak out loud, so during our live meets I am basically speaking to several silent avatar images on a screen. It's difficult to ascertain if students are understanding a concept or if they have a question since they are hesitant to speak out loud. One strategy that has worked for me to get my students to participate more in class is conducting social-emotional check-ins. I pose a risk-free question before we jump into content, like 'Who is your favorite musical artist?' and students can unmute themselves to speak or type their answer in the chat. This has helped me get to know my students and allows them to get to know each other a little better. The Google apps have been a valuable resource for me, particularly Docs, Slides, and Classroom. I create most of my student assignments in Docs, and it allows me to provide feedback to them in real time as they work on an assignment. I've also noticed that students really have opened up about themselves through their writing and through our written communication with this platform. The Slides app allows me to present content both synchronously and asynchronously, and Classroom provides a main platform where I can post the course material and meet with my students. Even with the challenges of distance learning, my students have managed to form a sense of class community and have been able to apply their academic skills, but perhaps most of all, they have learned the ability to adapt, troubleshoot, and succeed in unfamiliar learning circumstances."

> **Maslow before you Bloom! You must focus on the social-emotional side of learning.**

Brittany Mosher,
Postsecondary, University of Vermont, Vermont, USA

Part 1: Setting the Stage

"I started my position as an assistant professor of wildlife biology at the University of Vermont in October of 2019. All new faculty face challenges in their first year or two settling into the position, but as you know, I met some unforeseen challenges in that first year, too. I teach undergraduate ecology, wildlife biology, and conservation biology courses. In Spring of 2020, I was teaching a 25-student, 4-credit lab class in herpetology (the study of amphibians and reptiles) and co-teaching a 90-student, 4-credit lab course in conservation biology where we had weekly lab sections on building ecological models using spreadsheets. As a newbie, I was teaching each of these courses for the first time.

During our spring recess in March 2020, the decision was made to move to online instruction. I went to my office one last time, grabbed any textbook I thought might be useful, and loaded my collection of houseplants into my car. Who knew when I would return again!? (As of January 2021, I have been back to the office one time, in August, to change out textbooks and references for the fall semester.)

→ *Part 2: Lessons Learned*

"*Ask students to be your active learning partners:* The main lesson I have learned in online learning is to ask students to be your active partners in determining what does, and does not, work. A full semester is too long to wait to hear on course evaluations that the course was disorganized, that the instructor's microphone didn't work, or that students were completely and utterly overwhelmed. I had great success in polling my students weekly on what was working for them and what wasn't. Small changes on my end like posting slides before lecture, sending a weekly plan each Monday morning, and extending our weekly due date by a few hours were simple changes that seemed to make things much easier on my students. Once they realized that I truly was looking for their feedback, they became less shy about giving it, and I was rewarded by open, honest discussions where they learned the value of giving and receiving constructive criticism.

"*If it feels like busy work, don't do it:* My first impulse when we pivoted to online learning was to maintain everything we had planned to do but to switch it to an online format. Given that one of my courses was supposed to involve outdoor field trips, envisioning that change wasn't easy. What I ended up with was a list of assignments that felt overwhelming for students to tackle on their own. After scrutinizing each assignment against my learning outcomes, I found that some were busy work, while others could be modified to teach concepts, critical thinking, and other valuable skills. Now I try to approach every assignment and class this way. I heard so much feedback from students that faculty seemed to default to over-assigning work when we moved online. An overwhelmed student is one that is shut off to learning.

"*Get creative:* During Spring 2020, I could feel the stress and tension that my students were feeling about the state of the world. I felt it, too. Many students were seniors whose job prospects had just become very uncertain. I chose to give two options for the final project for the class—one was a more standard field notebook assignment, and one was an art assignment. Of 27 students, 15 selected the art assignment, and I was blown away by both their artistic skills and their ability to connect class concepts in new ways (visually, with music, through puns, etc.). View their creations on the 'UVM Field Herpetology' blog (bit.ly/uvmherpetologyblog). The projects were fun to grade, and students commented that it was rare that they could both learn something and decompress from the state of the world. This assignment is transferable to all disciplines (even technical ones!) and is one I will use in the future. The book *Teaching and Learning Creatively: Inspirations and Reflections* was a great resource to help open my mind to alternative assignments.

"*Your students are human:* 'Educating with compassion' became a motto of mine during the pandemic. In the past year, more than any other, students are dealing with huge emotional burdens. Some of my students have lost family members, have battled mental health, have been apart from their families, and more. I try to remember that I don't know what each student is going through and to give them the benefit of the doubt. Very few students are out to swindle us teachers; most are just asking for help in their own way. I try to make class an exciting and engaging place where they can open their minds and learn something new but understand when externalities lead to someone having a challenging day, week, or semester. Acknowledging these challenges has made students more willing to share with me when they need flexibility or support. Finding flexibility and support systems early on makes it possible for students to stay connected with class (even if at a different pace), rather than fading into the ether."

Keturah Rush,
Technology Integration Specialist,
Monticello School District, Arkansas, USA

"As the Technology Integration Specialist at Monticello School District for the past 11 years, I have never witnessed a year quite like 2020. We are very fortunate to have a plethora of technology devices, but we are still working our way to the higher levels (modification and redefinition) of the SAMR model [substitution, augmentation, modification, redefinition].

"We are 1:1 iPads kindergarten–fifth grade and 1:1 Chromebooks sixth–twelfth grade. Our district is not large enough to support a staff of virtual-only teachers; therefore, our teachers have face-to-face students as well as virtual students. The struggle is real! Even the 'tech savvy' teachers battle finding the time to make sure everything is connected, running, recording, volume up, camera connected, Wi-Fi working, and the list goes on and on. Synchronous learning is hard! It's hard for the student, hard for the parents, and hard for the teachers! In a perfect world, we would love to have a dedicated teacher for each class who focused solely on the virtual students. We know our virtual students still need the social and emotional connections with classroom teachers. We also know our teachers are overloaded trying to manage their face-to-face students, create blended lessons, and take care of their virtual students.

"Technology tools, such as Screencastify, Kami (kamiapp.com), and Book Creator, have been invaluable in the success of online learning. The ease of use for students and teachers alike makes all three of those resources top on our list. Tools like these that incorporate video and audio in lessons are a necessity for online learning."

> Understanding when to use synchronous learning and when to use asynchronous learning is key to designing successful online learning.

Sarah Hagans,
Digital Technology Teacher/Learning Offline Academy Teacher, Lincoln County Middle School, Stanford, Kentucky, USA

→ Background

"They say that you can't teach an old dog new tricks, but as a teacher who is closer to retirement than not, I find that each year is still a new year to learn new things. Many years ago, my teacher preparation program did a great job of not only encouraging us new teachers to incorporate technology into our teaching, but it also expected us to have a purpose for it in order to help students learn as well as prepare them for the ever-changing world of work. As part of my program, I was expected to learn new technology *and* have my students use it in natural ways as part of their own learning experience. As I began working in the classroom teaching Spanish, arts and humanities, or even coaching our Academic Team (a.k.a. Quiz Bowl), I did find ways to have students use technology, and I furthered my own study of it as well—something I have continued even to this day as a digital technology teacher.

2020—'A Year Like No Other'

"That was a quote we heard throughout the year, and it was the tagline that our principal had emblazoned on our staff shirts in the spring of 2020, but at the time, we didn't know that it would still hold true for the 2020–21 school year as well. As a result of the COVID-19 pandemic, in March our school began its first year of virtual course offerings.

"For us as a school, this first dive into virtual learning was a bit crude. I myself had a bit more experience than most in our school, since for the past two years I had tried my hand a little with flipped classroom practices, and several years earlier I'd taught my own distance learning course. These experiences helped give me a small edge as we began our journey as a school. I had begun to use some of these concepts in my regular classes already, but I and others of us using Google Classroom and even Hāpara had to alter how we were using these tools to better accommodate the needs of students working completely from home. We knew that we had to do more, so we started using additional tools like Zoom, Google Hangouts, Google Meet, Loom, Screencastify, and even social media all to teach and interact with our students. In the spring, our methods were like makeshift first aid efforts, and we learned through trial and error which tools worked best for different tasks. Students learned right along with us as they produced their own work. However, moving forward, we knew that we had to do better, and as it looked like the next school year would need a new approach to learning, we all began planning what that would look like.

"The spring of 2020 wasn't my first stab at online learning. Several years ago, during my first years of teaching, the principal from our high school approached me with a proposal to work with a student in credit recovery. This student had not fared so well in her Spanish I course at the high school, and as a senior, she was applying to colleges and wanted to redo the course to improve her chances of acceptance. However, there wasn't a course available in their school schedule that fit hers, so his request was if I could do an independent study with her. Given my own full middle school course load and coaching after school, I knew that it would be difficult, but I asked if they were willing to try something unconventional. I suggested that we could set up an online course where the student could receive all of her assignments, then we could meet in person once a week for tests and connections. In addition, I suggested evening office hours and online assistance, if needed. Both the principal and the student were up for this challenge. So, I created an online classroom using Nicenet—long before Google Classroom, Schoology, Seesaw, Canvas, Hāpara, or any of the other wonderful tools that we use today. However, even back then, it was a practical and successful way to reach students like mine who needed alternative learning pathways.

"Now, we have more versatile tools that are meant to engage students just like Nicenet did for my student way back when. From our experience in the spring of 2020, we learned that having a clear plan and a structure is crucial when students are learning from home in virtual environments, and consistency is key for a schoolwide approach. We learned that having a common foundation and common practices across grade levels, teams, and teachers was vital. As a middle school, we utilize interdisciplinary teams—each its own little mini-school family. However, we knew that even these different teams across grade levels needed some common structures and practices to make implementation and learning easiest for teachers, for students, and for families. We needed a common language and common understanding of how to do things so that students and families would benefit without so many difficulties.

"'The struggle is real' was a common phrase that we did not want to hear as much in the fall as we heard in the spring. In the spring, we were in 'survival mode,' building the plane as we flew it, using whatever tools that we had to do the best with what we could. We did not want a repeat of that. So, the summer provided an opportunity to reflect and take a more strategic approach for the fall. We all received training to build common structures and practices across disciplines, grades, and teams so that schoolwide, no matter which teacher a student had, they were getting some common expectations and supports. Because of this approach, our teachers have been able to use a common learning platform, common digital curricula, and common grading protocols for all students.

"Because the curricular materials were frontloaded, teachers had time to work on supplementing these foundational materials with additional support for remediation and for acceleration. Teachers began hosting live content coaching sessions that they also recorded and shared through the common platforms as well as expanding to Google Sites and QR codes. These teacher-made videos were created using Zoom, Loom, Screencastify, or other recording tools. Since coaching sessions were asynchronous for each department, teachers from other disciplines could even watch each other's sessions to get ideas and push each other to go further. Since the sessions were recorded, it also allowed students to watch the videos and work at a time that fit their needs. We learned that as middle schoolers, during the day many of them were babysitting younger siblings or going to alternate locations and could not always join sessions that would normally happen during school hours. So, the recordings of the live sessions were made available for after hours. We also started nighttime tutoring opportunities as well so that students could join a video chat or phone call to get help from a teacher who was on-call in the evening hours.

"All of these measures we put in place to better address the needs of not only our students but also our teachers. Not all teachers had a background or experience with distance learning. Many did not regularly use online learning environments like Google Classroom to share assignments or materials with students, and some still struggled with technology. However, gearing up for the fall meant summer training, planning, and continued learning throughout the school year—all to address the constant shifts in needs of all involved. My own summer training provided me with opportunities to learn about new (or forgotten) tools and resources that would come in handy while engaged in distance learning. I compiled and shared a list of these resources with my colleagues in case they might find some of them useful (bit.ly/TT4Teachers). But learning to use tools like these takes time, so our learning as teachers, just like our students, is ongoing, and our schedules during distance learning provide opportunities for us to do job-embedded professional learning as well.

"Just as we dealt with the changes to delivering curriculum and instruction to students, we also knew that we would need to address the social and emotional needs of our students. Students who had been in isolation were going to need different kinds of interaction and support—especially those living in less-than-supportive homes. And homes without internet or cellular data access for students to video chat or even text friends were going to be an even bigger challenge. So, we built in ways to address this with various structures: our mentoring component, our Learning Offline Academy for students without internet access who were learning from home, home visits—or 'porch visits'—for students on our watchlist, and small-group in-person opportunities for struggling students. Many of these measures we put in place at the start of the year, but some we had to implement after seeing a need as the school year continued. We also knew that many challenges of virtual learning would increase, especially as more and more families faced financial difficulties and couldn't afford internet access or had no one at home to provide structure for students who are less than motivated to keep up their studies on their own. Even our online learning curriculum underwent a makeover, all to meet the student needs in an ever-changing world of virtual learning.

"So, we continue to adapt—watching for issues and strategizing ways to overcome them. An upcoming challenge for us is the implementation of hybrid learning: how to best structure it so that all stakeholders benefit the best they can. With this implementation we have to navigate many challenges, including the fact that some students have the internet and some do not; some weeks students may attend twice a week, while others only once; some families have multiple students and may want or need them to attend on the same days. Our staff and students face these issues and more as the hurdle of hybridization comes into play. In addition, we face the ever-present obstacle of communication with families. Even with all of the many forms of communication already at our disposal—phone, text, email, Infinite Campus messaging, Google Classroom announcements, Remind (remind.com), websites, social media, SchoolMessenger

(schoolmessenger.com), Thrillshare (apptegy.com/thrillshare), newsletters, home visits, or even good old-fashioned letters—some students still slip through the cracks and are off the grid where communication is concerned—completely incommunicado. We try these multiple modes of sharing information, but even with all of these methods at our fingertips, we still have students and families who are unreachable. So, these challenges are ones we still continue to address. But, as we approach our second semester, we'll learn from our experiences from the past year and continue to triage so that our makeshift first aid efforts can continue to grow into a well-run, high-functioning, state-of-the-art virtual learning experience for our students so that they get our best efforts with the best service and experience we can provide.

➡️ *Takeaways*

"There has been a lot to learn from going virtual, and our learning continues. The structures that we have put in place are made up of many finely tuned details. But in the end there are some common, broader foundational actions that school leaders and teachers can take that can make virtual learning a bit more successful. Below are some of these basic takeaways from my experience:

- If you share students with other teachers, it is vital to collaborate. Work together to set up common structures and expectations for consistency and clarity. It'll make the learning experience for students and their families go much more smoothly if they see commonalities from teacher to teacher.

- If you share students, use the same learning platform for instructional materials and sharing information. For example, not only should each teacher use the same tool, something like Google Classroom, to share assignments, but they should also have similar layouts for their environments. This way, no matter whose space the students join, they know where to go to access their assignments and also how to get help.

- Share ideas on how to organize and structure your online learning environments so that they meet your students' needs. Think about their level of knowledge and experience. Then, create your layout based on their needs. Use images not only to add visual appeal to the space but also to direct student attention to different components.

- Put your contact information in an easy-to-access location for students and families, but also set expectations, or boundaries, for when and how to use those methods. Be clear about the days and times for your office hours but collaborate with other teachers to avoid conflicts. Teachers who share the same grade-level content can even pair up.

- Having common communication tools can also be helpful. If possible, select a method that all teachers can use and teach students how to use [it] from the beginning. Each teacher could manage this with a specific group of students (such as a homeroom, advisory, or mentoring group). Teach students the expected, or preferred, mode of communication—be it email, Google Voice, Remind, ClassDojo, or another tool. However, you should be prepared to use multiple modes in case some students and families have limitations. When sharing information, start with the preferred method but follow up using other methods of communication, if needed.

- Don't neglect your own learning. Set aside time to learn some new tools. Some could make your life easier once you learn them. Then, teach them to your students.

- Select tools that are user-friendly—for you, your students, and their families. Otherwise, you'll spend more time learning and teaching the tools than teaching the students.

- When teaching students how to do things, make your own how-to videos. It's okay to use ones that are already published online, if appropriate, but when students see their own teachers in their instructional videos, they tend to resonate more. Using tools like Screencastify, Loom, Zoom, or even Flipgrid or Google Meet can add a personal touch to the instruction. It may help to record the live sessions so that you are already in your teacher comfort zone.

- Build in systems for addressing student needs. Have a way to monitor and track needs. Then, have systems in place to provide assistance to students who struggle as well as those who excel.

- As a school, it's also important to set a schedule that works for families. If you need to stagger the schedule or offer evening hours for assistance to students who cannot work during the regular school day due to alternative living situations, set up those hours as well.

- Create systems to connect with students. Spend some time in the early days establishing relationships and rapport. During the first session, start by giving students time to just socialize; they probably need that time for release. Then, take time to establish protocols and norms for the sessions.

- Set regular times for students to engage in these informal connection activities. They can be video chats, interactive games, read-alouds, or other socialization activities for them to just spend time with one another. In Kagan structures, these are called 'teambuilding' and 'classbuilding' activities. When learning from home, these are sometimes the only times some students get to see or talk with students their own age—and at middle school, having time with their friends is so important.

- Postpone teaching course content for a while to establish these connections with students. Then, do some onboarding to acclimate students to their new learning environment before holding them responsible for any course content learning. They need to know how to do things before they should be held accountable for doing them.

- In all of this, don't forget the needs of the staff. Just like the students, staff need brain breaks as well. They get just as stressed and isolated as students. Just like the connecting activities that teachers do with students, staff should have opportunities to socialize virtually as well, if they are working apart.

- Then, underlying everything, is the need to adapt. Take time to periodically evaluate how things are going and constantly work to find solutions and improve. Find a critical friend or collaborative partner or team and find new ideas and new ways to address the needs that arise. Be ever vigilant and open to new opportunities and solutions. And as always, #learngrowpersevere!"

Summary

This section outlines the most important parts from the chapter:

- Online learning has no step-by-step instructions. Every online teacher has to find what works best for their unique mix of teaching style, content area, age of learners, and learner personalities.

- Apply the best practices shared to your unique learning environment.

Reflection

After reading "Chapter 20: Teachers Share Best Practices," reflect on how the content can be applied to your unique learning environment.

Share your reflections online using the hashtag **#TeachersGuideToOnline**.

What is your top takeaway from this chapter?

What will you apply to your teaching practice?

Chapter 21: Online Learning with Littles

One of the most common questions I received from educators over the course of 2020 was, "How do you teach and engage the youngest learners in a remote environment?" When planning this book, I knew there had to be a chapter devoted specifically to teaching primary-aged learners. However, I have never taught in the primary grades. I have been lucky to know some amazing educators who have allowed me to observe their primary classrooms and mentored me in all things "little." However, I knew that this experience would not do this chapter justice. I reached out to Traci Piltz, who is the queen of all things primary, and was thrilled that she agreed to write this chapter. Enjoy!

Online Learning with Littles by Traci Piltz

→ Introduction

I was so excited when Lindy invited me to guest author a chapter in this book about online learning with our littlest learners. After twelve years of teaching kindergarten, I have spent the past six years as a technology integration specialist for my district in Billings, Montana, helping kindergarten through second-grade teachers and students use technology to spark curiosity, create projects, and share their learning. In March, when we experienced emergency closures due to COVID-19, it became clear that our teachers needed more support in designing effective lessons and activities for young students learning online. I spent the spring and summer researching best practices for online learning, curating ideas, and creating activities, but it solidified for me this fall when I had the opportunity to apply what I learned as a remote first-grade teacher for our district. This chapter contains practical advice I have learned while teaching first graders fully online as well as some of my favorite lessons, digital tools, and early childhood educators to follow and learn from. Happy learning!

The big ideas for little learners:

- Communicate
- Simplify
- Engage
- Screen time and favorite digital tools

Communicate with and Support Families and Students

As mentioned near the beginning of this book, having a digital homebase is essential for online learning. Seesaw is the perfect tool to accomplish this for young learners:

- Easy login and simple interface

- Embedded creative tools allow students to create digitally and share hands-on learning with photo, video, and audio

- Connect family members to share student learning and easily communicate with the grown-ups who are supporting students at home

- *Huge* bank (we are talking tens of thousands!) of ready-to-use activities created by other teachers that you can assign to your students for *free*

In first grade, we use Seesaw for everything. Need to share the link to a Zoom meeting or YouTube video? Seesaw. Send a message to parents? Seesaw. Send a math assignment? Seesaw. Record a mini lesson? Seesaw. Having everything in one place makes it easy for students, families, and *you.* Seesaw has some fantastic supports for getting started in the training section of their website (web.seesaw.me/training-and-pd).

One of the largest challenges experienced by K–2 remote teachers in our district is families "helping" their students too much (try giving a reading assessment via Zoom with grandma whispering all the words to her granddaughter!). I found that giving families specific ways that they can help and support their learners significantly improved this situation. As online early learning educators, we need to recognize that the partnership between ourselves and the students' families is more critical than ever to our students' success. We can't be in the room with students, asking them the questions, helping them sound out words while writing, or checking their math strategies. I created this Family Resource Guide (bit.ly/firstgradefamilyguide) with tips for families, providing specific vocabulary and strategies they can utilize while helping their children learn. Make a copy and adapt for your own families!

Many of our young learners are pre-readers, so it's important to support them with audio and video as much as possible. When approving student work, I utilize audio comments and embedded video in Seesaw to provide feedback. I also utilize Screencastify or the screen record feature on the iPad (bit.ly/recordonipad) to make lots of screencasts and tutorials to share step-by-step instructions with my students. This is helpful not only for online learning but blended learning too! Utilizing audio and video lets teachers clone themselves to provide student support both in and out of the physical classroom.

Simplify and Use Learning from Home to Your Advantage

One of the first and most important lessons I learned while teaching first grade online was to *simplify*. In my kindergarten classroom, I liked to do all the things: the kids' artwork on beautiful bulletin boards, curriculum supplemented with fun seasonal and thematic units, projects created with a plethora of digital tools, food crafts, and field trips. As an online teacher, I learned that I couldn't re-create this experience, and I needed to stop focusing on what we *couldn't* do and instead focus on what we *could*.

My first graders enjoy being able to share what's happening around them and make connections to their own environments. I engage them with fun scavenger hunts, like these in Seesaw:

- Winter Scavenger Hunt (bit.ly/seesawscavengerhunt)

- Sounds Around Me Scavenger Hunt (bit.ly/soundsscavengerhunt)

I love these Playing with Words boards (bit.ly/wordboards) from Jessica Twomey and Christine Pinto, shared on their *Innovating Play* blog. These open-ended activities are optional each week and give students the chance to use items from around their homes to interact with letters and words in hands-on ways, then share what they make and learn with photos and videos. I make the playboards into Seesaw activities using our sight words for the week. For example, "Playing with Words: Names" Seesaw activity (bit.ly/wordboardsinseesaw).

Melisa Hayes, a remote second-grade teacher in Ohio, creates optional **STEAM** projects for her online learners to complete each week. [STEAM stands for science, technology, engineering, art, and math]. The projects utilize items easily found in their homes (a.k.a. "junk") to create innovative STEAM projects. An example is shown in *Figure 21.1*. Other ideas include designing a Giving Tree or creating 3D nametags, as shown in *Figure 21.2*. Students share their creations and learning on Flipgrid. I adapted her ideas into Seesaw activities, such as the "All about Me STEM Project," (bit.ly/allaboutmestem) where students build their names using items found in their homes that tell about themselves. In our classrooms, students don't have access to all of their toys, Legos, and other household

All About Me

Stem Project

Optional

Due on Friday

Your Task

Create and build your name out of materials that represent you! The

challenge part of this project is that your name must be as long as

you are tall! You can use PicCollage to organize your pics or whatever app you choose. Submit your pic thru Canvas:)

Examples of how to create your name may be

● Using legos or boxes if you ❤ to build

● Using hockey pucks if your favorite sport is hockey

● Using crayons if you love to be artistic

The possibilities are endless! I want you to have FUN with this project!

Figure 21.1: All about Me STEM Project • Source: Melisa Hayes. Used with permission.

Figure 21.2: 3D Nametags Example • Source: Melisa Hayes. Used with permission.

items, so design learning activities that allow them to utilize these unique assets during online learning.

Appreciate the small groups and breakout rooms in Google Meet and Zoom and use them to your advantage. In your classroom, you can pull a small group of students to your reading table, but you still have to monitor fifteen to twenty additional students in various centers and stages of learning around the room. While teaching small groups online, you have the opportunity to truly focus on individual or small groups of students and give them your full attention. My colleague, Hillary Gnerer, teaches a short lesson to all students in her small group, then sends them to their own "offices" (a.k.a. individual breakout rooms) to read, write, or work on math. She can then visit each breakout room to check-in, ask questions, have a student read to her, or conference together about their work.

I remind myself that my students' (and their families') capacity for learning at home isn't the same as it is at school. We focus on what is deemed critical for them to know, and I create lessons and activities that focus on these critical concepts and skills. I try to limit "extras" (e.g., the Play Boards and STEAM projects mentioned above) to one or two a week, because they are one more thing that falls on families' already-too-full plates. Even though I'd like to teach them a new app to make a creative project, I remember that I won't be there to help them access and troubleshoot the app, so maybe we can make that project using a tool we already know. Simplify what you're doing, prioritize what you're teaching, and use the benefits of online learning to your advantage.

Engaging Learners

When learning synchronously via a Google Meet or Zoom, I treat it like carpet or circle time in my physical classroom. Just as when we sit together on the carpet, I ask myself, "What are the students *doing* while I am teaching?" I don't ask my students to mute; I really like being able to engage in authentic conversations with them, and that's hard when they're muted. I ask that they be in a quiet spot, and if they're not, that they mute. Kindergarten teacher Ben Cogswell has some amazing resources for teaching these procedures that you can find on his website, "Coach Ben" (bit.ly/coachbenssite).

Young learners don't sit still very long and need to be engaged in the learning to get its full benefit. Since I can't share the pen with my students, I ask that they each have their own. They come to our Zoom meetings with a whiteboard or paper and markers (easier to see than pencil), and while I teach, they write: sight words, letters, sketches, math problems, and so on. They hold up their whiteboards to the screen so I can check their work. We interact just like we would in our classroom at carpet. I ask them to hold up fingers to show a number or indicate understanding of something, and they use hand gestures, such as the "Talk Moves" hand gestures shown in **Figure 21.3**, to show agreement, understanding, or the need for more information. Sometimes we use tools like Classkick (classkick.com), Pear Deck, or Nearpod that allow me to watch what the students are doing in real-time, but the simpler the better!

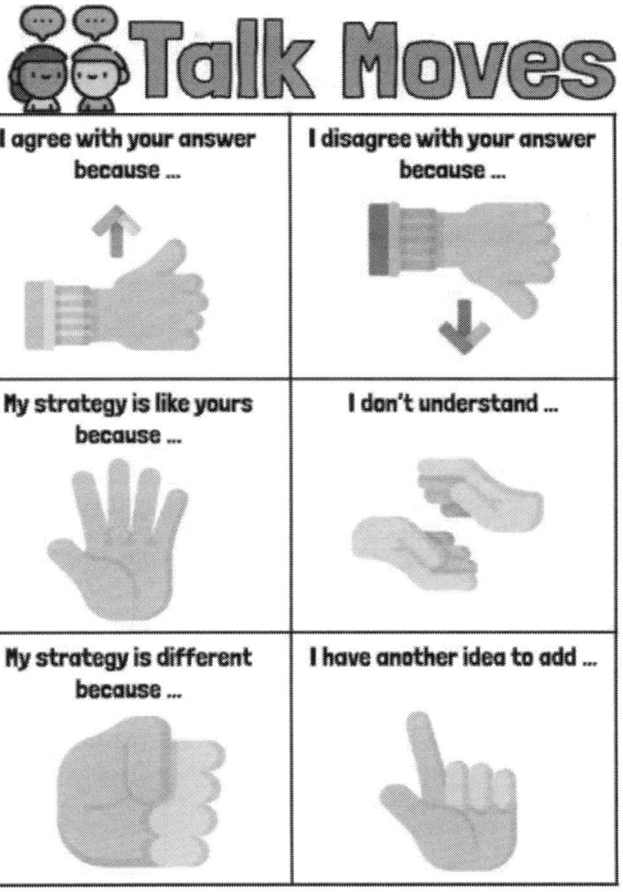

Building relationships with students is key to their learning success, and I was worried this would be more difficult in an online environment. However, I found that treating our online meetings like carpet time allowed me to interact with them authentically as I would in our classroom. I also began the year by scheduling individual video calls with each student just to chat and get to know them. They told me about kindergarten, what they liked (and didn't like) about learning online last spring, and some of their favorite things to do. I took notes so I could remember, reference, and incorporate their interests into our class activities.

Below are some of my favorite ideas for engaging students during synchronous learning:

Figure 21.3: "Talk Moves" Hand Gestures (found at intechgratedpd.org/vip)

- Give students the opportunity to teach something new to the class.

- Tap into a collaborative tool like Google Jamboard to share ideas in real time.

- Use a name spinner (I like wheelofnames.com) or sticks, just like you would in your classroom, to ensure equitable amounts of participation and sharing.

- Allow time at the end of your meetings for students to share stories or thoughts without taking instructional time.

You can find more in this ever-growing Wakelet collection (bit.ly/k3wakelet). My biggest concern was sacrificing precious teaching time (we have a really limited amount of "live" time with the students online) to build relationships and vice versa. I quickly learned you can do both. By incorporating authentic conversations and student interests into teaching and learning, I could build relationships while instructing my first graders.

When designing asynchronous activities, remember to focus on what's critical and limit the number of assignments you give them each day. Because online teachers don't have easy access to the resources we had in our classrooms, it can be incredibly time-consuming to re-create these. Try crowdsourcing these activities with your teaching partners; maybe one teacher creates the math assignments for the week, and another makes the reading activities. I was spending a gigantic chunk of my time making and assigning activities for my students, then reviewing and providing feedback on all of them. It was too much for me and too much for them. I found it important to scale back, and below is what I assign each day:

- Math lesson + one activity

- Fifteen minutes of ST Math (stmath.com)

- Language arts lesson + one activity

- Fifteen minutes of reading (a book they have or on Epic!)

- Reading group (each group twice a week)

- Writing lesson + submit a picture of their writing journal

I choose a certain number of activities each week to review and give thorough feedback on, but I don't give in-depth feedback on every piece of work. I don't do this when we're in the classroom; instead, I am strategic about what work I give feedback on.

Our district had a "pick up" time during the first few weeks of online learning when families could collect student workbooks, whiteboards, textbooks, and so on. I have also been putting together packets for families to pick up bimonthly with hands-on work like seasonal crafts, writing journals, and number practice. These aren't simply packets of worksheets but ways to practice cutting and pasting, number formation, and writing. I have also included styluses, as my students use iPads, and I think it's important that they have a stylus when writing letters and numbers. Families are invited to pick up these packets from a central location every other month; however, it has been a challenge to ensure all students receive these items. Some teachers provide a drop-off service to students to make sure they get the supplies they need. Students use these items daily to engage in hands-on work during our synchronous and asynchronous learning. Because so much of what they do is on their iPad screen, my first graders absolutely *love* getting to do math in their workbooks!

Screen Time and Digital Tools for Little Learners

Even before the pandemic changed the way we teach and learn together, I often heard concerns about screen time with our young learners. How much is too much? What is appropriate? I have long felt that the tasks completed on the screen are what's important; staring at a screen to consume content is different than engaging with the device to create, make, and do. My goal as a teacher of young learners has always been to utilize the device as a tool for them to learn and create.

This summer I attended a webinar hosted by the ISTE Early Learning Network, where they interviewed Chip Donohue. Mr. Donohue is Founding Director of the TEC Center at Erikson Institute and Senior Fellow at the Fred Rogers Center. He shared some fascinating insights into the idea of screen time and young learners. He recognized that these devices have become our lifelines for supporting human development and social-emotional needs and focused on cultivating media mentors (parents and teachers) for helping students use technology for learning. David Kleeman speaks of "ubiquitous interactivity," where "the concept of screen time has become meaningless in a world where screens bring entertainment, learning, discovering, communication, play, creation, and more."[80] Find more information and resources on the ISTE Early Learning Network website (bit.ly/isteearlylearning).

What does this mean to me as a teacher of littles?

> *It means that I recognize technology for the important tool that it is but remember that it's the tasks, interactions, and learning experiences I create that make it meaningful.*

---

80   David Kleeman, "Five Things That Haven't Changed (Much)," in *Exploring Key Issues in Early Childhood and Technology: Evolving Perspectives and Innovative Approaches*, ed. Chip Donohue (New York: Routledge, 2020).

I also intentionally build in opportunities to explore digital citizenship and work to be a media mentor to the parents of my students, helping them understand productive screen time and balance. Research shows that parents agree that media and technology enhance school readiness, using computer games, activities, and websites to enhance their children's math and literacy skills.[81] Some of my favorite resources to guide my use of technology and support parents are listed below:

- "What is a Family Media Use Plan?" infographic (bit.ly/familymediauseplan)

- "Smart Screen Time Tips" from PBS SoCal and Austin PBS (bit.ly/pbsscreentimetips)

While teaching digital citizenship to my students, I think it's important to embed these lessons authentically into our day-to-day work. However, some of the best resources I've discovered are the "Ruff Ruffman: Humble Media Genius" collection on PBS Learning Media (bit.ly/ruffmanmediagenius), as well as Common Sense Education's Digital Citizenship Curriculum (bit.ly/commonsensecurriculum).

Above all, while teaching young kids online, remember it's the relationships you form that are key. Be yourself, enjoy the small moments with your students, and be honest that this is new and you're learning too. I just received a card from one of my first graders and his family, and it said, "You are an amazing teacher, and you will always hold a special place in our heart." This is a stressful, unique, difficult situation, but I feel bonded to these kids and families in a truly special way as we navigate this experience together.

---

81   "School Readiness Survey" (SmartyPants Research, January 2014).

Summary

This section outlines the most important parts from the chapter:

- Implement these big ideas to support little learners: communicate, simplify, and engage.

- Seesaw is the perfect digital course homebase tool for young learners.

- Give families specific ways that they can help and support their learners.

- Don't try to re-create the face-to-face experience for young learners. Instead of focusing on what you *can't* do, focus on what you *can*.

- Simplify and focus on what is deemed critical knowledge.

- Ensure young learners are active to sustain engagement.

- When it comes to screen time, the tasks completed on the screen are what's important; staring at a screen to consume content is different than engaging with the device to create, make, and do.

Reflection

After reading "Chapter 21: Online Learning with Littles," reflect on how the content can be applied to your unique learning environment.

Share your reflections online using the hashtag **#TeachersGuideToOnline**.

What tip or strategy from teaching primary-aged learners can be applied to all ages of learners?

How can you support the families of young learners?

Chapter 22:
Teaching Students with Special Needs Online

As I dove into research on online learning, it became clear that there is little research on teaching students with special needs in a K–12 online learning setting.[82] Therefore, I decided the best approach to this chapter was to reach out to the collective. This chapter brings in the perspective of two special education teachers who will share their experiences of teaching students with special needs in an online environment. Happy learning!

Lynn Silbernagel,
Remote Life Skills and Independent Living, Grades K-5, Billings Public Schools, Montana, USA

"I am happy to share what I have learned so far about teaching special education remotely. My kiddos range from grades K–5, and I have both life skills and independent living students. The most common disability my kiddos share is a cognitive delay. However, they also share something *really* amazing! They all have an unparalleled excitement for learning and *that* makes teaching them pure joy.

"There are definite challenges with teaching remotely. My student caseload is three times what it would be in person. Therefore, the paperwork is completely overwhelming. Also, my students are mainly dependent on their parents for help logging on and keeping track of when to attend class. Thus, if their parents aren't engaged, my students don't have a fair shot at being engaged either.

"There are several things that work for me to help feel semi-successful during this remote teaching gig. One of them is having a consistent morning meeting. I offer that two times per week, and I almost always have a minimum of eleven of my eighteen kiddos attend. During the morning meeting, I share my screen while we dance around and sing to

---

82   Diana Greer, Mary Rice, and Bryan Dykman, "Reviewing a Decade (2004–2014) of Published, Peer-Reviewed Research on Online Learning and Students with Disabilities," in *Handbook of Research on K-12 Online and Blended Learning*, ed. Richard E. Ferdig and Kathryn Kennedy (n.p.: ETC Press, 2014).

various fun songs that also assist with academic goals at the same time. One of the kids' favorite singers is Jack Hartmann. My kids love him and get really excited about his songs. I primarily use music for the whole group to keep everyone engaged, and it works extremely well. I also read stories using a document camera, so the kids can see the pictures. I also include apps like Novel Effect (noveleffect.com) or use a flannel board to keep the story interesting! Novel Effect is a great app that has noises that correlate with the story while it's being read. I dance along with the kids, so it is really fun. We all get pretty goofy together. I've had some parents tell me that they didn't think their kids would be as engaged as they are, so that's been really neat to hear.

"I also have small groups where my kiddos are split into either the lion, zebra, or polar bear group. Each group meets twice per week via video call, and we work on more targeted skills. I still incorporate music to meet those skills. For instance, *Counting Superhero* is a song I use where we count to 100. The use of the song makes it much more fun for my kids!

"I also meet with every student one time per week to work on individualized goals. During the meetings, I make sure I call them by name and tell every one of them how happy I am to see them. At the end of the meeting, I always thank them and tell them how they made my day better by being at the meeting.

"I use several programs for the asynchronous part of teaching, including Seesaw, Epic!, ST Math, and Raz Kids (raz-kids.com). The remote program at my district has provided excellent training to help me set up these programs. Our technology integration specialist, Shelly Stanton, is outstanding and so supportive. Her technology classes and trainings have made teaching remotely much easier than I thought. I was actually really scared of the technology part of teaching remotely, as I didn't use a whole lot of it when I taught in-person. I had used some technology with the SMART Board, ST Math, but not much more. Now, I am sharing my screen with students and using my homemade green screen like a boss!

"I honestly think teaching remotely has helped me focus more on my students' individual goals and figure out how to target each in an engaging way since our time together is so limited. I really do love my job. My kiddos are the best in the world. It is the paperwork that seems impossible, but my students are amazing!"

Maslow before you Bloom! You must focus on the social-emotional side of learning.

Esther Jensen,
Remote Special Education Resource,
Billings Public Schools, Montana, USA

"Consistency—Students with special needs thrive on consistency, from scheduling to routines. It's important to be as consistent as possible when delivering and teaching on the remote platform. It also helps if the whole team is on the 'same page' to help with inclusion. I also feel students like to know what to expect from the teacher, so having a routine allows students some predictability.

"Relationships—Building relationships with any student helps show the student that the teacher cares about them. When the student feels that the teacher cares about them, the student is likely to do more for that teacher. I focus primarily on relationship building within the first two weeks. In every class session, I allow time for the students to talk amongst themselves or with me. I joke around, sometimes play a quick game, and so on. I have also created a weekly incentive where I will snail mail a positive note home, or even a small gift. If you are willing to put in the extra effort to build relationships, students in return will put in the extra effort for their schoolwork. It's amazing how a relationship can make or break a student's emotional state. Lastly, have fun and don't be a stick in the mud! If you are having fun, the student most likely is also having fun.

"Communication—Communicate, communicate, communicate! Communication helps build relationships and demonstrates consistency. Think of how, when, what, and stick to it! Are you going to communicate weekly? Daily? Biweekly? How are you going to communicate? Email, phone, message, or a letter in the mail? Lastly, what are you communicating and to whom? Parents love consistent communication or simply just communication in general. I email all my parents a weekly Google Form for their input (what is working? what is not working?). Always remind the parents to reach out to you for any reason. Respond as quickly as possible to emails, return phone calls, and so on. The quicker your response time, the quicker they seem to appreciate and respect you. I am not saying you have to respond at midnight, but make it a point to respond quickly and effectively. A good rule of thumb when having a conversation with parents about students is always start with the positive, then negative/concerns, and end on TWO positives!"

> Organization and consistency are critical to online learning.

Summary

This section outlines the most important parts from the chapter:

- There is little research on teaching students with special needs in a K–12 online learning setting.

- Relationship building is critical to student success.

- Students with special needs thrive on consistency.

- Communication helps build relationships and demonstrates consistency.

- Facilitate small-group and individual synchronous meetings in order to work on individual goals.

Reflection

After reading "Chapter 22: Teaching Students with Special Needs Online," reflect on how the content can be applied to your unique learning environment. Share your reflections online using the hashtag **#TeachersGuideToOnline**.

What is your top takeaway from this chapter?

What tip or strategy from teaching students with special needs can be applied to all learners?

Chapter 23: Leading Change

The major stakeholders in online learning are teachers, students, caregivers, and school leaders. So far, this book has shared the perspectives of three of these four stakeholders. Although the intended audience of this book is classroom teachers, I felt it was important to include the perspective of the last (but not least!) stakeholder: school leaders. After all, teachers need informed, supportive school leaders in order to accomplish meaningful online learning.

After reviewing the research on school leaders and K–12 online learning, once again it was discovered that there is little existing literature on the subject.[83] This was another area where reaching out to the collective was the approach to take. I invited Bill Bass to share the perspective of a school leader in COVID-19 times. How do you lead an educational institution through such a large change as moving from face-to-face to online learning?

Bill Bass is an international speaker and award-winning educator who currently serves as the innovation coordinator for instructional technology, information, library media, and federal programs for the Parkway School District in Chesterfield, Missouri, USA. As a district administrator, he is responsible for bringing innovative practice to the district, supports teachers and schools through systemic change, and strives to support digital learning for students at all grade levels. He is the past president of the ISTE board of directors, author of three books, and is often called upon to share his thinking with educators around the world.

Best Practices for School Leaders by Bill Bass

As we realized that the emergency closure of our schools was going to last longer than just a few weeks, we knew that we needed more than the temporary solution that we had developed to have students connect with their teachers online. At this point, we had already distributed hundreds of devices to our student population of 18,000 so that

---

83   Scott McLeod and Jayson W. Richardson, "School Administrators and K–12 Online and Blended Learning," in *Handbook of Research on K–12 Online and Blended Learning*, ed. Richard E. Ferdig and Kathryn Kennedy (n.p.: ETC Press, 2014).

they would be able to connect with our teachers using video conferencing platforms like Google Meet and Zoom, and we were developing partnerships with companies and local organizations like the public library to provide internet hotspots for our families without access at home. Taking care of access issues was actually one of the less complex issues that was currently facing us. In order for our students to continue learning and engaging with teachers, we knew that we had to support our teachers differently. In so many ways, our teachers had stepped up and met their students' needs through online learning opportunities, but for many of our teachers, this was uncharted territory. Many had never taught online and there was little time to get up to speed, but they were willing to figure it out and try to work through the issues for the sake of their students.

During those early weeks there was a large call by administrators and teachers all over the country to provide professional development on best practices for teaching online. My district was no different, and one of the decisions that we made was to scale our school days back to only four days a week, leaving that fifth day for teachers to engage in problem solving and professional learning and to figure out just exactly what it was going to take to keep learning alive in our students. We asked teachers to help each other by hosting thirty-minute sessions during that fifth day about topics that were important to them and where they found success. Over the course of a few weeks, our teachers and administrators hosted around sixty sessions a week to help each other and collaborate to serve our students better. Whether they were discussing how to use a specific online tool or revamping the curriculum to be sure that we were still able to meet our standards, these sessions gave my district the jump start it needed for teachers to be confident that they could weather this storm and still help their students. By providing the dedicated time, we were able to tap into the vast knowledge and experience of our entire teaching force and empower them to be the experts of the day. All sessions were recorded and made available to teachers so that, if they wanted, they could go back and review the sessions they could not attend.

As spring drew to a close and the school year was starting to wind down, there was still the great unknown about what school would look like in August. To prepare for an uncertain return to school, we wanted to learn from our experience in the spring and focus on helping teachers prepare for our return. Hence, the Parkway Distance Learning Hub became our go-to place for resources, strategies, and learning for the upcoming year. In the fall, we were committed to making sure that distance learning would continue to honor the rigorous, guaranteed curriculum our community expects and include more synchronous (live) learning opportunities. In order to help us grow from the emergency learning (eLearning) approach that we took in the spring into our fully developed distance learning approach, we identified six critical areas of focus. The Distance Learning Hub is designed for teachers to investigate, research, and participate within those six areas to prepare to engage students this fall.

- *Understanding your essential learning outcomes and priority standards*—Some students may come to us with gaps in their understanding, making it critical for us to prioritize the outcomes and standards that we will incorporate into our classes. This area provides structures and tools to help identify and design learning experiences for students around those prioritized outcomes.

- *Best practices in building an online community*—In person or virtually, we know that it's important for students to feel connected to their teachers and classmates. This area will help with strategies for building a community when students engage in distance learning.

- *Best practices in synchronous virtual learning*—An important component of distance learning is bringing students and teachers together at the same time. Synchronous instruction is a critical method of instruction utilized during distance learning. This area will highlight strategies and tools for bringing teachers and students together in real time.

- *Best practices in asynchronous virtual learning*—One of the benefits of distance learning is that activities and resources can be tailored to the individual needs of students and give them flexibility in their learning. During distance learning, providing instructional videos, resources, and clear instructions are of utmost importance. This area provides tips, tricks, and resources for designing and providing students with what they need for distance learning.

- *Best practices in assessment and feedback in an online space*—Feedback is essential for learning. During distance learning, the medium by which you provide feedback may be different than it is in your classroom. This hub focuses on the principles of effective feedback and provides helpful resources for formative assessment in a digital space.

- *Effective use of Parkway's online tools and resources*—We provide a variety of instructional and productivity tools that give teachers and students access to assignments, resources, and other digital materials. This area provides support and training for Schoology, Google, Zoom, and other tools teachers may find useful when engaging in distance learning with students.

One of the challenges for district and building leaders is to recognize that there are probably actually no "right" answers or approaches, just lots of compromises in order to try to keep the community safe. Leadership in this era requires thoughtfulness and deep, strategic reflection and planning. Over the course of the year, we provided many learning opportunities for teachers to learn how to utilize the online tools and find strategies that were going to work for them in their new instructional reality. With all of the demands of this unfamiliar environment, having the time to learn and plan was one of the biggest challenges to overcome. This need for time was exactly why we rearranged our schedules and made our school week four days long, reserving the fifth day for teacher learning. This allowed us to meet our teacher contracts as well as enhance our overall instructional skills. While we didn't require teachers to sign in or to have a certain number of participation hours of professional learning, it was a clear expectation that teachers should be prepared to provide high-quality, engaging instruction for our students. In this way, we chose to trust our teachers by giving them choice and opportunity and providing the time to collaborate, explore, and learn, thereby honoring the professionalism and integrity of those who work with our students.

Teacher Training Is Vital to Online Learning Success

Thank you to Bill for providing the perspective of a school leader helping prepare teachers for online learning. As he indicated, teacher training is vital to online learning success. Gurley indicates that how educators are prepared to teach impacts the quality of blended and online courses.[84] It is critical that online teachers receive sustained training and sufficient time to design effective online learning experiences.

---

84   Gurley, "Educators' Preparation to Teach."

Summary

This section outlines the most important parts from the chapter:

- The final stakeholder in online learning is school leaders.

- There is little existing literature on the subject of leading online learning in K–12 environments.

- School leadership in this era requires thoughtfulness and deep, strategic reflection and planning.

- Teachers need informed, supportive school leaders in order to accomplish meaningful online learning.

- Teacher training is vital to online learning success.

- Teachers need time to implement effective online learning.

Reflection

After reading "Chapter 23: Leading Change," reflect on how the content can be applied to your unique learning environment.

Share your reflections online using the hashtag **#TeachersGuideToOnline**.

 How can your educational institution support online teachers?

Chapter 24:
Parting Pep Talk

I can't let you walk away from the book without wrapping up a few final points.

Be a Lifelong Learner

When your job is to teach others how to learn, you must never stop learning. There are many learning opportunities to help teachers hone their craft. Social media is perhaps the best place for "do-it-yourself" professional development:

- Facebook has a group for every teacher. You can find groups with a broad focus (such as English teachers or primary teachers) or a specific focus (such as teaching middle school social studies online). Joining a Facebook group is a great way to connect with like-minded individuals for ideas, support, and feedback. Search Facebook for your interests, and you are bound to find a group to join or a page to follow.
- Twitter has a hashtag for every teacher. Hashtags are the key to conquering Twitter for learning purposes. Conduct a Twitter search for a topic of interest: online learning, virtual learning, teaching elementary online, and so on. Review the tweets for common hashtags. You may find #onlinelearning or #virtuallearning as common hashtags that you can now use to search Twitter and find information of interest. Once you find a few hashtags of interest, Twitter is a great source for **microlearning** or short bursts of content. Microlearning is becoming common for teacher professional development.
- TikTok is becoming a popular source of teacher microlearning. The great thing about TikTok is it works very similarly to Twitter with hashtags. You can search TikTok for the same hashtags you use on Twitter!

If you use any specific digital tools, check if the tool has a blog, online community, and/or certification program. This can be a great source of knowledge, ideas, and tips. If your school uses Google Workspace for Education, you may consider joining a Google Educator Group (bit.ly/googleedugroups) or earning your Google Certified Educator badge. If your school uses Microsoft 365 Education, apply for the Microsoft Innovative Educator (MIE) Expert program (bit.ly/microsofteduexpert).

Pep Talk

Don't try to create an online course overnight. Slowly build the course piece by piece. See what works, what doesn't work, and make small edits along the way.

Educators are very creative. You will find a way to teach things that you never would have thought could be taught in an online setting. Public speaking has been taught as a college online class since about 2000 (yes, that's twenty years)! I saw a video on Twitter of students practicing swimming techniques without a pool!

Remember, online learning can be fantastic!

Most of all, enjoy the process. Don't forget to have fun and focus on developing relationships with your learners. Don't forget:

If you take away one thing from this book, reading it will have been a successful learning experience."

As an educator, if you find this book helpful, **please consider leaving a review on Amazon (bit.ly/teachersguidetoonline)**. This will help get this knowledge in the hands of more educators.

Reflection

After reading "Chapter 24: Parting Pep Talk," reflect on how the content can be applied to your unique learning environment.

Share your reflections online using the hashtag **#TeachersGuideToOnline**.

? **What is one strategy from this book that you can implement into your teaching practice right now?**

? **How will you continue to hone your online teaching skills?**

Bring Lindy to Your School or Event!

Thank you for reading, and I hope you took at least one useful instructional strategy or tip away from the book. I would love to continue the learning at your school or event. I can work with your school to implement any of the strategies in this book, as well as other digital teaching and learning strategies. I can help with specific technology initiatives as well as pedagogical shifts. Some of my specialties include:

- Google Workspace for Education
- Microsoft 365 Education
- Online learning
- Blended and hybrid learning

- Personalized learning
- 1:1 implementation
- *Minecraft: Education Edition*
- Virtual reality
- Maker learning

No matter your focus, I always customize the learning goals to the needs of the school or event. What are your school's learning goals? Is your school currently conquering a technology initiative? *Please contact me in any of the ways below. I would love to chat!*

- **Website:** intechgratedpd.org
- **LinkedIn:** linkedin.com/in/lindyhockenbary
- **Email:** lindy@intechgratedpd.org

My style is to create learning experiences that are hands-on, applicable, and engaging. Get a peek of what educators and technology professionals have said about my training below:

"Lindy was amazing. She listened and understood what I wanted to accomplish with VR in my classroom and she tailored our session to my needs. She clearly researched and thought about the best practices and applications for the devices and my needs. I feel so much more confident moving forward. I'm incredibly grateful to her!"

— Candace Plaisance, Germantown Municipal School District, Tennessee

"We had our first-grade students draw monsters, made them from felt and they were darling. Then, we used the e-textile information from Lindy Hockenbary's presentation last summer and sewed LED sequins and battery packs into our monsters so their eyes, teeth, etc. would light up. So awesome! Then, the 7th graders wrote poems, recorded them on Flipgrid and downloaded QR codes that were attached to the monster. The kids were *so* excited (high school and elementary). It was such a fun STEAM project. Thanks for some great training Lindy Hockenbary!"

— Kim Knoche, Forsyth Public Schools, Montana

"Training classes with Lindy are exciting, informative and hands on! Lindy has done training for our customers who have purchased hardware from us. She is an engaging instructor who understands the pressures teachers are under and knows how to give time saving tips and great advice for really using technology in the classroom! I would highly recommend using her for any staff training!"

— Kim Dilliard, Lenovo Education Solutions Specialist at SYNNEX

Glossary

Accessibility checkers—software programs that flag common accessibility concerns, such as missing alt text for images

À la carte—a blended learning model where learners are in a traditional face-to-face learning environment but may take fully online courses in addition to their face-to-face courses

Alt text—text that describes an image

Artificial intelligence (AI)—the capability of a machine to imitate intelligent human behavior

Asynchronous learning—when learners complete work related to the course on their own schedule

Augmented reality (AR)—a technology that renders a digital image onto a user's view of the real world

Bitmoji—a personal avatar that can be customized to look like you

Blended learning—any combination of face-to-face learning and online learning

Bring your own device (BYOD)—a school device model where students provide a personal device

Cloud-based—when data is stored online (or in the cloud) instead of locally

Competency-based—when students advance based on their ability to meet proficiency or master a skill

Conditional formatting—a spreadsheet feature that allows the user to format cells that meet specific criteria or conditions

Course management system (CMS)—see *Learning management system*

Device agnostic—a tool that is not tied to a particular device and is accessible on any device or operating system

Differentiated learning—utilizes the differences and similarities among learners to provide learning options in terms of process, product, and/or content for *groups* of learners

Digital course homebase—the digital location where all communication for learning flows in and out

Document camera—technology that presents a real-time image to an audience

Easter egg—in terms of technology, a secret or hidden item or message

Elementary school—grades kindergarten–5 with students typically aged 5–11

Emojis—images used to express ideas and emotions

Enriched virtual—a blended learning model where learners complete most coursework online outside of a physical school building but also have supplemental face-to-face learning sessions with a teacher

Equity—making sure every student has the support they need in order to be successful

Face-to-face learning—learning that occurs with the learner and teacher in the same physical space

Flex—a blended learning model where learners move among learning activities according to their specific needs

Flipped classroom—a blended learning model where learners gain content knowledge via online coursework and lectures (usually at home), and face-to-face time is used for teacher-guided projects

Format—layout, design, or appearance

Formative assessment—assessment for learning

Forms—survey tools that allow you to set up questions that others can answer

Freemium—a digital tool that offers certain features for free and charges for premium features

Game-based learning—learning from or through a game

Gamification—adding game elements, such as points and leaderboards, to the learning experience

GIF—an animated image

Google Workspace for Education—Google's cloud-based productivity suite

Hashtag—a word or phrase preceded by a hash sign (#) to identify digital content on a specific topic

Higher education—continuing adult education, typically at universities or colleges

Hybrid learning—see *Blended learning*

Hyperdoc—an interactive digital lesson

Immersive Reader—an accessibility tool that customizes the reading experience for the user

Individual rotation—a blended learning model where learners rotate through stations on individualized schedules rather than in groups

Individualized learning—a learning environment where learners move at their own pace to accomplish the same learning goals

Inquiry-based learning—a model that utilizes curiosity to springboard learning

Instructional scaffolding—the process of adding certain supports for students when concepts or skills are first introduced

Internet bandwidth—the maximum amount of data that can be transmitted over an internet connection in a specific amount of time

Lab rotation—a blended learning model where learners rotate through stations, but the online learning component is completed in a specific location, usually a lab environment

Learning journal—a log of a learner's thoughts, reflections, notes, and more

Learning management system (LMS)—a software program designed to help you manage learning

Massive open online courses (MOOCs)—free online courses that typically have no limit on attendance

Metacognition—awareness or analysis of one's own learning or thinking processes

Microlearning—short bursts of content

Microsoft 365 Education—Microsoft's cloud-based productivity suite specifically for education

Naming convention—an agreed-upon format for naming things

One-to-one (1:1)—a school device model where all students are provided a school-issued device

Online learning—learning that occurs over the internet with no face-to-face interaction between teacher and learner

Operating system (OS)—software that supports the basic functions of a device

Personalized learning—learning that is tailored specifically to the needs, preferences, and interests of individual learners

Personally identifiable information (PII)—any information that can be used to identify, locate, or contact a student, including name, address, birth date, student ID, academic information, and health records

Postsecondary—see *Higher education*

Project assessments—hands-on projects that require students to apply knowledge

Project-based learning—a form of inquiry-based learning

Sans serif font—a font that does not have small lines (serifs) at the ends of characters

Screencast video—a video recording of your computer screen, usually including audio narration

Secondary school—grades 6–12 with students typically aged 11–18

Self-directed learner—a student who takes initiative and responsibility for their learning

Serif font—a font that has small lines at the end of characters

Single point rubric—a rubric with a single column that indicates expectations for proficiency

Standards-based—a way to measure student proficiency of course objectives

Station rotation—a blended learning model where learners rotate through stations with at least one station focusing on an online learning component

STEAM—an integrated learning approach to science, technology, engineering, art, and mathematics (see also *STEM*)

STEM—an integrated learning approach to science, technology, engineering, and mathematics (see also *STEAM*)

Student data privacy—the use, collection, handling, and governance of students' personally identifiable information

Student information system (SIS)—a tool that manages all student information and records

Style guide—outlines how the course will look

Summative assessment—assessment of learning

Synchronous learning—learning that happens together in real time

TAG—a feedback model that stands for tell something you like, ask a question, and give a suggestion

Teacher presence—design and organization, facilitating discourse, and direct instruction in order to reach meaningful and educationally worthwhile learning outcomes

Universal Design for Learning (UDL)—a framework that guides the learning design to ensure accessibility of learning to all

Video conferencing tool—software that allows two or more people to communicate via video using the internet

Web-based digital tool—software that works in a web browser and requires no downloads

Web browser—software that provides access to the internet, such as Google Chrome or Apple Safari

Zoombombing—disruptive intrusion into a video call by unwanted and uninvited guests

Bibliography

Anderson, Terry, Rourke Liam, D. Randy Garrison, and Walter Archer. "Assessing Teaching Presence in a Computer Conferencing Context." *Journal of the Asynchronous Learning Network* 5, no. 2 (2001). https://auspace.athabascau.can /handle/2149/725?show=full.

Arnett, Thomas. "In 2021, Teachers Hold a Key to Transforming Conventional Instruction." *Clayton Christensen Institute* (blog). Accessed February 10, 2021. https://www .christenseninstitute.org/blog/in-2021-teachers-hold-a-key-to-transforming -conventional-instruction/.

Bailenson, Jeremy N. "Nonverbal Overload: A Theoretical Argument for the Causes of Zoom Fatigue." *Technology, Mind, and Behavior* 2, no. 1 (2021). https://doi .org/10.1037/tmb0000030.

Bloom, Andrew, and Linnette Attai. *The ABCs of Student Data Privacy for Administrators.* McGraw Hill Education. Accessed November 18, 2020. https://cosn.org/sites /default/files/Platform_Student_Privacy_White_Paper.pdf.

Blum, Susan D. "Why We're Exhausted by Zoom." *Inside Higher Ed* (blog), April 22, 2020. https://www.insidehighered.com/advice/2020/04/22/professor-explores-why-zoom -classes-deplete-her-energy-opinion.

Cheung, Wing Sum, Khe Foon Hew, and Connie Siew Ling Ng. "Toward an Understanding of Why Students Contribute in Asynchronous Online Discussions." *Journal of Educational Computing Research* 38, no. 1 (2008): 29–50. https://doi.org/10.2190 /EC.38.1.b.

Clayton Christensen Institute. "Blended Learning Models." Accessed November 18, 2020. https://www.blendedlearning.org/models.

Diwanji, Prajakta, Bindu Puthur Simon, Michael Märki, Safak Korkut, and Rolf Dornberger. "Success Factors of Online Learning Videos." In *2014 International Conference on Interactive Mobile Communication Technologies and Learning*, 125–32. IEEE, 2014. https://doi.org/10.1109/IMCTL.2014.7011119.

Doolittle, Peter E., Lauren H. Bryant, and Jessica R. Chittum. "Effects of Degree of Segmentation and Learner Disposition on Multimedia Learning." *British Journal of Educational Technology* 46, no. 6 (2014): 1333–43. https://doi.org/10.1111 /bjet.12203.

Drexler, Wendy. "Personal Learning Environments in K–12." In *Handbook of Research on K–12 Online and Blended Learning*, edited by Richard E. Ferdig and Kathryn Kennedy, 447–66. n.p.: ETC Press, 2014.

Drouin, Michelle, and Lesa Rae Vartanian. "Students' Feelings of and Desire for Sense of Community in Face-to-Face and Online Courses." *The Quarterly Review of Distance Education* 11, no. 2 (2010): 147–59.

Fisher, Douglas, Nancy Frey, and John Hattie. *The Distance Learning Playbook, Grades K–12: Teaching for Engagement and Impact in Any Setting.* Thousand Oaks, CA: Corwin, 2021.

Fosslien, Liz, and Mollie West Duffy. "How to Combat Zoom Fatigue." *Harvard Business Review*, April 29, 2020. https://hbr.org/2020/04/how-to-combat-zoom-fatigue.

Garrison, D. Randy, and Martha Cleveland-Innes. "Facilitating Cognitive Presence in Online Learning: Interaction Is Not Enough." *American Journal of Distance Education* 19, no. 3 (2005): 133–48. https://doi.org/10.1207/s15389286ajde1903_2.

Gaudet, Pamela Livingston. *Like No Other School Year: 2020, COVID-19, and the Growth of Online Learning.* n.p.: Product Value Solutions, 2020.

Greer, Diana, Mary Rice, and Bryan Dykman. "Reviewing a Decade (2004–2014) of Published, Peer-Reviewed Research on Online Learning and Students with Disabilities. " In *Handbook of Research on K–12 Online and Blended Learning*, edited by Richard E. Ferdig and Kathryn Kennedy, 135-159. n.p.: ETC Press, 2014.

Guo, Phillip J., Juho Kim, and Rob Rubin. "How Video Production Affects Student Engagement: An Empirical Study of MOOC Videos." In *Proceedings of the First ACM Conference on Learning @ Scale*, 41–50. Association for Computing Machinery, 2014. https://doi.org/10.1145/2556325.2566239.

Gurley, Lisa E. "Educators' Preparation to Teach, Perceived Teaching Presence, and Perceived Teaching Presence Behaviors in Blended and Online Learning Environments." *Online Learning* 22, no. 2 (June 2018): 197–220. https://doi.org/10.24059/olj.v22i2.1255.

Hattie, John. *Visible Learning: A Synthesis of Over 800 Meta-Analyses Relating to Achievement.* New York: Routledge, 2009.

Healy, Nikki. "Keys to Success in Distance Learning." *Edutopia* (blog), August 21, 2020. https://www.edutopia.org/article/keys-success-distance-learning.

Hess, Karin K., Ben S. Jones, Dennis Carlock, and John R. Walkup. "Cognitive Rigor: Blending the Strengths of Bloom's Taxonomy and Webb's Depth of Knowledge to Enhance Classroom-Level Processes." ED517804 (2009). https://eric.ed.gov/?id=ED517804.

Hodges, Charles, Stephanie Moore, Barb Lockee, Torrey Trust, and Aaron Bond. "The Difference Between Emergency Remote Teaching and Online Learning." EDUCAUSE, March 27, 2020. https://er.educause.edu/articles/2020/3/the-difference-between-emergency-remote-teaching-and-online-learning.

ISTE. "ISTE Standards for Students." Accessed December 20, 2021. https://www.iste.org/standards/for-students.

Kleeman, David. "Five Things That Haven't Changed (Much)." In *Exploring Key Issues in Early Childhood and Technology: Evolving Perspectives and Innovative Approaches*, edited by Chip Donohue. New York: Routledge, 2020.

Krathwohl, David R. "A Revision of Bloom's Taxonomy: An Overview." *Theory into Practice* 41, no. 4 (2002): 212–18. https://doi.org/10.1207/s15430421tip4104_2.

Kumar, Swapna, Florence Martin, Kiran Budhrani, and Albert Ritzhaupt. "Award-Winning Faculty Online Teaching Practices: Elements of Award-Winning Courses." *Online Learning* 23, no. 4 (2019). https://doi.org/10.24059/olj.v23i4.2077.

Lee, Sang Joon, Sandhya Srinivasan, Trudian Trail, David Lewis, and Samantha Lopez. "Examining the Relationship Among Student Perception of Support, Course Satisfaction, and Learning Outcomes in Online Learning." *The Internet and Higher Education* 14, no. 3 (2011): 158–63. https://doi.org/10.1016/j.iheduc.2011.04.001.

McLeod, Scott, and Jayson W. Richardson. "School Administrators and K–12 Online and Blended Learning." In *Handbook of Research on K–12 Online and Blended Learning*, edited by Richard E. Ferdig and Kathryn Kennedy, 285–301. n.p.: ETC Press, 2014.

Menekse, Muhsin. "The Reflection-Informed Learning and Instruction to Improve Students' Academic Success in Undergraduate Classrooms." *The Journal of Experimental Education* 88, no. 2 (2020): 183–99. https://doi.org/10.1080/00220973.2019.1620159.

Miller, Katherine. "Bloom's Taxonomy and Webb's Depth of Knowledge." *Synergis Education* (blog), January 5, 2018. https://www.synergiseducation.com/blooms-taxonomy-and-webbs-depth-of-knowledge/.

Miller, Scott T., and Stephen L. Redman. "Improving Instructor Presence in an Online Introductory Astronomy Course through Video Demonstrations." *Astronomy Education Review* 9, no. 1 (2010). https://doi.org/10.3847/AER2009072.

Northcote, Maria T. "Lighting Up and Transforming Online Courses: Letting the Teacher's Personality Shine." In *Curriculum, Technology & Transformation for an Unknown Future. Proceedings ASCILITE Sydney 2010*, 694–98. Sydney: ASCILITE, 2010.

O'Neil, Carol A. "Introduction to Teaching and Learning in Online Environments." In *Developing Online Courses in Nursing Education*, 4th ed., edited by Carol A. O'Neil, Cheryl A. Fisher, and Matthew J. Rietschel, 1–10. New York: Springer, 2020.

Orsmond, Paul, Stephen Merry, and Kevin Reiling. "Biology Students' Utilization of Tutors' Formative Feedback: A Qualitative Interview Study." *Assessment and Evaluation in Higher Education* 30, no. 4 (2005): 369–86. https://doi.org/10.1080/02602930500099177.

PBLWorks. "What Is PBL?" Accessed December 28, 2020. https://www.pblworks.org/what-is-pbl.

Pearson, Elaine J., and Tony Koppi. "Inclusion and Online Learning Opportunities: Designing for Accessibility." *Research in Learning Technology* 10, no. 2 (2002). https://doi.org/10.3402/rlt.v10i2.11398.

Powell, Allison, John Watson, Patrick Staley, Susan Patrick, Michael Horn, Leslie Fetzer, Laura Hibbard, Jonathan Oglesby, and Su Verma. *Blending Learning: The Evolution of Online and Face-to-Face Education from 2008–2015.* International Association for K–12 Online Learning, 2015. https://aurora-institute.org/wp-content/uploads/iNACOL_Blended-Learning-The-Evolution-of-Online-And-Face-to-Face-Education-from-2008-2015.pdf.

Rello, Luz, and Ricardo Baeza-Yates. "Good Fonts for Dyslexia." In *ASSETS '13: The 15th International ACM SIGACCESS Conference on Computers and Accessibility*, Article 14. Association for Computing Machinery, 2013. https://doi.org/10.1145/2513383.2513447.

Roach, Virginia, and Linda Lemasters. "Satisfaction with Online Learning: A Comparative Descriptive Study." *Journal of Interactive Online Learning* 5, no. 3 (2006). https://www.ncolr.org/issues/jiol/v5/n3/satisfaction-with-online-learning-a-comparative-descriptive-study.html.

Şahin, Muhittin, and Halil Yurdugül. "Learners' Needs in Online Learning Environments and Third Generation Learning Management Systems (LMS 3.0)." *Technology, Knowledge, and Learning* (2020). https://doi.org/10.1007/s10758-020-09479-x.

Schlechty, Phillip C. *Engaging Students: The Next Level of Working on the Work.* San Francisco: Jossey-Bass, 2011.

"School Readiness Survey." SmartyPants Research, January 2014.

Sheridan, Kathleen, and Melissa A. Kelly. "The Indicators of Instructor Presence That Are Important to Students in Online Courses." *Journal of Online Learning and Teaching* 6, no. 4 (2010). https://jolt.merlot.org/vol6no4/sheridan_1210.htm.

Sinek, Simon. "How Great Leaders Inspire Action." Filmed September 2009 in Puget Sound, WA. TED video, 17:49. https://www.ted.com/talks/simon_sinek_how_great_leaders_inspire_action?language=en.

Spencer, John. "4 Ways to Craft Choice Menus in Distance Learning Classes." *John Spencer* (blog), May 6, 2020. https://spencerauthor.com/choice-menus/.

Swan, Karen. "Building Learning Communities in Online Courses: The Importance of Interaction." *Education, Communication, and Information* 2, no. 1 (2002): 23–49. https://doi.org/10.1080/1463631022000005016.

———. "Learning Effectiveness: What the Research Tells Us." In *Elements of Quality Online Education: Practice and Direction,* edited by John Bourne and Janet C. Moore, 13–45. Needham, MA: The Sloan Consortium, 2003.

Swan, Karen, Peter Shea, Eric Fredericksen, Alexandria Pickett, William Pelz, and Greg Maher. "Building Knowledge Building Communities: Consistency, Contact and Communication in the Virtual Classroom." *Journal of Educational Computing Research* 23, no. 4 (2000): 359–83. https://doi.org/10.2190/W4G6-HY52-57P1-PPNE.

Take Charge Today. "The Basics of Taxes." Accessed December 29, 2020. https://takechargetoday.arizona.edu/.

Titsworth, Scott, Joseph P. Mazer, Alan K. Goodboy, San Bolkan, and Scott A. Myers. "Two Meta-Analyses Exploring the Relationship between Teacher Clarity and Student Learning." *Communication Education* 64, no. 4 (2015): 385–418. https://doi.org/10.1080/03634523.2015.1041998.

Trespalacios, Jesús, and Jennifer Rand. "Using Asynchronous Activities to Promote Sense of Community and Learning in an Online Course." *International Journal of Online Pedagogy and Course Design* 5, no. 4 (2015): Article 1. https://doi .org/10.4018/IJOPCD.2015100101.

Underdown, Kimber, and Jeff Martin. "Engaging the Online Student: Instructor Created Video Content for the Online Classroom." *Journal of Instructional Research* 5 (2016): 8–12.

WebAIM. "Links and Hypertext." Accessed January 16, 2021. https://webaim.org /techniques/hypertext/.

Zacharias, Nugrahenny T. "Teacher and Student Attitudes toward Teacher Feedback." *RELC Journal* 38, no. 1 (2007): 38–52. https://doi.org/10.1177/0033688206076157.

Index